GRACE BEYOND THE GRAVE

GRACE BEYOND THE GRAVE

Is Salvation Possible in the After-Life?
A Biblical, Theological, and Pastoral Evaluation

Stephen Jonathan

Foreword by
Nigel G. Wright

WIPF & STOCK · Eugene, Oregon

GRACE BEYOND THE GRAVE
Is Salvation Possible in the After-Life?
A Biblical, Theological, and Pastoral Evaluation

Wipf and Stock
An Imprint of Wipf and Stock Publishers
199 W. 8th Ave., Suite 3
Eugene, OR 97401

www.wipfandstock.com

ISBN 13: 978-1-62564-496-1

Manufactured in the U.S.A.   05/16/2014

Contents

Foreword

THERE CAN BE FEW ministers or priests who do not identify with Stephen Jonathan's pastoral starting point for this inquiry into "grace beyond the grave." At the many funerals at which they might be called upon to preside, often for people who have little to do with the church, the anxious question of the bereaved as to the security in death of their loved one is one that many ministers would prefer to evade. At one level this is, of course, entirely understandable since what do we know and who are we to pronounce on such difficult and mysterious questions? At another level it is a probing test of a widely embraced Christian conviction, that there is a decision to be made in this life and before we die concerning our relationship to God, and that depending on how we do or do not answer that question lies our eternal destiny: heaven or hell. Logically, according to this pattern of thought, for those who do not die in faith there is little hope that the gift of eternal life awaits them. Yet logic is not always the best guide in navigating matters pastoral or theological, especially once we introduce the significant word "grace" into our vocabulary and thought world. Divine grace defies logic such that what we regard as impossible is by no means impossible for God.

There is no intention in the work that follows to deny or evade the Christian belief that ultimately human decisions are not inconsequential, in eternity if not also in this life. Yet what comes into question here is the word "ultimately." The human drama is not yet at an end, we are all still *in via*, the final judgment has yet to take place, there is still time and God is yet "patient with you, not wanting any to perish, but all to come to repentance" (2 Peter 3:9). What comes into question is whether the death of humans puts an end to any possibility of repentance once we integrate into this discussion the fact of the persistence of God in pursuing the divine will to save and the equal fact that although human beings may be bounded by death, God is not. Indeed in Christ God has made known his sovereignty *over* death. Why then should death, of necessity, be a point beyond which no other possibilities exist? And even if it be the case for some who have lived full and conscious lives, what of the vast multitudes whose lives have been cut short through abortion or miscarriage, infant and childhood illness or accident, mental incapacity or limitation, pogrom and holocaust, war and massacre, to say nothing of the unevangelized, the pre-Christian, and those who, even if they have "heard" the gospel have done so in a distorted and easily-rejected form?

It would be a strange and unthoughtful Christian to whom such questions have never occurred, and an inhumane one who would wish to give rigid and dogmatic answers without considering their weight. Many are dissuaded from pursuing the questions for fear of being thought unorthodox or "unsound." But thanks be to God that Stephen Jonathan here raises and addresses the questions with honesty, humanity, and devotion to Scripture and does so in a book which is fluently written, accessible, and beneficial for us all. The question of "grace beyond the grave" may exist not at the center of the Christian estate but at or around its periphery, but it is nonetheless one that bears upon the center and which, above all, affects the vision of God that is at its core.

Dr. Nigel G. Wright
Principal Emeritus, Spurgeon's College

Preface

A BOOK SO PROVOCATIVELY entitled *Grace beyond the Grave* will cause readers to want to categorize my theology and ecclesial background before they start to read in earnest. Where is this guy coming from? Is he a liberal, evangelical, fundamentalist, or something else? To which stream or denomination does he belong? Is he a theologian, pastor, lay leader, or is writing theology his equivalent of train-spotting or stamp-collecting? No offense intended to train-spotters or stamp-collectors! I must confess that these are the questions that I also ask when picking up a book from an unknown author.

Well, for those who might wish to label me, here goes: I became a Christian in 1977, aged eighteen, and then some years later trained for pastoral ministry in the Elim Pentecostal Church, UK. Following basic theological training in 1987, I commenced ministry in a city center church, before planting a church on a socially demanding housing estate. Having spent three years in church planting, I moved to Tamworth, a Staffordshire market town of eighty thousand, where I have led a team ministry for the last twenty-one years. In 1998, I gained a MTh with Manchester University and in 2011 a DMin degree with the University of Wales, Bangor. My research for that professional doctorate forms the basis of this book.

Given the pen-portrait above, some might wonder why someone like me should wish to write a book entitled *Grace beyond the Grave*, as by even raising such a question for discussion will cause some of my colleagues to dismiss me out of hand, whilst others will undoubtedly be intrigued at my desire to tackle the subject of posthumous salvation.

Having systematically taught through large sections of the New Testament in a quarter of a century of pastoral ministry, I have had a deepening consciousness that the sometimes mechanical answers to the more searching questions are often inadequate and some of the traditional interpretations need revisiting, especially with regard to salvation of those who have either not heard or not responded to the gospel in their earthly lives.

Maybe today, I am less willing to be as dogmatic on a range of subjects as I was in the earlier years of my Christian experience. Then, everything was black or white, but now, my own faith is more multi-colored and my world is not nearly as linear. Some fellow Christian believers, perhaps understandably, raise an eyebrow when I confess that I actually know less now than I did then! Maybe, my present less doctrinaire and rigid stance on a variety of subjects, theological and otherwise, has to do with both the mellowing of age and of the opportunity afforded me to reflect more on my Christian faith.

As mentioned, this book commenced life as a thesis for a professional doctorate, though there are some essential differences. Firstly, I am attempting to make the book generally more accessible in language and style than the original doctorate, though I recognize that there are some sections of this work, such as the detailed exegesis of chapter 3, that still require a quiet room and a certain level of concentration. Secondly, I have reduced the length of footnoted material with some of it finding its way into the main text. This will help the reader by not needing to "double-read" each page, moving from main text to footnotes and back again. However, I feel it is necessary to retain some footnotes for those who wish to chase up references for further study or to check my sources.

Chapter 1 of this book focuses on setting the scene contextually, emphasizing why the question of salvation beyond the grave is regarded as one of the most provocative theological issues of our day. Reasons for a revival of interest in the destiny of the unevangelized are appraised before laying down two theological axioms, namely God's universal salvific will, and the particularity and finality of salvation through Christ as foundational to this work. The second chapter provides an overview to the common approaches over the question of the destiny of the unevangelized, setting the subject of the postmortem opportunity for salvation in its wider context.

Chapter 3 evaluates the biblical passages which purportedly support or undermine the concept of posthumous salvation, concluding that there is no room for dogmatism either for or against it. It is argued that Canadian theologian, Clark Pinnock, is essentially correct in his claim that the scriptural evidence for postmortem opportunity for salvation is not abundant and that the strength of this view lies in its theological argument. Following the complexity of argument in chapter 3, chapter 4 is an easier read, and in my opinion is the key chapter of this book. Chapter 4 concentrates on a theological argument which has a close connection with the concept of postmortem opportunity, namely God's attributes, especially the relationship between divine love and justice. It is contended that it is theologically feasible to consider God's attributes of mercy and justice as complementary, rather than contradictory, with the concept of "restorative" justice being the preferred alternative to the more traditional position of "retributive" justice which is essentially punitive. It is further argued that this, in turn, is a position that helps to maintain the unity of God's nature and also supports the notion of postmortem opportunity for salvation.

Chapter 5 concentrates on the practical implications of posthumous salvation, arguing that it will not necessarily reduce the urgency for proclaiming the gospel, or cause unbelievers to procrastinate on making a decision for Christ. Furthermore, though it is accepted that utility does not establish truth, a belief in grace beyond the grave would enable clergy to offer comfort to the bereaved more effectively and to provide a more robust apologetic, where God is not viewed as capricious or unreasonable, and a gospel which offers the possibility of salvation beyond the grave is thought of as truly good news.

Grace beyond the Grave is not meant to be the last word on the matter of posthumous salvation—I would not be so arrogant—but I do hope that it will encourage a "grown-up" discussion among Christians, especially from the evangelical wing of Christ's church, who are my spiritual bedfellows and for whom I thank God, to theologically reflect upon one of the hottest subjects of our day, without reverting to name-calling or heresy-hunting. I trust and pray that this offering will both unsettle the comfortable and reassure the open-minded in equal measure.

Dr Stephen Jonathan (2014)

Acknowledgments

THIS WORK FOR ME has been a 'labor of love' over the last few years and an opportunity to explore a subject that ordinarily I would not have been able to research within the normal parameters of church pastoral ministry. Whilst I always believed that God is good, having completed doctoral research on the concept of *Grace beyond the Grave*, I now believe that he is considerably more wonderful than I ever imagined.

I am full of gratitude to those who have walked with me on my journey of theological research the last few years. Firstly, I wish to say a big "thank you" to Dr. Keith Warrington, my supervisor of doctoral research. Keith has been a good friend since we first met in 1984 and a colleague in ministry. Keith, however, did not "go easy" on me because of our friendship. There were times I felt I required a strong drink before opening the brown envelope containing his assessment of my latest piece of work. However, Keith's help, support and availability were invaluable throughout. I am also grateful for the opportunities that I had to present papers on my work to my doctoral peers at Regents Theological College. This always proved to be a worthwhile exercise and has helped to sharpen the end product.

I also wish to acknowledge the leadership team of the Tamworth Elim Church, with whom I serve as Senior Pastor, for their willingness to allow me to explore a subject that some might regard as provocative, if not controversial. I am so grateful for their kind offer of a three month sabbatical to research the subject of this book. Thank you also Martin, for your constant queries and intelligent discussion around posthumous salvation.

I am so blessed in belonging to a church family that mirrors the grace of God in real life and has allowed me to learn theology "on the ground." Much of what I have written in this work is birthed in the practical day to day work of being a pastor involved in counseling, evangelism, and other pastoral duties.

Dr. Richard Massey, formerly Principal of Birmingham Christian College (formerly Birmingham Bible Institute), has also been a friend, mentor and such a wonderful encouragement to me. Richard has diligently read through my work, offering his wisdom, advice and a "steady hand" and has, on many occasions, kindly given of his time to chat through my work.

I appreciate the love and friendship of Terry and Helen Salih, friends for over three decades, for their allowing me to explore this subject on our evenings out at the Ferrer's Arms, and for Terry's avid reading of this work. Also, deep appreciation to our three, now adult, children, David, Siân and Andrew, and son-in-law Dan, who have all helped me re-assess my theology in the light of their sometimes penetrating questions and postmodern world-view, often without realizing the impact of their own words. Andrew has painstakingly worked as my copy-editor. I continue to be amazed at his diligence and astuteness, working on a script that is far removed from his own scientific background. You are a star!

Last, but certainly not least, I thank Julie, my wife and best friend, who has put up with piles of books and theological papers around our house, but more so for allowing me to get my desire for doctoral study and then this book "out of my system." Julie has demonstrated the patience of Job, especially on the occasions when I needed to study and write at the expense of being more husbandly. In the earlier days of this research Julie bore the brunt of what appeared to her as my grappling with new and not always "orthodox" ideas, yet she continued to support me in all my questioning and re-examining of our long held, more "traditional," understanding of the Christian faith.

Whilst I am indebted to all of those mentioned above, it is important to emphasize that the conclusions of this work are not necessarily theirs.

1

Introduction

ONE SUNDAY MORNING a few years ago, a young South African member of our church collared me following the worship service. "Steve, I work with this guy who refers to himself as an Evangelical Christian, but he believes that there is opportunity for salvation beyond this life," said Walter disbelievingly. I probably have scores of conversations with our church family following a Sunday morning church service, but this short exchange is memorable as it set me off on a course that I could not have anticipated in my wildest dreams. Walter followed up the statement about his work colleague with a question: "Steve, do you have any Bible verses that I could share with him to show him that he is mistaken?" Immediately, I quoted the first two that came to mind, not forgetting that this was a hurried conversation at the front door of our church with half a dozen other folk waiting in line to shake the pastor's hand before they vacated the building. I said, "Look up the story of Lazarus and the rich man in Luke 16:19–31 and also read Hebrews 9:27 which states 'It is appointed unto men once to die but after this the judgment,'" which I quoted from my memory of the King James Version. Walter seemed happy enough with my answer, though I must confess that I was less so, and I walked away from that momentary exchange with two immediate thoughts. Firstly, I asked myself, were there any other Bible verses or passages that supported the argument? Secondly, did the Bible texts I quoted actually support the belief that our lives on earth alone offer the opportunity for salvation? To tell you the truth, I felt a little unnerved.

That very simple and innocuous question inquiring if this life is the only arena for salvation set me on a journey that would call into question many of my deeply held convictions. To say the least, the months and years that followed were anything but comfortable as I grappled with the fear that this question would unravel the whole of my Christian faith. The other, not insignificant, problem was my needing to fulfil a promise I made at my ordination to teach God's truth faithfully to those for whom I had the "care of souls" as a church pastor. After all, how could I teach on areas of doctrine that I was privately questioning? How was I to hold onto my integrity? Throughout this time, the words of an older colleague in ministry remained at the forefront of my consciousness: "Lose your integrity, and you've lost everything!" and I knew he was right. I simply couldn't play-act, as for me a preaching-teaching ministry is founded on a deep faith commitment to biblical truth. To say that my internal wrestling was unsettling would have been an understatement indeed. Now, about eight years on from that innocent question from my friend Walter, I have come to a place of "theological rest" where I don't feel as though I am being torn in two between long-held and sincere views and those gut-wrenching questions that caused the foundations of my evangelical heritage to be shaken. By "theological rest" I don't mean that I have come to a place where there are no more questions, or to a place where I feel that I am right and everyone else is wrong, or to a position of dogmatism and inflexibility in my present thinking. I, like everyone else, am on a journey, a voyage of experiential discovery with my God and Savior. I admit that it's a bit scary on times, not being able to hold on to some of my former certainties, but I find it is a place which is more real, where God is not reduced to a formula, or where I have an answer for most things. This has been replaced by a God who is more transcendent, more mysterious, and whose ways and thoughts are so much higher than mine. I suppose, the reason I have written the last couple of sentences is to explain that *Grace beyond the Grave* is a part of my own spiritual journey, and not about some guy who loves controversy and feels the need to debunk traditional ways of understanding God's offer of salvation, irrespective of how misguided some of my readers will think I am.

Is there grace, or salvation, beyond the grave for those who have either not heard or have heard but not responded to the Christian gospel this side of death? These are hugely important questions that many church leaders are grappling with as they interpret the biblical text in the light of the daunting reality that the vast majority of people alive on earth now, and who have ever lived, have not made a conscious decision to embrace the Christian gospel or accept Christ, and of this number, most have lived and died in the religion into which they were born.[1] The World Christian Encyclopedia states that of the estimated 181 million people alive in AD 100, 1 million were Christians with 60 thousand unreached people groups at that time. By

---

1. Hick, *God Has Many Names*, 44. Hick suggests that this number is 98–99%.

AD 1000 it is estimated that there were 270 million people, 50 million of whom were Christians with 50 thousand unreached groups. In 1989 it was estimated that there were 5.2 billion people alive with 1.7 billion Christians and 12 thousand unreached groups. In addition to these large numbers of unreached people groups, there are incalculable numbers that lived prior to the Incarnation who never heard of the Israelites or of God's covenant with them, not to mention children who died before having opportunity to hear the gospel.[2]

The popular view, certainly amongst evangelicals, is that of restrictivism,[3] which means that salvation is restricted to where the gospel message is proclaimed and subsequently accepted.[4] Whilst this view is not found in the doctrinal statements of many evangelical institutions, for most it is an "unwritten article of faith."[5] And if restrictivism is true, then it would appear to disqualify the unevangelized, those with learning difficulties who might not be able to make a cognitive response to the gospel, and those who die in early childhood. The subject of infant salvation has a long history of debate, and is an area of research in its own right, and for that reason will be outside the remit of this book.[6]

Furthermore, restrictivists claim that any alternative view is a disincentive to evangelism,[7] yet some Christians might suggest that restrictivism itself is a greater hindrance to the reception of the gospel message by unbelievers, for some would say that this view portrays the Christian God as arbitrary, uncaring, and unjust, and not the God who defines himself

---

2. See Sanders, *What About Those*, 9.

3. Unger, "Destiny," *Direction*, 54–63.

4. Restrictivism is the term preferred by Sanders (see Sanders, *No Other*, 37–79). Other terminology, including exclusivism and particularism, is also used and the benefits, or otherwise, of these terms will be discussed in more detail in chapter 2. However, I shall adopt the term "restrictivism" as exclusivism can technically also include universalism (the belief that all will ultimately be saved). Sanders (*What About*, 12–13) states, "In the literature on religious pluralism, exclusivism designates the view that Christianity offers the only valid means of salvation . . . Though exclusivism affirms the particularity and finality of Jesus, it does not necessarily entail restrictivism, since some exclusivists are universalists, while other exclusivists affirm an opportunity after death for salvation."

5. See Sanders, *No Other*, 22–23.

6. Strange, *Possibility*, 302. Strange challenges this view and argues that not all who would be classified as restrictivists actually believe that young children and the mentally incapable are among the damned. For an excellent summary of the issues, see Sanders, *No Other*, 287–305.

7. Boettner, *Reformed Doctrine*, 119; Nash, "Restrictivism,"105–39, [134–6]; Borland, "Theologian Looks," 11.

as "Love" in the pages of the New Testament.[8] Clark Pinnock argues, "The implication of popular eschatology is that the downtrodden of this world, unable to call upon Jesus through no fault of their own, are to be rejected for eternity, giving the victory to the tyrants who trampled them down. Knowing little but suffering in this life, the unevangelized poor will know nothing but more and worse suffering in the next. Popular eschatology simply does not add up."[9]

Foundational to *Grace beyond the Grave*, and my earlier doctoral thesis, is my experience of pastoral work in an Evangelical/Pentecostal church, involving teaching, counseling, and mission—all three areas having a bearing on this subject. In more recent years, I have had a growing awareness that more orthodox or traditional theology is often formulaic, especially when dealing with salvation, evangelism, and bereavement.

Following that penetrating question asked by my friend Walter, I turned to a book entitled *No Other Name* by John Sanders that addresses alternatives to the restrictivist position as a start point. Unconvinced by both restrictivism and universalism, Sanders offers a critique and evaluation on alternative wider hope views, namely, universal evangelization before death, eschatological evangelization (also known as future probation; posthumous salvation; postmortem evangelization[10]), and inclusivism, which will all be discussed later. Sanders defines these wider hope views as affirming that "God, in grace, grants every individual a genuine opportunity to participate in the redemptive work of the Lord Jesus, that no human being is excluded from the possibility of benefiting from salvific grace."[11] Sanders's book is regarded as a seminal text in this area. His sixth chapter focuses on posthumous salvation,[12] which provided me with key biblical texts, theological considerations, leading defenders, evaluation, and historical bibliography. In his later book, *What about those who have never heard?*, he continues the discussion with contributions from two other scholars, each making a case for their own view (inclusivism, restrictivism, and postmortem evangelization).

Other contemporary theologians have also accepted the possibility of death as not being the seal of one's ultimate destiny. These include Gabriel

---

8. See 1 John 4:8, 16, God is not only described as loving in his actions, but love is his very essence.

9. Pinnock, *Wideness*, 152.

10. Fackre, "Divine Perseverance," 71–95 [73].

11. Sanders, *No Other*, 131.

12. His preferred term is "eschatological evangelization."

Fackre, Clark Pinnock, Donald Bloesch, and Nigel Wright[13]—all evangelical scholars. Pinnock is regarded as somewhat of a maverick,[14] and has enticed scholarly reaction in response to his work, thus providing further theological sources for this subject,[15] though his views on postmortem opportunity are not necessarily representative of other advocates of this view, as shall be shown later. There are others, contemporary and historical, evangelical and liberal, who also favor the view of posthumous salvation as a valid answer to the question of the fate of the unevangelized. Their contributions to this subject will be included in the course of this work, though my main focus is upon the views within evangelicalism.

Setting the scene contextually

In a pastoral setting, some of the most difficult questions of all are linked to the death of a loved one, especially when the person's Christian faith was uncertain. For many relatives, there is an uneasy hope that "things will be okay" and that God will benignly smile upon their loved one, offering warm acceptance into his eternal presence. Not many clergy would dare to contradict such optimism, even if they privately believed differently. They would often allow such hope on the basis of agnosticism; after all, who really knows where a person might have stood in regard to his or her faith in God? It is a matter for God alone; besides if such optimism helps the family's grief, then a dose of pragmatism is not such a bad thing. It is certainly better than the bleaker option. Moreover, such needless and unnecessary distress to the family would potentially provide reason to barrack the Christian faith.

When the question of an eternal resting place is put more directly to clergy, there are many ways in which the question is deflected or conversation exited without the need to convey a pessimistic reply to the family and friends of the deceased. The following are some typical responses that arise from my experience in pastoral ministry and through countless conversations with colleagues about such issues. I have no intention of suggesting that these "clergy responses" are anything other than sincere. These are also typical survival strategies for Christians who have lost unsaved loved ones:

13. Fackre, *Christian Story*, 219–21; 229–41; Fackre, "Scandals," 32–52; Fackre, "Divine Perseverance," 71–95; Pinnock, *Wideness*, 168–72; Pinnock and Brow, *Unbounded Love*, 94. See comments in Chapter 2, Conclusion, regarding a proper understanding of Pinnock's view on posthumous salvation; Bloesch, *Essentials*, 2:226–7; Bloesch, "Descent," 313–5; Wright, *Radical*, 98–99.

14. Strange, "Clark H Pinnock," 311–26.

15. One such major example is Strange, *Possibility.*

- Communicating that God is a God of both love and justice, using Abraham's words "Will not the Judge of all the earth do right?" (Gen. 18:25). This throws the decision back onto God with a hopeful agnosticism. The bereaved are consoled by the fact that God is just, always makes the correct decision, and by the truth that God loves the deceased more than anyone else does, including the grieving family.

- To encourage the bereaved that faith "as small as a mustard seed" (Luke 17:6) is all that God requires. Just as people were saved from death by looking at the bronze snake that Moses lifted up in the desert, all one needs to do is look to Jesus for eternal life (John 3:13–15).[16]

- To remind the grieving family that many people make an eleventh hour decision to receive Christ. This happened to the thief on the cross next to Jesus and undoubtedly to many others (Luke 23:32–43).

- Where a person once attended church, even though that might have been for a brief period in his or her life, the source of encouragement would be again on God's eternal and unconditional love and preservation declaring that no one should be plucked out of God's hand (John 10:28–29). This would also assume that the person had made a response to God during this period of his/her life.

- God will look favorably upon the person's response to the revelation that they had. In more theological parlance, general revelation is potentially salvific.[17]

- In the case of children, that God will suffer little children to come to him (Mark 10:13–16).

Whilst many of the above replies are given in all sincerity as a pastoral response to the grieving, many more contemplative clergy remain privately ill at ease over the superficiality of their consolation and question whether there are better answers and a better theology than they presently embrace.

Aware of this pastoral dilemma, Eric Stoddart, who reflects upon the difficulties for clergy in trying to offer comfort to the bereaved of the unsaved, suggests the need for a bespoke theology.[18] He refers to the funeral itself where the vicar has the challenge of maintaining integrity between what s/he would preach ordinarily from the pulpit and what s/he might say in the funeral chapel. Indeed, the very words of the committal itself which contain the phrase "in sure and certain hope of the Resurrection from the

---

16. This argument is proposed by Kendall, *Once Saved*, 19–20.

17. This issue will be discussed in more detail in chapter 2 and in Appendix A

18. Stoddart, "Bespoke," 20–22.

dead" are a statement of assurance which s/he might regard as inappropriate for the deceased.[19] Some clergy might add "for those that love the Lord," or the like, following the above statement, which would go unnoticed by all but those most sensitive to the vicar's dilemma. Such a subtle sidestep often helps the minister to keep his theological integrity whilst offering some pastoral comfort.[20] Stoddart also argues that there is "a dissonance between the rhetorical requirements of the evangelistic sermon and the pastoral concerns of the house-call to the bereaved. Publicly acknowledging the breadth of this grey area . . . would be perceived as blunting the gospel or, in the eyes of some of his congregation, 'going liberal.'" He also insightfully adds, "this can be exacerbated when influential lay-leaders in a congregation, who do not have to conduct funerals of 'the lost,' disregard any conflict between rhetorical and pastoral considerations."[21]

Revival of interest in the destiny of the unevangelized

In more recent times, there has been an upturn in scholarly interest in the fate of those who have never heard. Okholm and Phillips claim that "the debate within the evangelical academy regarding salvation and the unevangelized is intense and fierce, dominating all other discussions. And it should be, for this debate is momentous. In large measure the future of evangelical theology and world missions will be shaped by its outcome."[22] Similarly, Pinnock claims that the meaning of Christ's lordship in a pluralistic world "is one of the hottest topics on the agenda of theology," stating his conviction that "this issue is second to none in importance to Christian theology."[23]

However, this resurgence of interest upon the unreached peoples in our world lacks the emotional subjectivity of having, for example, to answer a grieving widow's earnest question regarding her husband's salvation when she is aware that during his lifetime he made no conscious decision to follow Christ, even though he might have had opportunity to hear and respond. Although the subject of the unreached is not precisely the same issue as the

19. There are varieties of statements. In the Ministers' Manual used by Elim Pentecostal pastors, the words are "in sure and certain hope of the Resurrection to eternal life . . ." (see Bradley, *Manual*, 50).

20. The Ministers' Manual used by Elim pastors actually changes the committal more significantly, both by not referring to the deceased as a *brother/sister in the Lord* and by extracting any words of hope of the Resurrection to eternal life and other such sentiments, see Bradley, *Manual*, 51.

21. Stoddart, "Bespoke," 22, see also footnote 16.

22. Okholm and Phillips, *Four Views*, 12.

23. Pinnock, *Wideness*, 7.

pastoral one mentioned, the contemporary debate around the wider hope views is a step in the right direction in challenging the restrictivist position and thus helping to sharpen theological responses within the pastoral context.

Globalization

Millard Erickson claims that "one of the burning issues of the present day is the extent of salvation, occasioned by increasing cultural and religious pluralism in what have formerly been 'Christian' nations, and by the discussion of the fate of those who never hear the gospel of Jesus Christ."[24] Globalization is a major contributor to present day interest in the unevangelized. Erickson correctly argues that for "much of history of the world, most people lived their entire lives without coming into contact with individuals of drastically different persuasions or cultures."[25] In the nineteenth century, at a time when international travel was not commonplace, the gospel was taken to the mid-Pacific Sandwich Islands and thousands of Hawaiians were converted, causing the disquieting question: "What will happen to our ancestors who have not heard the gospel?" The returning missionaries brought back with them this question to the theologians of New England in the late 1880s, resulting in the controversial Andover Theory of Future Probation (or posthumous salvation).[26]

However, due to today's easy access to international travel, immigration (where migrants bring their customs, language, and religion with them), television, and the advent of the World Wide Web, western Christians are exposed to people of other cultures and faiths in a variety of ways. Furthermore, many countries belong to trading-blocs or form strategic alliances, resulting in greater racial and cultural awareness.[27] Such proximity brings with it the challenging question of their salvation. It is indeed an easier thing to make generalized statements about people of other faiths that once were removed and detached, but now, the "alien and stranger" has become a next door neighbor or the parents of one's child's friend or a work colleague. What is more, one frequently finds oneself impressed by the way they might practice their religion, bring up their children, or by their work ethic. When their devotion, sincerity, and ethical lifestyle is observed, the

24. Erickson, "Fate," 3.

25. Erickson, "Fate," 9.

26. Fackre, "Divine Perseverance," 71; see also Field, "Andover Theory," 461–75; Taylor, "Future Probation"; Smyth, *Andover Heresy*.

27. Pinnock, *Wideness*, 9.

sweeping generalizations concerning their fate at the Judgment becomes, for some, more problematic and uncertain.

A changing world

Associated with the revival of interest in the fate of the unevangelized created by globalization is the advance of a postmodern worldview with its critical questioning of truth claims and metanarrative (the "big stories" about life, the universe, and everything that not only includes the belief systems of the world's religions but also the scientific and secular systems such as Marxism). O' Donnell argues that "metanarratives are rejected because they are impossible or incomplete. They also tend to be rigid and dogmatic, and have often used terror and force to keep themselves in power. Think of Christianity's legacy with the Inquisition and burnings at the stake, or fundamentalist Islam with its beheadings and amputations. Secular ideologies can have Gulags and firing squads too. Even materialistic views of science can be mocking and dismissive to people with spiritual beliefs in a so-called enlightened age."[28] Metanarratives are frequently coupled with doctrinaire, totalitarian systems which are intolerant to any ideology other than their own. Such apparent intolerance and dogmatic assertions of truth by Christianity, or any other ideology, causes suspicion and cynicism over such claims in an age when relativism or "political-correctness" is the dominant and prevailing virtue in Western societies. Tolerance of other people's opinions, beliefs and practices, unless illegal, is paramount, particularly the views of the marginalized or disenfranchised. Okholm and Phillips note that in this culture "religious beliefs amount to little more than matters of personal taste, on a par with one's preference for ice cream or movies."[29] Against this postmodern backdrop, to insist on a restrictivist message of salvation being possible only through a conscious decision made for Jesus Christ, with its corollary of the unevangelized being lost, is odious and repellent to the postmodern mind-set. Pinnock is undoubtedly correct to say that "in this climate any diversity of choice is tolerable except one: the mentality that believes that some choices are right and others wrong, some beliefs true and others false. That cannot be tolerated."[30]

---

28. O'Donnell, *Postmodernism*, 125.

29. Okholm and Phillips, *Four Views*, 9.

30. Pinnock, *Wideness*, 9–10.

More recent challenges

Pluralism

The subject of the fate of the unevangelized has received much recent attention due to outspoken pluralists,[31] such as John Hick and Paul Knitter, challenging the long-accepted restrictivist view.[32] Hick's views are summarized as follows:[33]

1. Christianity is a minority religion and failing to keep pace with the population growth.

2. The place where one is born correlates with what one believes, which according to the restrictivist view would preclude the majority of the world's population from salvation.[34]

3. The moral quality of other religions is not inferior to Christianity.[35]

4. Phenomenologically, the same religious experience is found in different religions.[36]

Hick challenges traditional orthodox theology, claiming that the "eternal destiny of the large majority of the human race is at stake," and maintains that "the unacceptable aspect of the old exclusivist view that non-Christians are eternally lost, or eternally tormented in hell, is its dire implication concerning the nature of God." He asks, "Is it compatible with the limitless divine love that God should have decreed that only a minority of human beings, those who have happened to be born in a Christian part of the world, should have the opportunity of eternal life?"[37] However, Hick's rejection of Christianity's claim to have a unique knowledge is mildly ironic as such a statement itself claims "privileged access to knowledge, insight and understanding."[38]

Hick calls for a Copernican revolution in theology of religions away from the older Ptolemaic view. His vivid illustration refers to a time when

31. Pinnock rather expressively writes, "The challenge of religious pluralism has gotten the theological pot boiling," see Pinnock, *Wideness*, 11.

32. Hick, *God Has Many Names*. Hick came to his views from earlier fundamentalist beliefs; Knitter, *No Other Name*.

33. See Erickson, "State," 27–28.

34. Hick, *God Has Many Names*, 44, where Hick suggests that the number is 98–99%.

35. Hick, "Pluralist View," 27–91 [39].

36. Hick, *God Has Many Names*, 62–66.

37. Hick, "Pluralist View," 45. See Wright, *Radical*, 18.

38. See Wright, *Radical*, 18.

it was believed that all the heavenly bodies revolved around the earth (Ptolemaic view), but as it later became known and accepted, the sun, not the earth, is the center of our planetary system (the Copernican view). Before the Copernican view of the sun at the center became the accepted view, the concept of epicycles was added to the Ptolemaic understanding of the universe in order to make sense of new astronomical knowledge that did not seem to fit anymore into the old system. These epicycles were manufactured so that the Ptolemaic view would continue to work and in time became more and more complex and contrived. Finally, the Copernican view was adopted by the scientific community. Hick likens the present theology of religions in these terms, in that, he claims, at the center should be God and not Christ, for when Christ is at the center, one is left with having to make various maneuvers in order to make sense of everything. He claims that the various theological attempts at making sense of the two apparently conflicting propositions of "outside of Christianity there is no salvation" and "outside of Christianity there is salvation" are unsatisfactory.[39] His answer is for a Copernican shift in theology. He writes, "It must involve a shift from the dogma that Christianity is at the center to the thought that it is *God* who is at the center and that all the religions of mankind, including our own, serve and revolve around him."[40]

What pluralists like Hick and Knitter appear to overlook is that in their desire to affirm the doctrine of God's love and salvation for the whole world, they have taken their understanding of God as Love from Christianity. A loving God who desires the salvation of the world is not found in Buddhism, Hinduism, or Islam, but is especially mediated through the ministry of Christ. Gavin D' Costa questions, "How credibly can Hick expound a doctrine of God's universal salvific will if he does not ground this crucial truth in the revelation of God in Christ, thereby bringing Christology back onto centerstage?"[41] Pinnock rather eloquently agrees, stating, "What happens is that liberals climb up the ladder of Christology to arrive at a God defined as loving personality, and then think that they can kick the ladder away, hoping that no one will notice and nothing will be affected. The sleight of hand involves retaining the word *God*, in the sense in which Jesus embodies him, and then dropping belief in the Incarnation while hoping that nobody would notice that the 'theo' of theocentric was Christologically defined."[42]

39. He is essentially referring to the efforts of Vatican II and wider hope views. See Hick, *God Has Many Names*, 30–37.

40. Hick, *God Has Many Names*, 36.

41. D' Costa, *John Hick's Theology of Religions*, 103.

42. Pinnock, *Wideness*, 45.

Within Roman Catholicism

The official position of the Roman Catholic Church for many years was Cyprian's famous maxim of "*Extra ecclesiam nulla salus*" (outside of the church there is no salvation), meaning that salvation was tied in with being a communicant member of the Roman Catholic Church and receiving the benefits of its sacramental system.[43] Whilst the *extra ecclesiam* formula was officially preserved, in practice it has gradually developed into a more inclusivist position.[44]

Pope Pius IX distinguished between those whose ignorance was conscious and those whose ignorance was invincible. Ignorance is invincible if a person could not remove it by applying reasonable diligence in determining the answer. Whilst underscoring the old formula, he was reluctant to limit God's mercy to those, who through no fault of their own, remain outside of the Roman Catholic Church.[45] In 1949, more than a decade before the Second Vatican Council, Father Leonard Feeney, a prominent Jesuit priest, defended three lay teachers who had been dismissed from Boston College for teaching that those who are not explicitly members of the Roman Catholic Church will be damned. An unrepentant Feeney was eventually ex-communicated in 1953, thus showing a changing climate of tolerance within the Catholic Church, even before Vatican II.[46] An official statement on this issue was provided by the Pope who wrote to Cardinal Cushing, archbishop of Boston, stating, "For someone to obtain eternal salvation it is not always demanded that he is . . . incorporated as a member of the Church, but what is absolutely required is that he should adhere to it by wish and desire." This wish and desire might be implicit, for "where a man labors under invincible ignorance God also accepts an implicit wish . . . for it is contained in that good disposition of the soul whereby a man wishes to conform to the will of God."[47]

What was implicit before Vatican II was elaborated and officially adopted at that Council. Whilst reaffirming *extra ecclesiam nulla sallus*, the

---

43. Walis, "Epistle 72," n. 21.

44. Erickson, *How Shall*, 103.

45. Dezinger, *Sources*, 1716–7, as cited by Erickson, *How Shall*, 41. Erickson suggests that this represented a shift in Catholic teaching as previously the *extra ecclesiam* formula focused on the status of heretics and schismatics, those who consciously and willingly rejected the Catholic tradition.

46. Congar, *Wide World*, 102, n. 1, as cited by Erickson, *How Shall*, 104, who ironically comments, the "one who held that there is no salvation for those outside the church was himself expelled from that church."

47. See Neuner and Roos, *Teaching of the Catholic Church*, 244, as quoted in Erickson, *How Shall*, 104.

Council broadened its understanding of the membership of the church.[48] That is, the church acknowledged degrees of membership: firstly there are the Catholic faithful who are "professing and practicing communicants of the Roman Catholic Church" who are said to be "fully incorporated into the society of the church." The second category includes those who are linked to the church, namely non-Catholic Christians. This group is said to honor the sacred Scriptures which are taken as their norm for belief and action, believe in the Trinity, are consecrated by baptism, receive from God his gifts and graces, but are not fully incorporated into the church as are communicant Catholics. The third group includes those who have not received the gospel, but who are said to be "related in various ways to the People of God." Included within this category are Jews, to whom the covenants and promises were given and from whom Christ was born, and those who acknowledge the Creator, which would include Muslims who profess to hold the faith of Abraham.[49] Also in this group are those who, through no fault of their own, do not know of Christ or his church, seek God and endeavor to live by the dictates of their consciences and those who without blame on their part have no unequivocal knowledge of God but attempt to live a good life by his grace.[50] The concept of "no salvation outside the church" is therefore to be understood in the light of there being such degrees of membership in the church, with Vatican II making explicit what was previously comparatively implicit in the Catholic consciousness.

Two leading Roman Catholic theologians have supplemented the work of Vatican II on the destiny of the unevangelized, namely Karl Rahner and Hans Küng. Rahner's concept of "Anonymous Christians" is founded on his twin beliefs of the necessity of being a member of the church and of God's desire to see everyone saved. Rahner states that this can only be done by acknowledging that all people are capable of being members of the church. The degrees of church membership range from the explicitness of baptism to "a non-official and anonymous Christianity which can and should be called Christianity in a meaningful sense, even though it itself cannot and would not describe itself as such."[51] Erickson defines anonymous Christians as "people who do not have an explicit, overt, or conscious Christian faith. So far as others know, or even as they themselves know, they are not Christians. Yet they are actually Christians and participate in God's grace."[52]

---

48. Abbott, *Document*, 33–35.
49. Erickson, *How Shall*, 109.
50. Erickson, *How Shall*, 108–10, who quotes, Abbott, *Document*, 32–37.
51. Rahner, *Theological Investigations*, 6:391.
52. Erickson, "State," 29. Rahner declares that it would be wrong to claim that every

Hans Küng questions whether it remains possible to proclaim the *extra ecclesiam* principle (ecclesiocentric view) in the light of the relative minority of Christianity in the world.[53] Küng prefers a theocentric view (God's plan of salvation) over the ecclesiastic view, focusing on a "positive reassessment of the significance of the world religions in relation to God's universal plan of salvation."[54] Whilst Rahner attempts to expand the meaning of church to include non-Christians, Küng disagrees believing that the starting point for the discussion is God's plan of salvation and not the church.[55] He claims that just as every human being is under God's grace and can be saved, every world religion is also under God's grace and can be a vehicle of salvation. Küng argues, "A man is to be saved within the religion that is made available to him in his historical situation. Hence, it is his right and his duty to seek God within that religion in which the hidden God has already found him." This is permissible until such a time as he is confronted in an existential way with the revelation of Jesus Christ.[56]

At this stage, the focus of this work has been to demonstrate the more recent developments which have contributed to the revival of interest in the destiny of the unevangelized and not to argue the strengths and weaknesses of such views.

Within conservative Protestantism

The pluralist challenge of advocates like Hick has often resulted in creating a hostile response from conservatives. The majority of evangelicals are uncompromising restrictivists, and according to Pinnock, many are becoming more resolute in resisting a change in their thinking.[57] James Davison Hunter claims that about two thirds of evangelical college and seminary students in the United States believe that all unevangelized will be damned

person is an anonymous Christian irrespective of whether he accepts grace. "Anyone who in his basic decision were really to deny and reject his being ordered to God, who were to place himself decisively in opposition to his own concrete being, should not be designated a 'theist,' even anonymous 'theist'; only someone who gives—even if it be ever so confusedly—the glory to God should be thus designated," Rahner, *Theological Investigations*, 6:394–5.

53. Küng, "World Religions," 25–26.

54. Erickson, *How Shall*, 115, referring to Küng, "World Religions," 31–36.

55. Although he is comfortable with the inclusion of Protestant Christians.

56. Küng, "World Religions," 52.

57. Pinnock, *Wideness*, 12. For example, Borland, "Theologian Looks," 3–11; Sproul, *Reason to Believe*, 47–59; Dowsett, *God, That's Not Fair!*; Fernando, *Christian's Attitude*; Nash, "Restrictivism," 107–39.

to hell.[58] However, not all evangelicals have reacted or responded to the challenge of the unevangelized in this way as some have been willing to dialogue and openly explore the possibility for alternative answers.[59] Alongside the radical pluralism, and the conservative reaction to it, is another track, a middle way between two extremes, a "megashift in Christian thinking" which provides a greater appreciation of the wideness of God's mercy and awareness of his salvific purpose in the world which replaces the old pessimism.[60] This track is often referred to as the "wider hope" which embraces a range of theological positions and affirms that God graciously grants all people a genuine opportunity to receive salvation through the work of Christ. The wider hope views differ on the nature and timing of the opportunity for salvation, namely whether a person is aware that their salvation is in and through Jesus Christ and whether the opportunity of salvation extends beyond the boundary of death.[61]

The destiny of the unevangelized has become a theological battleground amongst evangelical Christians in the latter part of the twentieth century. By the latter part of the 1980s, the topic of the fate of the unevangelized was often found in theological journals,[62] and given a prominent place at evangelical gatherings such as the Evangelical Affirmations conference held at Trinity Evangelical Divinity School in May 1989.[63]

Sanders states that he experienced this heated reaction to his article entitled *Is Belief in Christ Necessary for Salvation?*,[64] as well as the acrimonious reaction that Clark Pinnock received in response to the paper he presented on this topic in the 1989 Evangelical Theological Society national meeting.[65] Partly, the reason for this adverse reaction is due to there not being a single "evangelical view" on this subject,[66] and neither has there been a consensus nor a definitive position in the history of the church. Erickson reminds us that "no official council has ever given . . . authoritative ruling that was

---

58. Hunter, *Evangelicalism*, 34.

59. Pinnock, *Wideness*, 12, for example, lists, C. S. Lewis, J. N. D. Anderson, Colin Chapman, Charles Kraft, Stuart Hackett, John Sanders. Pinnock himself is perhaps the most powerful advocate for change in this area.

60. Pinnock, *Wideness*, 12.

61. Sanders, *No Other*, 131.

62. Illustrative of this are the consecutive articles by Millard Erickson in *Bibliotheca Sacra*: Erickson, "Fate," 3–15; Erickson, "Is There Opportunity," 131–44; Erickson, "Is Hell," 259–72; and Erickson, *How Shall*.

63. Sanders, *No Other*, 24.

64. Sanders, "Is Belief," 241–59.

65. Sanders, *No Other*, 20, see fn.15.

66. McVeigh, "Fate," 370–9.

given to such doctrines as the Person of Christ and the Trinity" and whilst certain elements of the doctrine of salvation were examined, the questions of the ultimate destiny of the lost, the duration of punishment, and, more importantly for this book, the question of how many will be saved, did not receive attention.[67]

Two foundational theological axioms

As previously discussed, there has been a significant challenge from those who advocate pluralism to surrender any claim for the uniqueness of Christ, contending that Jesus is just one of many ways to salvation. There are those, like Hick, who would argue that insistence upon the necessity of belief in Christ as requisite for salvation is both arrogant and intolerant. Whilst the challenge of pluralism has placed the subject of the unevangelized more firmly on the evangelical agenda, it is outside the scope of this book to interact philosophically or apologetically with the pluralist challenges. *Grace beyond the Grave* is written essentially within the parameter of evangelical Christianity, placing emphasis on two theological axioms from which the discussion on the unevangelized arises, namely God's universal salvific will (universality) and the particularity and finality of salvation (particularity) which is through Christ. It is also important to recognize one's "control beliefs" that guide and control the way that one might approach a subject like the destiny of the unevangelized. Control beliefs are those larger convictions that guide one's thinking and approach to the smaller issues. I write as an evangelical and would acknowledge the following control beliefs: Christ alone, grace alone, faith alone, and Scripture alone. That is, that salvation is only possible through the finished work of Christ, that God's free grace is appropriated by faith, and that the Bible is the final authority for faith and practice.[68] The challenge is to understand how both axioms can be held together in tension. That is, how can God love the entire world and truly desire the salvation of all, whilst at the same time offer salvation exclusively through Jesus Christ of whom most humans, in time and place, are ignorant?

67. Erickson, "Fate," 13.

68. See Sanders, *No Other*, 31–34; Pinnock, Wideness,18; Erickson, *How Shall*, 134–5; Knitter, *No Other Name?*, 90–96.

Universality

The first theological axiom is God's universal salvific will, though some conservative Christians would protest to this axiom, as those from a Reformed tradition believe in both election and limited atonement. Strange, contends (correctly) that "no Reformed theology . . . can hold to a belief in universal accessibility because in Reformed theology, the gift of salvation is given only to those predestined to be saved . . . all positions that affirm universal accessibility come from within the Arminian and postconservative evangelicalism."[69] Sanders, however, states, "Most contemporary evangelicals espouse unlimited atonement,"[70] a view that is accepted for the purpose of this book. For an excellent defense of God's universal salvific will and a comprehensive appraisal of the Calvinist perspective see Pinnock's *The Grace of God and the Will of Man*. On the subject of salvation for those who have never heard, it is important to understand whether God actually desires the salvation of all, or not. If he does, does God then do everything within his power to bring about the salvation of all? Further questions which are logically linked ask if God is capable of passively allowing large numbers of his creation to perish and whether he gets glory from the damnation of sinners, as some theologians maintain.[71]

The answers to such questions determine whether one should be optimistic or pessimistic with respect to those who have not heard. Boettner affirms that those who have not heard the gospel message of Christ are lost, stating, "Those who are providentially placed in the pagan darkness of western China can no more accept Christ as Savior than they can accept the radio, the airplane, or the Copernican system of astronomy, things concerning which they are totally ignorant. When God places people in such conditions we may be sure that He has no more intention that they shall be saved than He has that the soil of northern Siberia, which is frozen all year round, shall produce crops of wheat. Had he intended otherwise, he would have supplied the means leading to the designed end."[72] Whilst his point of what is, or, what is not, known and accepted in western China is debatable, even in 1954 when his book was written, the thrust of his argument, which most evangelical Christians would find disturbing, is nevertheless clearly conveyed. Boettner's view is an affront to many more sensitive Christians

69. Strange, *Possibility*, 306.

70. Sanders, *No Other*, 30.

71. See Gregory MacDonald, *Evangelical Universalist*, 21, who refers to a Calvinism that portrays God as displaying the glory of his justice in his treatment of the damned. See Bray, "Hell," 23, as an example.

72. Boettner, *Predestination*, 120.

who would not believe that God's universal salvific will is frustrated by accidents of birth.

Elton Trueblood questions whether such a morally shocking "scheme" is a live option for thoughtful Christians. He writes: "What kind of God is it who consigns men and women and children to eternal torment, in spite of the fact that they have not had even a remote chance of knowing the saving truth? What sort of God would create men and women in love, only to irrationally punish the vast majority of them? A God who would thus play favorites with his children, condemning some to eternal separation from himself while admitting others, and distinguishing between them wholly or chiefly on the basis of the accidents of history or geography, over which they had no control, would be more devil than God."[73]

Often quoted verses that refer to universality include: "The Lord is not slow in keeping his promise, as some understand slowness. He is patient with you, not wanting anyone to perish, but everyone to come to repentance" (2 Pet. 3:9), and "For God has bound all men over to disobedience so that he may have mercy on them all" (Rom. 11:32). However, God's universal plan of redemption does not rest on isolated texts, but is to be found throughout the Scriptures, starting in the Garden of Eden with the promise of a future deliverance, where we are told that the woman's seed will crush the serpent's head, referring to the future deliverance from the effects of the Fall (Gen. 3:15). Following the Flood, God enacts a covenant that includes the promise of future universal blessing. The rainbow was the sign which extended to all humanity, not just to a special people (Gen. 9:8–19). God then decides to initiate his plan for salvation of all peoples through the calling of Abraham. Even here, the focus is on God's universal restorative purposes as God promises, "I will bless those who bless you, and whoever curses you I will curse; and all peoples on earth will be blessed through you" (Gen. 12:3). Abraham's calling should not be viewed as the calling of a particular people for special benefits while others were overlooked, but as the calling of a people who were to become God's instrument of salvation to the world. From the earliest chapters of the Old Testament, salvation history's objective is the healing of the nations. Abraham was chosen for the sake of the world and not just for his own sake. Pinnock argues that the Old Testament doctrine of election remains essentially unchanged in the New Testament, that is, a calling to be God's chosen people as a servant community and not a selection of certain individuals to be saved. He further states that Augustine's reinterpreted biblical doctrine of election as a special redemptive privilege rather than a unique vocation was a disaster in the history of

73. Trueblood, *Philosophy*, 221.

theology. He asserts that "it manages to make bad news out of good news" and "it casts a deep shadow over the character of God."[74]

There are many texts scattered throughout the Old Testament which reveal that God's redemptive plan is for the whole world and not just Israel. The book of Jonah is a poignant testimony to God's universal salvific will. The message is that God cares for the Ninevites and desires to save them, despite Jonah's reluctance and lack of enthusiasm for his mission (Daniel 4:1–3). The Assyrians were a hideously cruel nation and enemies of Israel, but God is willing to forgive them as they repent. Jeremiah also declares God's unbiased dealings with the nations: "If at any time I announce that a nation or kingdom is to be uprooted, torn down and destroyed, and if that nation I warned repents of its evil, then I will relent and not inflict on it the disaster I had planned" (Jer. 18:7–8). This text again shows the impartiality and universality of God's grace. Pinnock is correct in stating that "the elect are not a sign of damnation to the others but a sign of God's saving purposes for the world."[75]

The theme of universality is continued in the pages of the New Testament. Jesus' message of the kingdom of God had, at its center, God's unlimited mercy and grace to those who did not deserve it. Jesus repeatedly reached out to the undeserving and disenfranchised, offering forgiveness and healing. He was accused of being a friend to sinners (Matt. 11:19) by having table fellowship with those who were so regarded by the religious establishment. In response to accusations by the teachers of the law that Jesus "welcomes sinners," Jesus told the three parables of a lost sheep, a lost coin, and a lost son, confirming the point of God's great generosity to them (Luke 15:1–31). The message is unmistakable, for God is just like the prodigal son's father who reaches out beyond all expectation to a son who had apparently forfeited his father's benevolence.

Furthermore, Jesus is one who reached across the cultural and racial divide bringing God's love to those outside the household of Israel. Jesus commended the faith of the Roman centurion maintaining that he had not found "anyone in Israel with such great faith" (Matt. 8:10; Luke 7:9). He spoke with a woman from Samaria, leading her to leave her errant ways and acknowledge Jesus as the Savior of the world. Since those to whom she testified confessed Jesus as Savior of the world, it can be safely assumed that this was her testimony also (see John 4:42). Jesus also favorably told a story of a Good Samaritan who had a compassionate attitude to a man who had been beaten and robbed and, by inference, questioned the morality of a Jewish

74. Pinnock, *Wideness*, 24–25.
75. Pinnock, *Wideness*, 29.

priest and a Levite who passed by the needy man (Luke 10:25–37). Furthermore, Jesus applauded the faith of the Canaanite woman who requested that Jesus have mercy on her demon-possessed daughter (Matt. 15:21–28). The so-called Great Commission also shows Jesus' outlook and attitude to non-Jews: "Therefore go and make disciples of all nations, baptizing them in the name of the Father and of the Son and of the Holy Spirit, and teaching them to obey everything I have commanded you. And surely I am with you always, to the very end of the age" (Matt. 28:19–20; see also Mark 16:15). Similarly, the promised Spirit was to be the agent of mission to the world. Jesus informed his disciples, "But you will receive power when the Holy Spirit comes on you; and you will be my witnesses in Jerusalem, and in all Judea and Samaria, and to the ends of the earth" (Acts 1:8). Throughout the rest of the Book of Acts the continuation and fulfilment of this prophetic announcement is witnessed as the church extends throughout the Roman Empire. As one ventures through the pages of both Old and New Testaments, one becomes patently aware that any claims for elitism and exclusivity are to be rejected, as the theme of God's universal salvific will is clearly evident.

Particularity

The second axiom of particularity and finality of salvation through Christ is to be held in tension with universality. *Finality* refers to the "full and authoritative revelation of who God is and what God desires. There is no revelation that will surpass him."[76] Finality is taught in passages such as:

- "The Son is the radiance of God's glory and the exact representation of his being, sustaining all things by his powerful word." (Heb. 1:3).

- "Jesus answered: 'Don't you know me, Philip, even after I have been among you such a long time? Anyone who has seen me has seen the Father. How can you say, "Show us the Father"?'" (John 14:9).

Particularity refers to the person of Jesus as the particular and unique being whom God assigns as Savior of the World. Salvation is through Christ and no one or nothing else, evidenced in the following texts which are only for illustrative purposes:

- "Salvation is found in no one else, for there is no other name under heaven given to men by which we must be saved." (Acts 4:12).

- "Jesus answered, 'I am the way and the truth and the life. No one comes to the Father except through me.'" (John 14:6).

76. Sanders, *What About*, 10.

- "Whoever believes in him is not condemned, but whoever does not believe stands condemned already because he has not believed in the name of God's one and only Son." (John 3:18).

- "For he has rescued us from the dominion of darkness and brought us into the kingdom of the Son he loves, in whom we have redemption, the forgiveness of sins." (Col. 1:13–14).

Texts often quoted to jointly support universality and particularity include:[77]

- "For God so loved the world that he gave his one and only Son, that whoever believes in him shall not perish but have eternal life. For God did not send his Son into the world to condemn the world, but to save the world through him" (John 3:16–17), which is a text that holds together both axioms of universality (the *world* and *whoever*) and particularity (*in him* and *through him*).

- "This is how God showed his love among us: He sent his one and only Son into the world that we might live through him," (1 John 4:9).

- "And we have seen and testify that the Father has sent his Son to be the Savior of the world," (1 John 4:14).

- "That God was reconciling the world to himself in Christ." (2 Cor. 5:19).

- "He is the atoning sacrifice for our sins, and not only for ours but also for the sins of the whole world," (1 John 2:2).

- "This is good, and pleases God our Savior, who wants all men to be saved and to come to a knowledge of the truth. For there is one God and one mediator between God and men, the man Christ Jesus, who gave himself as a ransom for all men," (1 Tim. 2:3–6).

The first axiom of universality would be challenged mostly by restrictivists, especially by those who hold the Reformed position. The second axiom of particularity would receive most opposition from liberals who would defend the universality of God's salvific will but jettison a high Christology. Throughout this book, both axioms will be held equally in order to discover a better way forward, theologically and pastorally.

Chapter 2 will scan the alternatives to restrictivism (namely, inclusivism, universal evangelization before death, "middle knowledge," classical universalism, and posthumous salvation) though the main focus of this book will be centered on the belief that opportunity for salvation exists

---

77. These Bible references are merely illustrative and not meant as an in-depth survey.

beyond physical death for those who have not heard the gospel and also to those who have previously rejected the gospel in life. This view will be evaluated biblically, theologically, and practically in the following chapters.

2

Common Approaches to the Destiny of the Unevangelized

THIS CHAPTER WILL PROVIDE an overview of the common approaches to the destiny of the unevangelized and will also demonstrate how posthumous salvation relates to other positions. Fackre likens the present conversation on the destiny of the unevangelized as similar to the Christological controversies of the first four centuries, in that it took considerable time for a clear and accepted picture to develop to understand Jesus as one who is "truly God, truly human and truly one."[1] Following the works of Race and D' Costa, the threefold typology of exclusivism, inclusivism, and pluralism is today the most common way of approaching the question.[2]

Overview of the common approaches

Exclusivism

This view asserts that Jesus is the only Savior of the world and it is not possible to attain salvation apart from explicit knowledge of him. Exclusivism contends that Jesus is both an ontological and an epistemological necessity[3]—that is, people can only be saved through him and his Atonement

---

1. Fackre, "Divine Perseverance," 72.

2. Race, *Christians and Religious Pluralism* and D' Costa, *Theology and Religious Pluralism.*

3. Okholm and Phillips, *Four Views,* 16, regard the term *exclusivism* as so prejudicial that it precludes true dialogue because exclusivism has been associated with "arrogance, intolerance, dogmatism, and close-mindedness." They also regard the label

(*ontological*) and they also need to exhibit knowledge of him through faith (*epistemological*).

Sanders writes, "In the literature on religious pluralism, exclusivism designates the view that Christianity offers the only valid means of salvation." He further clarifies that "although exclusivism affirms the particularity and finality of Jesus, it does not necessarily entail restrictivism, since some exclusivists are universalists, while other exclusivists affirm an opportunity after death for salvation."[4]

Exclusivism can be divided into four subgroups: restrictivism, universalism, universal opportunity, and posthumous salvation.

Restrictivism

This view advocates that the possibility of salvation is "restricted to those who have heard the gospel and have made a conscious decision to accept it."[5] Erickson lists a set of six characteristics to be found in what he calls the "traditional view of Christianity"[6]:

- All humans are sinners, guilty before God and under divine condemnation.

- Salvation is only through Christ and his atoning work.

- Belief is necessary to obtain the salvation achieved by Christ. The church therefore has a responsibility of taking the gospel to unbelievers.

- Adherents of other religions are spiritually lost apart from Christ.

- Physical death brings an end to the opportunity to exercise saving faith in Christ. "The decisions made in this life are irrevocably fixed at death."

- All humans will be separated at the final judgment on the basis of their relationship to Christ.

According to this view, God's "general" revelation of himself through creation leaves all people without excuse, but to be saved one needs "special" revelation of Jesus Christ and his redemptive work. Within the concept of

---

restrictivism as detrimental as it gives the impression of an "arrogant elitist club." Their preferred term is *particularism*.

4. Sanders, *What About*, 12–13. This book retains the differentiation between restrictivism and exclusivism.

5. Boyd and Eddy, *Across*, 180.

6. Erickson, "The State of the Question," 23–24. It is noteworthy that the concept of posthumous salvation agrees with all except point 5.

restrictivism, there are varied classifications, which include: *hard restrictivism, pessimistic agnosticism*, and *optimistic agnosticism*. Hard resrictivism asserts that "God does not reveal himself redemptively through other means than . . . through his children's missionary activity to a lost world."[7] The pessimistic agnostic stance confirms the necessity of special revelation, but leaves the difficult question of salvation of the unevangelized in the hands of a God who is merciful and righteous, though not holding out much hope for them.[8] The optimistic agnostic viewpoint affirms that though there are "optimistic hints" in the Bible there is no warrant from Scripture that God will save the unevangelized and it would be wrong to presume such.[9] Packer demonstrates this position, stating, "Living by the Bible means assuming that no one will be saved apart from faith in Christ, and acting accordingly."[10] Whilst admitting that not all restrictivists are "hard" or indeed "Reformed," the restrictivist view strongly implies that the majority of people, in history and geography, will be lost.[11]

7. Lindsell, *Christian Philosophy of Missions*, 117.

8. Geivett and Phillips, "A Particularist View," 211–70, demonstrate this kind of pessimistic agnostic viewpoint, though they acknowledge the possibility of exceptions in very special circumstances.

9. Okholm and Phillips, *Four Views*, 21–22.

10. Packer, "Evangelicals," 121–3. Strange's typology/classification of positions is yet more comprehensive. He differentiates between positions of *particular accessibility* and *universal accessibility*. See Strange, *Possibility*, 307–21. Under his section on particular accessibility viewpoints, he includes: Reformed "hard" restrictivism, which affirms both belief in God's particular salvific will (election) and God's salvific provision (limited atonement), a position that Strange admits is logically coherent but offensive to many; Reformed "agnostic" restrictivism (as explained above); Reformed "soft" restrictivism, which admits that God sovereignly can illuminate whom he wills according to his pleasure in extraordinary circumstances; John Piper's Reformed *Preparatio Evangelica* (see also Universal Opportunity before death) where the gospel is divinely directed by angels or humans to those who are already searching for the truth from the general revelation they've received; Implicit-Faith view; "soft" inclusivism / "opaque" exclusivism, though I have followed Sanders and Pinnock who have classified this view as Inclusivism in their typologies; Non-Reformed Restrictivism, which allows for both axioms of God's salvific will and particularity in Christ. This latter view would concede that God has a desire to save all persons, but his will is frustrated by the failure of evangelization, therefore, claiming that although God desires all to be saved, he has limited himself in the way that salvation is mediated. Strange claims that he knows of no published evangelical who argues along this line.

11. Some believe that this is more than an implication and that Jesus himself taught that this would be so e.g. Matthew 7:14.

Universalism

I have placed universalism in the category of exclusivism as Christian universalists regard Jesus as both ontologically and epistemologically necessary. Parry and Partridge assert that under the heading of "strong" universalism are three subdivisions,[12] namely:

- a non-Christian version of universalism, where all people shall attain to the ultimate good.

- pluralistic universalism which argues that all religions lead to the same goal.

- Christian universalism, which is placed firmly within the orthodox Christian tradition.[13]

It is this third type of universalism that is being referred to here which embraces both axioms of God's universal salvific will and the particularity and finality of salvation which is through Christ. Scholars, such as Strange, believe that universalism is "untenable for evangelicals" though not all agree.[14] For example, Robin Parry, a.k.a. Gregory MacDonald, argues forcefully for the feasibility of being a committed universalist and an evangelical, in his aptly named book, *The Evangelical Universalist*.[15] This is also the subject matter for Parry and Partridge in their *Universal Salvation?* and for the Evangelical Alliance in *The Nature of Hell (ACUTE)* report that maintains that universalism is a largely non-evangelical view[16]—although there were signs that it was beginning to have some influence in evangelicalism at the turn of this century.

Christian, or classical, universalists are divided on two crucial issues, namely:

---

12. Parry and Partridge, *Universal Salvation?*, xxi, and Hilborn, *Nature of Hell*, 27–28. Though the latter classifies into: pluralistic universalism of Ernst Troeltsch and John Hick; inclusivistic universalism of Paul Tillich, John Macquarrie, and Jürgen Moltmann; hopeful universalism of J. A. T. Robinson and Jan Bonda. Trevor Hart makes the distinction between pluralist universalism and Christian universalism in "Universalism: Two Distinct Types," in Cameron, *Universalism*, 1–34. Fowler speaks of three categories, namely, philosophical universalism, pluralistic religious universalism, and Christianized religious universalism, in Fowler, James, "Universalism," 1–3. He uses the word "Christianized" because he feels that to use "Christian" for this belief system is a misnomer and oxymoron.

13. Also referred to as Classical Universalism, see e.g. Sanders, *No Other*, 81.

14. Strange, *Possibility*, 297.

15. Gregory MacDonald is a pseudonym for Robin Parry. The pseudonym was taken from Gregory of Nyssa and George MacDonald, both influential universalists.

16. Hilborn, *Nature of Hell*, 27.

- the matter of human freedom: some universalists are deterministic, asserting God's all-powerful and sovereign will overrules human freedom, bringing it into submission to the divine will. Schleiermacher is the most well-known advocate of this view.[17] According to Bauckham he was the first great theologian of modern times to teach universalism and a "predestination as absolute as that of Augustine and Calvin."[18] Most universalists reject this deterministic view and contend that eventually all human beings will freely accept God's gracious offer of salvation.[19]

- what happens to the unevangelized on the other side of the grave: some believe that there will be a remedial constituent of hell before they leave for eternal bliss (restorationists), whilst others reject this concept of hell altogether (ultra-universalists).[20]

Though much could be said on this subject in respect of arguments, for and against, philosophically, theologically, and biblically, it essentially remains outside the limited scope of this book. For further reading see Cook who deals with this question and asks whether posthumous salvation will lead by implication to universalism, which might in turn be recognized as an evangelical option in a few decades time much in the way that the "unmentionable" doctrine of conditional immortality became acceptable to evangelicals.[21] He further argues for the rational consistency of Pinnock's position who believes in posthumous salvation, but is not a universalist. Gray, in response to Cook, supports the notion that a person cannot freely and rationally choose hell, once its nature is clear, and where hell is understood to be a place of continuing sin.[22]

Universal Opportunity (before death)

According to Sanders's typology, this proposition can be further divided into three views:[23]

17. Schleiermacher, *Christian Faith*, paras. 117–20, 163.
18. Bauckham, "Universalism," 50.
19. Sanders, *No Other*, 82.
20. Sanders, *No Other*, 82.
21. Cook, "Is Universalism," 395–409.
22. Gray, "Post-Mortem Evangelism," 141–50.
23. Sanders, *No Other*, 151–2. These views have two control beliefs in common, namely, (i) that one needs to accept the gospel message, or be judged on the way they would have responded should they have heard it; (ii) that a person's final destiny is sealed at, or before death, not after death.

- God will send the gospel to all those who seek him. It is believed that God will not condemn anyone to hell without having first had the opportunity to respond to the gospel, so all those who are seeking God's truth through the light they have been given will be sent a messenger from God with the gospel message of Christ. This might be through people, angels, or dreams. Piper's Reformed *Preparatio Evangelica* appears to be the same concept under a different name.[24] This view regards general revelation as insufficient for salvation, though it does prepare the way for the seeker to be provided with explicit knowledge of Christ which is necessary for salvation. Biblical examples often quoted include: how God arranged for Philip to be his messenger to the Ethiopian eunuch who was seeking God (Acts 8:26–40), and the way in which Peter was sent to the Gentile Cornelius who was a devout man who believed in God, but did not know of Christ and the gospel (Acts 10:1–48).

- All people will have an evangelistic encounter with Christ at the moment of death, which is principally a Roman Catholic position. The "Final Option" theory, as it is known, teaches that all people have an opportunity at the moment of death to respond to Christ. Those who hold this view, including Cardinal John Henry Newman, who endorsed it, believe that this encounter happens at the moment of death when the soul is separated from the body for the first time, and not after death.[25] Hick contends that this theory "empties the present life of its religious significance and gives meaning to death by depriving this life of its meaning."[26]

- God will judge the unevangelized on the basis of how they would have responded to the gospel should they have heard it in their lifetime. This view is called *middle knowledge* (or Molinism[27]), because it is situated between two other types of divine knowledge, namely: God knows all the possibilities of what *could* happen in any given situation and what *will* happen. This view holds that God also knows what *would* happen in any situation, including the decision a person would make if they had heard the gospel in their lifetime. A key text in this concept

24. Strange, *Possibility*, 316, refers to John Piper, *Let the Nations*, 135–45.

25. see Fairhurst, "Death and Destiny," 324.

26. Hick, *Death*, 238.

27. Molinism, named after sixteenth-century Jesuit theologian Luis de Molina. Contemporary philosophers that defend it include: Alvin Plantinga, Alfred Freddoso, Thomas Flint, and William Lane Craig—see MacDonald, *Evangelical Universalist*, 26, n. 38.

is (Matt. 11:21–23) "Woe to you, Korazin! Woe to you, Bethsaida! If the miracles that were performed in you had been performed in Tyre and Sidon, they would have repented long ago in sackcloth and ashes. But I tell you, it will be more bearable for Tyre and Sidon on the day of judgment than for you. And you, Capernaum, will you be lifted up to the skies? No, you will go down to the depths. If the miracles that were performed in you had been performed in Sodom, it would have remained to this day." Sanders states that the "concept of middle knowledge is used . . . both to allow salvation of the unevangelized and to rule it out."[28] He cites Goodman as an example of the former and Craig as an example of the latter. Goodman believes that a person might be saved without any commitment or act of trust in God for salvation as it would be dependent upon God's foreknowledge, being independent of human decision or will. Craig maintains that no one is saved this way.[29] The view of Goodman allows for universal accessibility of the gospel. However, it takes the decision away from the person and places it with God, thereby denying that an act of faith is necessary.[30] As for Craig, it is debatable whether his view supports universal opportunity for salvation at all. Sanders astutely comments that "Craig gives every evidence of being a restrictivist attempting to relieve God of blame for not giving all people an opportunity to hear of Jesus the Savior."[31]

Posthumous salvation

This section aims to explain the concept of posthumous salvation, which is the main focus of this book, by providing an overview of its rationale in preparation for a more in-depth biblical and theological analysis and evaluation in the following chapters. Posthumous salvation is included under the category of exclusivism as it holds fast to both the ontological and epistemological necessity of Christ and his Atonement. That is, there is no salvation apart from Christ and one also needs to exhibit knowledge of him through faith to receive salvation. It is to be distinguished from both Purgatory and

---

28. Sanders, *No Other*, 167–70.

29. On this subject see Craig, *Only Wise God*, and "No Other Name," 176; George Goodman is cited by J. Oswald Sanders in *How Lost*, 62.

30. Their concept of Middle Knowledge would also take this view outside of exclusivism, the idea that Jesus Christ is both an ontological and epistemological necessity. See also Altstadt and Wan, *Salvation of the Unevangelized*, who include this view under inclusivism rather than exclusivism, probably due to the fact that there is no conscious decision of faith on the part of the unevangelized.

31. Sanders, *No Other*, 174.

universalism. Purgatory, in Roman Catholic theology, is a place where those who die at peace with the church are purified prior to heaven and therefore do not require evangelizing.[32] The distinction between posthumous salvation and universalism is that the postmortem opportunity offered does not necessarily result in salvation as it does with universalism. Advocates of posthumous salvation believe that the offer of salvation can be rejected as well as be accepted. The similarity between posthumous salvation and universalism is that both affirm the universal salvific will of God and that death is not a barrier to the possibility of salvation. As mentioned previously, the question of whether the concept and offer of posthumous salvation will lead to universalism is outside the scope of this book.

BRIEF HISTORY

Posthumous salvation, although marginal to mainstream Christianity, has had a long history, being advocated in the early church by such as Clement of Alexandria, Origen, Hermas, Hilary of Poitiers, Gregory of Nyssa, and Ambrose.[33] However, the doctrine of posthumous salvation was marginalized until the late nineteenth century before re-emerging on the fringes of orthodox Christianity.[34] Field claims that this "truth was hidden in the Middle Ages by the doctrine of Purgatory, which is only a caricature of it," causing the Reformers to reject it due to their aversion to the doctrine of

32. Boettner, "Purgatory," 897; see also Hilborn, *Nature of Hell*, 20–24.

33. Erickson, "Is there," 131–44, [131]; Wilson, "Stromata," Book 6, Chapter 6; Origen, *Contra Celsum* 2.43, Origen here suggests that Christ's sojourn in Hades was similar to his time on earth, where sinners were able to repent; *Shepherd of Hermas*, *Similitude* 9, Chapter 16; Though Hilary believed that a person is judged at death and dispatched to either Abraham's bosom or to punishment (Comm. Ps. 2:49), he also held out hope for the possibility of God's mercy after death (Comm. Ps. 51.23); Gregory's *On the Soul and Resurrection* is presented as a dialogue with Macrina, whom he refers to as "The Teacher." She takes the story of the Rich Man and Lazarus story and reinterprets it in a universalist manner; Ambrose, *De Fide* 3.14.111; cf. 3.4.27–28. See also Boyd, *Across*, 187; Hudson, *Future Probation*, 74.

34. Even Martin Luther raised the question of its theological credibility. Luther was insistent that faith was required for God to save, but he also wrote, "It would be quite a different question whether God can impart faith to some in the hour of death or after death so that these people could be saved through faith. Who could doubt God's ability to do that?" Luther, "Letter to Hans von Rechenberg," 54. Luther himself answered, "That God could do so could not be denied, that God does so cannot be proved." Luther, *Dr. Martin Luthers Briefe*, 455, as quoted by Taylor, "Future Probation," 156. As will be observed from some of the following "more dated" references, the discussion of future probation was at its peak in the late nineteenth century.

Purgatory.[35] Furthermore, Taylor asserts that "one of the most virulent doctrinal controversies in the nineteenth century was the battle over the dogma of Future Probation, or salvation after death" and that it was debated in a host of denominational papers "from Catholic to Adventist" where this view became "the test case for orthodoxy in evangelical churches."[36] The Andover Theological School in Massachusetts became the ideological center for the belief in future probation.[37]

Taylor states that the two strands of future probation thought came to America from Great Britain and Germany. The British strand came through the writings of Anglicans like Herbert Luckock, Edward Plumptre, and Frederick Maurice.[38] She states that the British debate also extended to the Baptists causing Charles Spurgeon to resign from the Baptist Union in Great Britain because some of its members believed in future probation.[39] The German rationalism strand came through biblical exegetes and theologians who included Johann P. Lange, Isaac Dorner, and Philip Schaff.[40] The so-called Andover Theory of Future Probation taught that "all men are sinners and under condemnation, lost by reason of sin, but that a gracious dispensation has been provided for the sinful race by the Incarnation and Atonement of Christ; that Christ died for every man, and that faith in the Lord Jesus Christ is absolutely essential to salvation."[41] Therefore, according to Field, "if Christ died for every man, and faith in Christ is absolutely essential to salvation, then it follows, as a necessary inference, that the offer of this salvation will be made to every man before the final judgment."[42] Leckie, writing in 1918, quite remarkably states that "the majority of evangelical teachers at the present day hold some form of the doctrine that is called 'Future Probation.'"[43] Erickson maintains that in recent years posthumous

---

35. Field, "Andover Theory," 473.

36. Taylor, "Future Probation," 153.

37. See Smyth, *Andover Heresy*.

38. Luckock, *Intermediate State*, 183–208; Plumptre, *Spirits in Prison*; Taylor, "Future Probation," 156.

39. Taylor, "Future Probation," 156, refers to "The Facts about Mr. Spurgeon," 4.

40. Lange, *Peter*; Smyth, *Dorner on the Future State*; Dorner, *System of Christian Doctrine*, 130–5; Taylor, "Future Probation," 156–7.

41. Field, "Andover Theory," 461–3, emphasizes that there were other theories of future probation after death that he did not believe were in harmony with orthodox doctrines such as those that taught that humans will never come to a fixed state of good or evil.

42. Field, "Andover Theory," 463.

43. Leckie, *World to Come*, 94.

salvation "has experienced something of a resurgence of interest" with orthodox and evangelical Christians expressing an interest in this view.[44]

Rationale for Posthumous Salvation

Destinies are not necessarily determined at death

Proponents of posthumous salvation assert that final destinies are not necessarily sealed at death, but opportunity for salvation is possible for many
beyond death and up until the time of the final judgment. This is a view
that cuts across the understanding of most Evangelicals and Catholics, who
view the moment of death as the dividing line beyond which no hope for
salvation exists. That is, up until one's dying breath, just like the thief on
the cross next to Jesus who reached out to him in his last moments and was
given the promise of paradise, opportunity for salvation exists, but not one
moment after death. Traditionally, death terminates all hope as destinies are
understood to be sealed at this point. Yet, according to Boyd, "Why should
we assume that death is an insurmountable obstacle for the Lord when his
most definitive act involved defeating the one who had the power of death
and overcoming the grave (Heb. 2:14)?"[45] He continues, "Because of his
Resurrection, Jesus now holds 'the keys of Death and Hades' (Rev. 1:18). If
someone died whose heart was not irreversibly set against Christ, it seems
natural to assume that Christ would be willing and able to continue trying
to win that person over."[46] Field argues that it is the final judgment and not
death that is the end of opportunity for salvation. He contends that "we
have neglected the eschatology of Scripture, and made death the judgment,
and death the coming of Christ."[47] Lange makes the same point in his commentary, writing, "Holy Scripture nowhere teaches the eternal damnation of
those who died as heathens or non-Christians; it rather intimates in many
passages that forgiveness may be possible beyond the grave, and refers the
final decision not to death, but to the day of Christ."[48]

Davis asks whether it is possible that certain people would respond
positively to God's love after death who had not responded positively during
their lives. Whilst recognizing that his conjecturing is without clear biblical
warrant, he believes that this is possible for "Christ has the power to save

44. Erickson, "Is there," 131.
45. Boyd and Eddy, *Across*, 186.
46. Boyd and Eddy, *Across*, 186.
47. Field, "Andover Theory," 469.
48. Lange, *First Epistle*, 75.

human beings wherever they are, even in hell" and that some who "hear the gospel hear it in such a way that they are psychologically unable to respond positively. Perhaps they heard the gospel for the first and only time from a fool or a bigot or a scoundrel. Or perhaps they were caused to be prejudiced against Christianity by skeptical parents or teachers." He continues, "Whatever the reason, I believe it would be unjust of God to condemn those who did indeed hear the good news but were unable to respond positively. This is why I suggest that even in hell, people can be rescued."[49] Davis, however, distances himself from universalism by claiming that he sees no need for a second chance for those "who have freely and knowingly chosen in this life to live apart from God."[50] Pinnock, like Davis, raises the question of the fate of those who have heard the message of Christ only in inadequate ways. He deliberates on the fate of the person who knows the name of Jesus, but associates it with Zionism, if they are Muslims, or with Auschwitz, if they are Jews, thereby causing them to reject Christ most vehemently. He claims, "One can hardly say that they know the Good News and have rejected it."[51] Wright contends that those who are deprived of the opportunity to respond to Christ in life are provided that opportunity postmortem, but "this is not so much a 'second chance' as a first opportunity."[52] However, he continues by emphasizing that the language of "chances" which suggests "barely minimal ways of satisfying 'fair play'" are not always helpful as it does not accurately portray the grace of God which extends to undeserving human beings. Wright expands his reference to "chances" by emphasizing that "the key question . . . is not so much whether human beings can be redeemed beyond death as whether God's search for his fallen creatures is thwarted by death or continues beyond it."[53]

Advocates of posthumous salvation differ in their views regarding the *duration* and the *extent* of any future probation. Firstly, regarding the *duration*, some contend that the future probation will continue throughout all eternity allowing everlasting opportunity for repentance and faith in Christ as Savior. It would appear that the logical counterargument of this view would allow for a perpetual possibility of apostasy from God, to which

---

49. Davis, "Universalism," 183–4.

50. Davis, "Universalism," 184.

51. Pinnock, *Wideness*, 174.

52. Wright, *Radical*, 99. Bloesch, "Descent," 313–4, claims that the "descent doctrine affirms the universality of the first chance, an opportunity for salvation for those who have never heard the gospel in its fullness" and not to be confounded with the doctrine of a second chance.

53. Wright, *Radical*, 99.

Kellogg argues that such a doctrine "finds few advocates."[54] Field agrees, stating that "the idea that man never, in all the future, comes to a fixed state of good or evil . . . does not seem possible to reconcile with the teachings of Scripture on the final judgment."[55] Others argue that although opportunity for salvation will extend beyond the grave, there is a time of opportunity beyond which it will "be forever too late to be saved."[56] Cochrane asserts that "a man's state may thus be fixed long before death" and contends that "the limit to probation is not arbitrary. It is a limit of character, reached by the sinner himself in the spontaneous course of sin. It may or it may not coincide with the moment of death. It may, perchance, be reached afterwards. It certainly may be reached before. It is a spiritual limit rather than a temporal one" fixed by the state of the soul rather than by a moment in time.[57] Furthermore, Kellogg claims that those who believe in the possibility of salvation after death, yet deny universalism, are distinguished by their belief that any such future probation will have a limit.[58] Secondly, regarding the *extent* of future probation, some believe that all who die impenitent, irrespective of whether they have previously heard the gospel, will have the opportunity for salvation after death, whether unlimited or limited.[59] This view is often referred to as "second chance." Others believe that future probation is offered just to the unevangelized who have not had the opportunity to trust in Christ during their lifetimes, but not to those who have had previous opportunity.[60]

Advocates and opponents use the Bible to support their arguments for or against posthumous salvation yet come to quite opposite conclusions. These Scriptures will be critiqued in chapter 3. A theological and pastoral evaluation will be made in subsequent chapters.

The necessity of explicit faith in Christ for salvation

Furthermore, most proponents of posthumous salvation believe that explicit faith in Christ is an essential element in salvation and if one has not had the opportunity to make such an explicit response before death,

54. Kellogg, "Future Probation," 229.

55. Field, "Andover Theory," 462.

56. Kellogg, "Future Probation," 226.

57. Cochrane, *Future Punishment*, 222.

58. Kellogg, "Future Probation," 231.

59. Frame, "Second Chance," 991–2, refers to Origen, Schleiermacher, Dorner and Godet.

60. For example, Pinnock, *Wideness*, 168–72.

then a merciful God who always acts justly will give opportunity beyond the barrier of physical death.[61] Proponents of posthumous salvation do not believe that general revelation is sufficient for salvation, corresponding with restrictivists in contending that explicit faith in Christ as revealed through special revelation is necessary for salvation. However, they differ in that restrictivists believe that such explicit faith in Christ is required before death whereas supporters of posthumous salvation allow for salvation after death. Both positions challenge the inclusivist "implicit faith" position. Fackre in *The Christian Story* states that "the texts of the New Testament . . . overwhelmingly assert faith to be an explicit confession and not a covert one."[62] Lindbeck writes, "saving faith cannot be wholly anonymous, wholly implicit, but must be in some measure explicit: it comes, as Paul puts it, *ex auditu*, from hearing (Rom. 10:17)."[63] Bloesch agrees, affirming that "outside of Christ and faith in his atonement there is no salvation either in this life or in the life to come," stating that it is pernicious to believe that anyone can be saved apart from explicit faith in Christ.[64] He further argues that "the natural knowledge of God is sufficient neither for a valid understanding nor for salvation but only for condemnation."[65] However, it could be claimed that since Bloesch allows for a postmortem opportunity for salvation, his view on general revelation is more "palatable" to many Christians than that of restrictivist theologians, who neither allow for implicit faith nor for postmortem opportunity.

Lutheran theologian Carl Braaten concurs with the belief in the necessity of saving faith coming through hearing about the grace of Christ and not through general revelation. Braaten states, "If, traditionally, Roman Catholic theology has taught that 'outside of church there is no salvation,' Lutheran theology has taught that 'outside of Christ there is no salvation.'"[66] Demarest comes to this same conclusion by arguing for the inadequacy of general revelation. He claims, "General revelation elicits the anxious interrogation, 'What shall I do to be saved?' It prompts the question and poses the difficulty, but it cannot provide the solution."[67] He acknowledges that people, including those of other religions, can have genuine contact with God through general revelation, yet "the light they . . . possess is too frag-

---

61. Leckie, *World to Come*, 95–96.

62. Fackre, *Christian Story*, 232–3. Fackre gives evidence by listing 177 texts.

63. Lindbeck, *Nature of Doctrine*, 57.

64. Bloesch, *Essentials*, 2:230.

65. Bloesch, *Future of Evangelical Christianity*," 121.

66. Braaten, "Lutheran Theology," 122.

67. Demarest, *General Revelation*, 70.

mentary and distorted to illumine the path that leads to a saving knowledge of God."[68] Sanders disagrees, claiming that "God uses general revelation to mediate his salvific grace,"[69] as does Richardson who contends that, "all revelation is saving revelation" and that "the knowledge of God is always saving knowledge."[70] Sanders adds, "This does not mean that it is revelation which does the saving. Neither special nor general revelation save or condemn: it is *God* who saves or condemns."[71]

The discussion of the merits of general revelation with regard to mediating salvific grace will be discussed in more detail in Appendix A, but for now it is sufficient to say that all advocates of posthumous salvation agree with restrictivists in that explicit faith in Christ is necessary for salvation.

Often linked to the belief in the necessity of explicit faith is the belief that explicit rejection of Christ is the only ground for condemnation.[72] For example, Berkhof states that "The fundamental principle of which this theory [posthumous salvation] rests, is that no man will perish without having been offered a favorable opportunity to know and accept Jesus. Man is condemned only for the obstinate refusal to accept the salvation that is offered in Christ Jesus."[73] Passages that are used to affirm that unbelief is the only reason for condemnation include: Matthew 10:32–33; 12:31–32; Mark 16:15–16; John 3:18, 36; 15:22; 16:8–9; Romans 10:9–12; Ephesians 4:18; 2 Thessalonians 1:8; 2 Peter 2:3–4; 1 John 4:3. However, Berkhof claims that these only prove that faith is necessary for salvation which is not the same as proving that a conscious rejection of Christ is the only basis for condemnation.[74]

Frame agrees, "John 3:18 and similar passages teach that Jesus is the only way to salvation, but not that disbelief in him is the only ground for condemnation; we are condemned for all our sin, including our corporate sin in Adam."[75] Berkhof argues that rejection of Christ is not the only sin that condemns humans as by their nature they are lost and under condemnation quite apart from any actual sins that they commit. Sanders also remains unconvinced that such passages teach what Fackre and others claim, yet declares that should Fackre be able to make the case that the only reason

68. Demarest, *General Revelation*, 259.

69. Sanders, *No Other*, 233.

70. Richardson, *Christian Apologetics*, 127.

71. Sanders, *No Other*, 233.

72. Berkhof, *Systematic Theology*, 692–3.

73. Berkhof, *Systematic Theology*, 692.

74. Berkhof, *Systematic Theology*, 693.

75. Frame, "Second Chance," 992.

why anyone should be consigned to eternal condemnation is for explicitly rejecting Christ, then he would have an excellent argument for posthumous salvation.[76] However, it might be argued that proponents of posthumous salvation do not need to make the case as it is not, as Sanders, Frame, and Berkhof appear to imply, dependent upon the view that the only basis for condemnation is an explicit rejection of Christ. All that is required is to provide biblical evidence that death is not the end of probation. Sanders quite succinctly claims that the reasoning behind posthumous salvation is:

1. salvation is universally accessible.

2. explicit knowledge of Christ is necessary for salvation.

3. the only reason that a person is condemned is for rejection of Christ.

Based on this foundation, he claims that it is not unreasonable to conclude that the unevangelized have some opportunity to respond to Christ after death.[77] However, if (3) was straightforwardly replaced by the belief that death is not the end of one's probation, this would eliminate the need for advocates of posthumous salvation to "make the case." In fact, the need to prove that explicit rejection is the only reason for condemnation (a view that has brought criticism from opponents) is excluded.

Although Boyd does not refer to explicit rejection of Christ as the only reason one might be condemned, he does make reference to the freewill defense theodicy, which raises similar issues. That is, in essence, evil exists in the world because God has created a world where creatures have the freedom of choice, and freedom of choice might mean that they would choose evil over love. Boyd states that if this theodicy is accepted then no one can enter God's love without choosing it and conversely no one can be excluded from God's love without choosing it either. He argues, "If even one person could automatically go to heaven without choosing it, the entire freewill defense falls to the ground. Yet many people obviously die without having made a resolved choice for or against God. The postmortem evangelism position is the most natural way of reconciling the need for choice with the fact that in this life choice is often unavailable to people."[78]

Associated with the view that explicit faith in Christ is required for salvation is God's need to discern a person's response. Pinnock maintains that the logic behind posthumous salvation "rests on the insight that God, since he loves humanity, would not send anyone to hell without first ascertaining

---

76. Sanders, "Response to Fackre," 102–6 [104].

77. see Sanders, *No Other*, 180.

78. Boyd, *Across*, 208.

what their response would have been to his grace."[79] Although Pinnock does not here refer to Open Theism, it would appear that this statement is founded upon Pinnock's views on the subject of God's omniscience. In essence, he believes that God does not know what humans will choose until they make their choice. Pinnock has moved beyond the usual Arminian understanding of God's foreknowledge, where God foreknows what choices humans will make, to a position which essentially abandons God's omniscience of all future events.[80] By his own admission, Pinnock is not a truly representative advocate of posthumous salvation, for his understanding of this view is to be held alongside his more dominant inclusivist views on the faith principle.[81] His view on posthumous salvation is, in essence, a postmortem confirmation of the direction of one's faith in God through general revelation. Pinnock states that "decisions in this life set the soul's direction in relation to God, and fuller revelation after death enables the person to pick up where things left off and decide once and for all whether to journey toward or away from God." Furthermore, his Open Theism view, in abandoning God's omniscience, is not a logical precursor to belief in posthumous salvation, nor necessarily typical of others who embrace the opportunity for salvation after death.

Inclusivism

This position advocates that Jesus Christ is the only Savior of the world but it is possible to be saved through Christ without having explicit knowledge of him. That is, one can be saved by placing faith in God on the light that one has received through general revelation. Anderson claims that this would be required in the most elementary principle of justice.[82] Thus, Jesus is ontologically necessary but not epistemologically necessary for salvation, meaning that one can be saved through Christ without knowing the details of Christ or his redemption.[83]

The inclusivist believes that God has not left himself without witness in the world and that salvation of the unevangelized is made possible according to the revelation, though partial, one has of God and his message. That is, a person may be saved on the basis of Christ's work as s/he responds in faith to God. Restrictivists often refer to general revelation as being

---

79. Pinnock, *Wideness*, 168.

80. Pinnock, "God limits His Knowledge," 146, 157.

81. Okholm and Phillips, *Four Views*, 148; Pinnock, *Unbounded Love*, 94–95.

82. Anderson, *Christianity and World Religions*," 146.

83. See Boyd, *Across*, 179.

insufficient to save, but enough revelation to cause the unevangelized to be without excuse. Dale Moody asks, "What kind of God is he who gives man enough knowledge to damn him but not enough to save him?"[84] Anderson concurs, asking, "Might it not be true of the follower of some other religion that the God of all mercy had worked in his heart by his Spirit, bringing him in some measure to realize his sin and need for forgiveness, and enabling him, in the twilight as it were, to throw himself on God's mercy?"[85]

This so-called "faith principle" (that one is saved by faith not by the amount of knowledge one has of God and his ways[86]) is key to inclusivist thinking. In response to the restrictivist opinion that one needs a full understanding of the life and ministry of Christ in order to be saved, inclusivists argue that it is God who saves, not what one knows of the Christian faith and that people are saved by God if they respond in faith, irrespective of how limited their knowledge might be. It was Campbell Morgan who insisted that "no man is saved because he understands the doctrine of the Atonement. He is saved, not by understanding it, but because he fears God, and works righteousness. Oh, the glad and glorious surprise of those ultimate days when we find that there will be those who walked in the light they had, and wrought righteousness, and were acceptable to him; not because of their morality, but by the infinite merit of the Cross, and by the fact that they yielded themselves to the light they possessed."[87] Anderson poignantly asks, "Does ignorance disqualify for grace? If so, where in Scripture do we have the exact amount of knowledge required set out? For *assurance*, no doubt, knowledge is required, but for grace it is not so much knowledge as a right attitude towards God that matters."[88] Inclusivists claim that it would be unthinkable for Jesus, who prayed for his persecutors who had treated him so cruelly: "Father, forgive them, for they do not know what they are doing" (Luke 23:34) to leave the unevangelized without hope and condemn them even though they might not have even heard of his name.

Ryrie makes a valid point in stating that "the *basis* of salvation in every age is the death of Christ; the *requirement* for salvation in every age is faith; the *object* of faith in every age is God; the *content* of faith changes in the various dispensations."[89] Ryrie states that the object of faith of people, like

---

84. See Moody, *Word of Truth*, 59.

85. Anderson, *Christianity and World Religions*, 148–9.

86. Hebrews 11:6 states that "without faith it is impossible to please God, because anyone who comes to him must believe that he exists and that he rewards those who earnestly seek him."

87. Morgan, *Acts of the Apostles*, 281, as cited by Sanders, *No Other*, 224.

88. Anderson, *Christianity*, 99.

89. Ryrie, *Dispensationalism Today*, 123, as cited by Sanders, *No Other*, 44.

Abraham, who lived a couple of millennia before Christ, is God, yet the content of Abraham's saving faith, was that he believed that God would give him a son (Gen. 15:6 "Abraham believed the LORD, and he credited it to him as righteousness" which Paul quotes in Romans 4:3 and in Galatians 3:6 in his argument on justification by faith). Abraham did not have a detailed understanding of Christology, he simply believed what God had said to him which Paul translates into saving faith. He was saved through Christ, but the content of his faith was a trusting relationship with the God who had revealed himself to Abraham. Restrictivists, like Nash, sometimes treat inclusivist understanding of faith with a measure of disparagement, claiming that the object of faith, Jesus, is unimportant to inclusivists and that they have a faith which is nebulous and lacking in biblical content.[90] This indictment is often reactionary and unfair.[91]

Pre-Messianic believers did not know about Jesus, his life, his atoning work, his death or Resurrection, yet in the pages of the New Testament they are spoken about as heroes of faith who had entered into a trusting relationship with God. Anderson asserts that pre-Messianic believers' "knowledge was deficient, their assurance was fitful, but their forgiven status identical with ours."[92] Strong views the possible salvation of the heathen as being through the same "faith principle" that saved Old Testament believers. He writes, "The patriarchs, though they had no knowledge of a personal Christ, were saved by believing in God so far as God had revealed himself to them; and whoever among the heathen are saved, must in like manner be saved by casting themselves as helpless sinners upon God's plan of mercy, dimly shadowed forth in nature and providence. But such faith, even among the patriarchs and heathen, is implicitly a faith in Christ, and would become explicit and conscious trust and submission, whenever Christ were made known to them."[93] This argument is challenged by restrictivist theologians, like Henry, who claim that to compare Old Testament believers with the

90. Nash, "Restrictivism," 113–5.

91. Nash, "Restrictivism," 107–39. This is an example of a restrictivist theologian who is hugely derogatory to theologians of other viewpoints (inclusivist and posthumous salvation). Nash's attempt to make a case for restrictivism against chapters written by Sanders and Fackre is quite embarrassing as he chooses simply to attack the views of his opponents without making a constructive case for his own view. Both authors rightly challenge him over his "extended polemic against alternative views rather than a developed statement of restrictivism" (see Sanders "Response to Nash," 140–9, and Fackre, "Response to Nash," 150–6). Fackre rather provocatively suggests that "perhaps no careful case is made for restrictivism . . . because it is so difficult to do so persuasively."

92. Anderson, *Christianity*, 99.

93. Strong, *Systematic Theology*," 842.

unevangelized overlooks the fact that the former benefited from special (not general) revelation. Henry further claims that this point is not sufficiently answered by inclusivists.[94]

Neither is it merely the Israelites who are commended for their faith, for there also exists true faith outside of the nation of Israel, often referred to as "holy pagans," people who were theologically well-informed,[95] which would include Job,[96] Melchizedek,[97] Lot,[98] Abimelech,[99] Jethro,[100] Rahab,[101] Ruth[102] and the Queen of Sheba.[103] Perhaps the most often quoted example used by inclusivists is Cornelius who was a God-fearing uncircumcised Gentile who prayed regularly and became a follower of Christ. It is claimed that Cornelius received salvation before Peter had arrived to present him with the fullness of salvation that comes from a personal relationship with Christ.[104] Inclusivists often make the distinction between believers and Christians. In Cornelius's case, it is claimed that he was a believer before Peter's visit and later became a Christian through Peter's proclamation of the gospel. Inclusivists contend that not all believers are Christians, but all

94. See Henry, *God, Revelation and Authority*, 369.

95. Pinnock, *Wideness*, 92–93.

96. The Lord's own testimony of Job was that "there is no one on earth like him; he is blameless and upright, a man who fears God and shuns evil" (Job 1:8).

97. Christian anthropologist, Don Richardson has documented many cases where God was redemptively at work with people groups prior to their introduction to the gospel message. He calls this spiritual insight the "Melchizedek factor," see Richardson, *Eternity in Their Hearts*. Melchizedek was a pagan priest who declared a blessing on Abraham. He was said to be a priest of "God Most High" (Gen. 14:18; Heb. 6:20—7:28), worshipping the same God as Abraham, though seemingly without the special revelation that Abraham received.

98. 2 Pet. 2:7 ". . . Lot, a righteous man, who was distressed at the filthy lives of lawless men."

99. See Gen. 20, where Abimelech's fear of God is in stark contrast to Abraham's fear of man.

100. Exod. 2:18, Jethro, a priest of Midian, is referred to as Reuel, meaning a "friend of God."

101. Heb. 11:31; Jas. 2:25 which refer to the former prostitute Rahab as both a hero of faith and as an example of one who was considered righteous.

102. Ruth, a Moabitess, whose friendship of Naomi, her Jewish mother-in-law, is celebrated as a picture of faith and piety in the Old Testament book that bears her name.

103. 1 Kgs 10:1–10; Matt.12:42; Luke 11:31. The Queen of Sheba made a connection between the wisdom of Solomon and the God he served. Jesus used her as an example to condemn the people of his day who had not recognized him.

104. See Acts 10. Both Luther and Calvin agree with this verdict—see Luther, *Lectures on Galatians*, 210, and Calvin, *Institutes*, (Beveridge, "John Calvin," 3.17.4)—though many restrictivists regard Cornelius as an unbeliever before Peter's visit, undermining the inclusivist argument, see for example, Erickson, *How Shall*, 137.

Christians are believers and are usually cautious in not diminishing the importance of the proclamation of the gospel in its fullness, which is only found in Jesus Christ.

Inclusivists would challenge Cyprian's *extra ecclesium nulla salus* as they believe that there is salvation outside the church, but not outside of Jesus Christ. In this, they highlight the work of the Trinity in salvation, in which the Father loves all his creation and desires their salvation, the Son has made salvation possible for all through his redemptive work and the Spirit reaches out universally seeking the lost. That is, "God is free to work universally in various cultural, temporal, geographical and religious contexts."[105] Furthermore, inclusivists recognize the cosmic pre-incarnate work of Christ in revelation, which finds its root in the Logos Christology of the early Church Fathers.[106] Following Vatican II, inclusivism has become the dominant view amongst Roman Catholic theologians and is a growing force amongst evangelicals. Its leading supporters have included: John Wesley, G. C. Morgan, Bernard Ramm, C. S. Lewis, J. N. D. Anderson, John Sanders, Clark Pinnock, and N. T. Wright.[107]

Perhaps one of the most memorable literary illustrations for inclusivism is found in C. S. Lewis's *Chronicles of Narnia: The Last Battle.* Lewis speaks of a man named Emeth who had been brought up in a country where the chief god was Tash. Emeth fought gallantly against Narnia and its God Aslan (the Christ-figure) whom Emeth believed was evil. One day Emeth was welcomed into Aslan's kingdom. The following dialogue ensues:

> "I fell at his feet and thought, Surely this is the hour of death, for the Lion (who is worthy of honour) will know that I have served Tash all my days and not him . . . But the Glorious One bent down his golden head and touched my forehead with his

105. Sanders, *No Other,* 237.

106. It is believed that the supreme revelation was found in the days of Jesus' earthly ministry, but this is not the sole revelation of the Son of God. It is claimed that this "logos Christology" was a forerunner of modern day inclusivism. Many early Christians believed that the Son of God was actively involved in revealing truth and righteousness in some aspects of paganism, for example, Justin Martyr understood the *sperma* (seed) of the universal logos to be present in all, so that all have a measure of divine revelation. See Wilken, "Religious Pluralism," 379–91, and Dupuis, "The Cosmic Christ," 106–20; Justin Martyr, *Second Apology,* chapters 8, 10, 13, as cited by Sanders, *No Other Name,* 239–40.

107. Wesley, *Works,* 6:286; 7:196–9, 258, 353; Morgan, *Acts,* 280–1; Ramm, "Will All Men Be Finally Saved?," 21–33; Lewis, *Last Battle,* 164–5; Anderson, *Christianity,* chapter 5; Sanders, *What About*; Sanders, *No Other*; Pinnock, *Wideness*; Pinnock, *Unbounded Love*; Wright, "Towards a Biblical View," 57. This list is merely illustrative. For a more comprehensive list/historical bibliography, from the first to twenty-first centuries, see Sanders, *No Other,* 267–80.

tongue and said, Son thou art welcome. But I said, Alas, Lord, I am no son of Thine but the servant of Tash. He answered, Child, all service thou hast done to Tash, I account as service done to me . . . I take to me the services which thou hast done to him, for I and he are of such different kinds that no service which is vile can be done to me, and none which is not vile can be done to him. Therefore if any man swear by Tash and keep his oath for the oath's sake, it is by me that he has truly sworn, though he knows it not, and it is I who reward him. And if any man do a cruelty in my name, even though he says the name Aslan, it is Tash whom he serves and by Tash his deed is accepted . . . But I said also (for the truth constrained me), Yes I have been seeking Tash all my days. Beloved, said the Glorious One, unless thy desire had been for me thou wouldst not have sought so long and truly. For all find what they truly seek."

Pluralism

The challenge of pluralism to the restrictivist position was briefly referred to earlier in chapter 1. Pluralism is a view that "Jesus is only one of many saviors available in the world's religions," making Jesus neither "ontologically nor epistemologically necessary for salvation."[108] It argues that other religions are salvific and since this is a view that has been universally rejected by evangelical Christians it remains outside the scope of this book, falling outside the axiom of the finality and particularity of Christ. Pluralism also rejects fundamental doctrines such as the Trinity, the deity of Christ, the Atonement, and the Resurrection, amongst others.

Conclusion

This chapter has sought to introduce the subject in its wider context, setting the parameters of whether grace is available beyond the grave and whether this life is the only arena for salvation.

This subject in its broadest sense, that is, not just the subject of posthumous salvation but of the possibility of salvation to the unevangelized *per se*, is one of the most challenging and provocative subjects in theological studies in the twenty-first century, with, according to Fackre, "no 'knockdown' argument for any one position." Fackre further contends that "we

---

108. Boyd, *Across*, 179.

have to search the Scriptures and be in conversation with one another."[109] Whilst an in-depth evaluation and critique of the various wider hope views contained in this chapter is a subject of great interest, it is beyond the remit of this book, yet I believe that all the wider hope views offer something to the ongoing conversation and are a step in the right direction in challenging the more traditional and widely accepted view of restrictivism.

The various views have points of agreement as well as disagreement. For example, inclusivism joins with restrictivism against the view of posthumous salvation in emphasizing that individual destinies are sealed at the moment of physical death. The view of posthumous salvation agrees with restrictivism and against inclusivism in that a knowledge of the gospel and explicit faith is required for salvation, though they disagree whether this explicit faith must take place before physical death. Inclusivism and posthumous salvation agree against restrictivism that God makes salvation available to all people everywhere in time and space. However, unlike most proponents of the individual theories, I would be more prepared to view the wider hope views as complementary to each other rather than as competitors in the race to find the one supreme answer to challenge the restrictivist position.[110]

Clark Pinnock is a theologian who, at face-value, appears to hold both the views of inclusivism and posthumous salvation simultaneously. Nash claims that these two positions are "logically incompatible,"[111] although Carson does not agree with Nash on their incompatibility. Carson simply states that he cannot understand why anyone would want to hold both views simultaneously. He argues, "If faith that is consciously focused on Jesus is not necessary for salvation, why should people be offered a further chance beyond death? Alternatively, if a further chance is offered beyond death, with the structure of the gospel clearly presented, why should people be thought disadvantaged if they do not hear the gospel in this life? We begin to suspect that we are not dealing with a well thought out theological synthesis."[112] Pinnock's rationale for combining both views is "that decisions in this life set the soul's direction in relation to God, and fuller revelation after death enables the person to pick up where things left off and decide

109. Fackre, "Divine Perseverance," 72.

110. For example, see Sanders, *What About*, 56–61; 102–6. Fackre and Sanders present their views of posthumous salvation and inclusivism respectively and are then invited to critique the other's views. Whilst this is the *raison d'être* of the book, it is still possible to hold one's convictions yet in a complementary rather than exclusive way.

111. Nash, *Is Jesus the Only Savior?*, 149.

112. Carson, *Gagging*, 299–300.

once and for all whether to journey towards or away from God."[113] Pinnock further clarifies his position, stating, "I do not hold to evangelism for the unevangelized after death, as Fackre and Bloesch do. Rather, I contend that those who have had faith in God during their earthly lives, as Hebrews 11:6 indicates, are 'believers,' even if they are not Christians; and I hold that after death, these people encounter the reality of God's grace in Christ for which they had longed."[114]

Essentially, Pinnock's view of posthumous salvation is understood through the lens of his dominating inclusivist understanding.[115] However, Pinnock's intermediate position on posthumous salvation is weak and adds little to the debate. One would imagine that most inclusivists would believe in a postmortem encounter with Christ for all those saved through their response to general revelation anyway, for such an encounter would be inescapable! All Pinnock appears to be claiming for such a postmortem encounter is that unevangelized believers would have their knowledge of God updated when they enter his presence.[116]

All those who hold wider hope views contend for God's universal salvific will, that he is a God who truly desires the salvation of all his creation and will do all within his power to achieve that objective. If this is so, then could it not be that those who hold inclusivist views are correct, but so are those who believe in postmortem salvation, and so are those who believe in universal opportunity before death? Basically, the God of Love will use any and every means of getting his will done. Surely one does not need to choose one view over another. For some, as the Ethiopian eunuch (Acts 8:26–40), God brought alongside him Philip who showed him the way, but it is unlikely that God always chooses to do that. Maybe, there are others who have responded to the light they have been given and truly trusted in God who are later welcomed into the eternal kingdom where their knowledge of Christ is made perfect. Furthermore, is it not possible that for those who have not responded to the partial, dim and diffuse light of general revelation to have opportunity to bow the knee before the Lord who is revealed in his full glory the other side of the grave? Could not all these views be held in tension and as complementary to one another? Would not the "Hound of Heaven" use every available means to bring his loved ones home? Whilst

---

113. Pinnock, *Unbounded Love*, 94–95.

114. Okholm and Phillips, *Four Views*, 148.

115. He deals with "Postmortem Encounter" in *Wideness*, 168–75, but only in conjunction with the "faith principle" of inclusivism.

116. See Pinnock, *Wideness*, 172.

this argument might appear appealing to some, there is no theologian, that I am aware of, who explicitly makes this case.

Lastly, this book is focused upon just one of the wider hope views in preference over the others, namely posthumous salvation. Is this because it is more theologically or biblically credible? Or, do other views have less to commend them? The answers to these questions are twofold. Firstly, the posthumous salvation view has been written about less than its more widely acknowledged relative, inclusivism, in more recent times, although it appears that this view was more widely known and debated in the late nineteenth century. Secondly, the focus of this book has pastoral implications, and the view of posthumous salvation, if biblically and theologically credible, would provide answers that no other view could. As inferred earlier, much of the recent debate has focused on the unevangelized and largely ignored the pastoral theology aspect, which tends to be more subjective. That is, it is one thing to establish a strong polemic in discussing the salvation of those who are the "unknowns" of some far-reached part of the world, but it is another thing altogether to provide real answers to the difficult questions of bereaved families in one's parish ministry. For example, the universal opportunity before death concept does not work for a grieving widow, as it is patently obvious to her that her dearly loved husband did not turn to Christ before death; therefore he cannot have been a spiritual seeker in the first place. Neither does the concept of middle knowledge offer much comfort as, apart from the contextual difficulty of attempting to explain such a philosophical idea to a grieving wife, it offers no assurance that her husband would have responded to the gospel message had he been presented with it. The omniscient God alone knows the answer.

The inclusivist position offers little hope too, especially if her husband had had opportunity to respond to the gospel message, or at least, he did not appear to have any spiritual inclination to the light given to him, indicating again that there is little hope for his salvation. Agnosticism really helps no one in these circumstances. Restrictivism would encourage the grief-stricken wife that her husband might have turned to the Lord in his last moments on earth, but then again, he might not have, and maybe there is nothing to suggest that he did.

However, the concept of posthumous salvation, if theologically and biblically acceptable, offers hope that he might respond to Christ beyond the grave, bringing comfort and consolation in that her dearly loved "departed" will have opportunity to bow the knee in submission and praise to God. Her husband, unrestricted by sin or partial revelation, will indeed meet the God who has always, and will forever, love him, face to face, and be invited to acknowledge and confess the Lord Jesus Christ, the only Savior of the world.

If posthumous salvation is true, this is not only truly good news, but also provides clergy with an apposite pastoral response to the large majority of bereaved they serve.[117]

117. For further discussion on this subject, see chapter 5. Furthermore, posthumous salvation, arguably, offers the most cogent answer to the death of an infant of all the views presented. For example, inclusivism, which relies upon one's response to general revelation is irrelevant in the case of infants as they would not have had the opportunity to respond to the light of general revelation. The question of infant salvation, has had a "long and controversial history," Sanders, *No Other*, 287. For an excellent summary of the issues, see Sanders, *No Other*, 287–305, and for a list of bibliographical and historical surveys, see his footnote 1. Essentially, there have been three proposals. Firstly, that only some are saved, whether they are those who have been baptized according to some sacramental churches, or the elect, according to some Calvinists. The second view is by far the most popular in today's churches of all persuasions, claiming that all who die in infancy will be saved. The third view suggests a probation after death, whereby infants are allowed to grow and mature and accept Christ, a belief that was propounded as early as the fourth century by Gregory of Nyssa, see Dyer, "Unbaptized Infant," 147.

Biblical Evaluation of Posthumous Salvation

Introduction

Following the general introduction to the subject of this book in chapter 1, chapter 2 focused upon the common approaches to the destiny of the unevangelized, also providing an overview of posthumous salvation and outlining the main facets of this position. The rationale for the belief in posthumous salvation was summarized, emphasizing that (i) one's eternal destiny is not necessarily determined at death, but allows for opportunity for salvation beyond the grave, and that (ii) explicit faith in Christ is necessary for salvation.[1] Chapter 3 will now provide an overview on what is, or at least is perceived to be, the biblical arguments for and against posthumous salvation.[2] Theological perspectives will be explored in chapter 4.

This present chapter will firstly evaluate texts that are used by proponents of posthumous salvation in claiming that Christ descended to hell and offered salvation to those there. According to Erickson, the 1 Peter 3:18—4:6 passage plays a crucial role in their argument, though Erickson's

1. The question of whether one's faith needs to be explicit will be raised in Appendix A where it will be argued that inclusivism and posthumous salvation are not mutually exclusive in this respect, as proponents of inclusivism and posthumous salvation often argue, but are actually wider hope bedfellows.

2. Sanders, *No Other*, 178–88, categorizes three kinds of biblical text in support of posthumous salvation, namely, as texts that teach: (i) a person must possess explicit knowledge in Christ to receive salvation; (ii) a person will only be condemned to hell through explicit rejection of Christ and the gospel. As discussed in chapter 2, Sanders's emphasis that posthumous salvation rests heavily on this belief is questionable and unnecessary, for all one needs to believe is that God is just and fair and desires all to have access to the offer of salvation. Thus, the argument moves from biblical exegesis to theology; (iii) Christ's descent to hell and his preaching of the gospel there.

assertion itself will be shown to be arguable.[3] Furthermore, this chapter will also include other biblical passages that are commonly used to support the belief that a person's eternal destiny is not determined at death.[4] Conversely, the most often quoted proof-texts used by opponents of posthumous salvation are Luke 16:19–31 and Hebrews 9:27.[5] The selected texts in this chapter which question the duration of one's opportunity for salvation will be evaluated through the grammatico-historical method of interpretation, largely on account of this being the method that is most used by evangelical scholars writing on this subject. Bray declares that grammatico-historical criticism relies heavily on exegetical principles and the belief that the meaning of a word is determined from its context and usage elsewhere. Furthermore, it aims to discover the meaning of the passage as both originally intended by the author and as would have been understood by the original recipients and therefore is the most valuable hermeneutical tool for this exercise.[6]

The temptation of venturing beyond biblical passages which deal with, or at least are perceived as dealing with, death being the end of one's opportunity for salvation, will be resisted as outside the scope of this chapter. The associated subjects of the Second Coming, hell, wrath, and judgment are quite distinct to the question posed by this book on whether opportunity for salvation exists beyond the course of this life. It is accepted that one might believe in God's wrath, divine judgment, and the existence of hell, in whatever form that they might be understood, and still believe in posthumous salvation. Furthermore, the prospect of posthumous salvation

3. Erickson, *How Shall*, 165.

4. In addition to apparent "descent" passages (1 Pet. 3:18—4:6; Eph. 4:8–10; Acts 2:27; Rom. 10:6–7), Matt. 12:32 (Anyone who speaks a word against the Son of Man will be forgiven, but anyone who speaks against the Holy Spirit will not be forgiven, either in this age or in the age to come) and 1 Cor. 15:29 which refers to a "baptism for the dead" will be evaluated to determine whether Jesus actually communicated forgiveness of sins in the "age to come" in the manner that some proponents of posthumous salvation would argue, and to ascertain whether Paul endorsed posthumous baptism. Nash, "Restrictivism," 128, a severe and determined critic of any view that is not restrictivism, claims that supporters of posthumous salvation apparently appeal to five major texts (1 Pet. 3:18—4:6; Acts 17:31; 2 Tim. 4:8; 1 John 4:17; and John 5:25–29) to support their theory. More specifically, Nash is critiquing Fackre's position, and challenges his use of these texts as lacking in serious exegesis.

5. See, for example, Berkhof, *Systematic Theology*, 693; Erickson, "Is there," 141, who also quotes Psalm 49 and Revelation 20:11–15; Grudem, "Christ Preaching Through Noah," 203–39 [230]; Feinberg, "1 Peter 3:18–20," 303–36, [326]. 2 Cor. 5:10 "For we must all appear before the judgment seat of Christ, that each one may receive what is due to him for the things done while in the body, whether good or bad," which is sometimes used to indicate that one's conduct in this life, and not after death, is what determines our final award at the judgment, will also be evaluated.

6. Bray, *Biblical Interpretation*, 354.

is not necessarily to be associated with universal salvation, as it remains a possibility that even should it be accepted as a biblical/theological option, it does not necessitate that everyone will accept God's posthumous offer of salvation.

Biblical passages used in support of posthumous salvation

As stated above, the biblical texts evaluated in this chapter are limited to those that deal with the belief that death ends a person's opportunity for salvation. In this regard, the most often quoted verses in support of posthumous salvation are the "descent to hell" passages, especially 1 Peter 3:18—4:6.[7] Some proponents of this view claim that Jesus, between his death and Resurrection, descended to Hades and proclaimed the gospel to the dead, many of whom subsequently repented and were led out of Hades.[8]

---

7. For example, Leckie, *World to Come*, 90–93; Erickson, *How Shall*, 165–75; Fackre, "Divine Perseverance," 81–84; MacCulloch, *Harrowing*, 45–65.

8. Leckie, *World to Come*, 93, is typical of this position, stating, "Peter's reference to the ministry of Christ in the Underworld thus remains the earliest and most important of those utterances which show . . . that it [early Christian thought] did not object to the idea that some of the dead might hear good tidings and be delivered from the Prison-house of Souls." Beasley-Murray (*Baptism*, 258–9) concurs, asserting that "the primary lesson in the writer's mind is to exemplify the universal reach of Christ's redeeming work and the divine willingness that all should know it. The preaching of Christ between his cross and his Easter is intended to prove that the wickedest generation of history is not beyond the bounds of his pity and the scope of his redemption, hence there is hope for *this* generation, that has sinned even more greatly than the Flood generation in refusing the proclamation of a greater Messenger of God." Cranfield ("Interpretation," 372) makes a similar claim by affirming that there is a "hint within the Canon of Scripture," although ambiguous and obscure, that Christ was active as the Savior of the world between Good Friday afternoon and Easter morning. He further suggests "that those who in subsequent ages have died without ever having had a real chance to believe in Christ are not outside the scope of His mercy and will not perish eternally without being given in some way . . . an opportunity to hear the gospel and accept Him as their Saviour." MacCulloch (*Harrowing*, 50) not only asserts the same, but proclaims that many other interpretations are ingenious and were "arrived at because the plain meaning of the passages conflicted with the interpreters' views of the nature of life beyond the grave, or of the impossibility of enlightenment or pardon there." Pannenberg (*Apostles' Creed*, 95) similarly declares that "salvation from future judgement is still made available to those who during their lifetime encountered neither Jesus nor the Christian message." Pinnock (*Wideness*, 169) likewise, though not as assured, considers the Petrine passage to provide the scriptural support for posthumous salvation, stating, "It *seems* to have some [scriptural support] in Peter's word about the Gospel being preached to the dead, where the text *sounds as if* the dead are given opportunity to respond to Christ." Italics mine.

The majority of scholars however have not held to the above position of Christ's descent and preaching in Hades.[9] Nash, for example, announces the danger in attempting to use unclear and controversial texts to ground any key theological concept.[10] Sanders similarly makes reference to the obscurity of a text whose precise meaning has been the subject of debate for nearly two millennia. He believes that although Christ on his descent to hell did preach, he did not preach evangelistically. Rather, it was for the purpose of those who died with a faith commitment to God though he acknowledges that he, like others, does not have an air-tight argument.[11] Jobes also asserts that this "intriguing passage is fraught with problems that obscure its interpretation—text-critical problems, grammatical ambiguities, lexical uncertainties, theological issues, as well as the question of what literary and theological backgrounds the author is assuming."[12] Even so, Jobes emphasizes that the interpretation of such an obscure and ambiguous passage should be governed by its immediate context within the letter.[13]

Erickson offers wise advice, contending that if the Petrine "descent" passage is to be used as a scriptural foundation for posthumous salvation then two steps are required. Firstly, it is necessary to demonstrate that the passage actually teaches that Christ preached the gospel to those in Hades during the interim period between his death and Resurrection, and that he provided them with a genuine opportunity for salvation. Secondly, provided the first step can be proved, it is then necessary to demonstrate that the offer of salvation made by Christ on that occasion is available to all persons who live and die in subsequent generations.[14]

1 Peter 3:18–20 — Christ preached to the 'spirits in prison'

> "For Christ died for sins once for all, the righteous for the unrighteous, to bring you to God. He was put to death in the body but made alive by the Spirit, through whom also he went and

9. Erickson, *How Shall*, 172.

10. Nash, "Response to Fackre," 97.

11. Sanders, "Response to Fackre," 105–6.

12. Jobes, *1 Peter*, 237. For a survey of this passage's history of interpretation see Dalton, *Christ's Proclamation*, 15–41; Reicke, *Disobedient Spirits*, 7–51; Feinberg, "1 Peter 3:18–20," 309–12.

13. Jobes, *1 Peter*, 237. That is, its link with 3:13–17 and the claim that it is better to suffer for doing good than for doing evil, and 3:22, which emphasizes that even though Christ suffered unjustly for doing good, that suffering was not the defeat that it appeared, but was a victory over angels, authorities, and powers.

14. Erickson, *How Shall*, 165–6.

preached to the spirits in prison who disobeyed long ago when God waited patiently in the days of Noah while the ark was being built. In it only a few people, eight in all, were saved through water."

As previously stated, this passage is viewed as both the most important and controversial text used in support of posthumous salvation by many commentators.[15] The divergence of opinion on how this passage is to be interpreted is caused by the way one answers the following questions. Although many commentators raise the issues, Grudem's analysis of the questions and possible answers is particularly succinct, and for that reason will be used to provide a structure to the discussion in this section, though I do not necessarily agree with all of Grudem's conclusions.[16]

1. Who are the spirits in prison?

    a. Unbelievers who have died?

    b. Old Testament believers who have died?

    c. Fallen angels?

2. What did Christ preach?

    a. Second chance for repentance?

    b. Completion of redemptive work?

    c. Final condemnation?

3. When did he preach?

    a. In the days of Noah?

    b. Between his death and Resurrection?

    c. After his Resurrection?

---

15. For example, Sanders, *No Other*, 185; Erickson, "Is there," 144. Those who use this passage to support the notion of posthumous salvation link 3:19 "spirits in prison" with the "dead" in 4:6 ("For this is the reason the gospel was preached even to those who are now dead, so that they might be judged according to human standards in regard to the body, but live according to God in regard to the spirit"), though most contemporary interpreters do not link these verses, see Achtemeier, *1 Peter*, 291; Banstra, "Making Proclamation,"120–4; Dalton, *Christ's Proclamation*, 42–51; Davids, *First Epistle of Peter*, 154; Elliott, *1 Peter*, 730–1; Hillyer, *1 and 2 Peter, Jude*, 122; Kistemaker, *Peter and Jude*, 163–4; Michaels, *1 Peter*, 237–8.

16. Grudem, "Christ Preaching Through Noah," 203.

Types of interpretation

Feinberg claims that "one could hold to any number of positions and not be thought to be on the fringe."[17] When one takes into account all the possible answers to the above questions, there arises a number of possible positions,[18] namely:

A. Christ "in spirit" preached through Noah repentance and righteousness, when he was building the ark, to those who were unbelieving humans then on earth, but are now "spirits in prison" (in Hades).[19]

B. After Christ died, he went and preached to people in Hades, proclaiming a message of repentance and righteousness, offering them a chance to repent and believe for salvation.[20]

C. Following Christ's death, he went and preached to people in Hades declaring that he had triumphed over them and that their condemnation was final.[21]

---

17. Feinberg, "1 Peter 3:18–20," 312.

18. Both Grudem and Erickson highlight the following five positions [A–E] identically (see Erickson, *How Shall*, 168; Grudem, "Christ Preaching Through Noah," 204–6), though Erickson does offer a further alternative of Pannenberg's view that preaching to the "spirits in prison" should not be being taken literally, but symbolically, conveying the idea that redemption is universal in its extent or influence. Pannenberg (*Jesus: God and Man*, 272) speaks of the "increasingly mythological conception of Jesus' preaching in the realm of the dead or in hell" in relation to the statement in 1 Peter. He further claims that "it is not, like the crucifixion, a historical event." Erickson, 171, questions Pannenberg's theology, claiming that it stands outside the authority of both biblical and ecclesiastical tradition. Pannenberg's is a minority view and for that reason will not be considered in this overview. Sanders, *No Other*, 184–6, makes reference to a seventh view [F], though he lists just four, what he considers, main views [A, B, E, F]. See also Feinberg, "1 Peter 3:18–20," 307 who recognizes viewpoint [F].

19. See Augustine, Letter 164 to Evodius, *Letters, 156–210 Epistulae*, 69–71; Aquinas, T. "Christ's Descent," art. 2, reply to obj. 3. This view was frequently dismissed because Augustine, who first proposed it, took "in prison" metaphorically to refer to the "darkness of ignorance" in which the unbelievers lived, see Grudem, "Christ Preaching Through Noah," 205. Grudem interprets "spirits in prison" in terms of those who were unbelieving humans *then*, but are *now* "spirits in prison." Apart from this difference, it would appear that Grudem and Feinberg have essentially followed Augustine's argument.

20. See Fackre, "Divine Perseverance," 81–84; Cranfield, "Interpretation," 369–72; Leckie, *World to Come*, 93; Beasley-Murray, *Baptism*, 258–9.

21. Reicke, *Disobedient Spirits*, 44–45, lists several seventeenth-century supporters of this view. He refers to it as the orthodox Lutheran theory.

D. Following Christ's death, he went to proclaim release to people who had repented just before they died in the Flood. Christ led them from imprisonment in Purgatory to heaven.[22]

E. After Christ died, or between his Resurrection and ascension, Christ descended into Hades and proclaimed his triumph over the fallen angels who had sinned by marrying human women before the Flood.[23]

F. Following Christ's death, he went to proclaim release to the Old Testament believers in Hades and led them to heaven.[24]

Whilst it is not possible to provide a comprehensive study or a detailed exegesis of this biblical passage in the space available, I wish to question whether the view of Christ going to preach to the inhabitants of Hades inviting them to repent and receive salvation [B], which many proponents of posthumous salvation use as a key text, is the most credible or convincing solution. Each view will be evaluated in the light of the three questions raised by Grudem in an attempt to ascertain their strengths and weaknesses and subsequently the credibility of the Petrine text being used in supporting the concept of posthumous salvation. A detailed evaluation of the merits, or otherwise, of each option is beyond the limits of this book.

Evaluation of the alternatives

WHO ARE THE "SPIRITS IN PRISON"?

The first question relates to whether those referred to as "spirits in prison" (1 Pet. 3:19) were humans or angels. The word "spirits" (*pneumasin*) can refer to both angelic spirits or humans depending on the context.[25] It would

22. This view has been common amongst Roman Catholic interpreters. See Reicke, *Disobedient Spirits*, 42–44; Dalton, *Christ's Proclamation*, 30–31.

23. Grudem ("Christ Preaching," n. 5, 204) claims that this is probably the dominant view today, primarily because of the influence of Selwyn's commentary (see Selwyn, *First Epistle of Peter*) and also the work of Dalton. This view rests heavily upon the extra-biblical Jewish tradition of Enoch going to proclaim a message of condemnation to disobedient angels, in 1 Enoch, being well-known to Peter's readers.

24. Sanders, *No Other*, 183–4, argues that there were two main schools of thought that developed in the early church with regards to the purpose of the descent as giving salvation to the dead. Firstly, Christians such as Ignatius of Antioch, Irenaeus, and Tertullian limited the dead to OT patriarchs and prophets [view F]. Secondly, those who held that Christ released any who desired salvation from the realm of hell, which was the view preferred by Clement of Alexandria, Origen, Athanasius, and others [view B].

25. For human spirit, see Matt. 27:50 "And when Jesus had cried out again in a loud voice, he gave up his spirit"; Luke 23:46 "Jesus called out with a loud voice, 'Father, into

appear that many contemporary commentators claim that the word "spirit" is never used to refer to the human spirit without further specification or definition from the context, though others, like Grudem, disagree with this claim.[26] Kelly, for example, argues that "it is highly improbable that *spirits* denotes the spirits of dead human beings."[27] However, Grudem argues that 1 Peter 3:19 is not an example of *pneumasin* being used without definition from its context, for the "spirits in prison" are those "who disobeyed long ago when God waited patiently in the days of Noah while the ark was being built" (1 Pet. 3:20).

Therefore, to understand the context of "spirits in prison" it is necessary to examine four defining phrases in verse 20, namely:

- who disobeyed.
- in the days of Noah.
- when God waited patiently.
- while the ark was being built.

Firstly, the Genesis narrative indicates that it was human beings who disobeyed God. In Genesis 6:5–13, which precedes the command to build the ark, human sin is identified as the cause for God deciding to flood the world. God does not state that he is sorry that he has made angels, but is sorry that he has made man (v. 6), for it is not the violence and wickedness of the angels that provokes God's wrath, but the violence and wickedness of humans (vv. 5, 11, 12, 13), and consequently, God decides to blot out humans, not fallen angels (vv. 6, 13). The New Testament testimony affirms, with reference to the Flood, that it was the people who disobeyed, not angels. For example, Matthew 24:37–39[28] and Luke 17:26–27 emphasize

your hands I commit my spirit'"; Acts 7:59 "While they were stoning him, Stephen prayed, 'Lord Jesus, receive my spirit'"; for angelic spirit (or demon), see, Matt. 8:16 "When evening came, many who were demon-possessed were brought to him, and he drove out the spirits with a word and healed all the sick"; Matt. 10:1 "He called his twelve disciples to him and gave them authority to drive out evil spirits and to heal every disease and sickness."

26. Selwyn, *First Epistle*, 199; Dalton, *Christ's Proclamation*, 147: Davids, *First Epistle*, 140; Elliot, *1 Peter*, 656; Kelly, *Epistles of Peter and of Jude*, 154; Kistemaker, *Peter and Jude*, 143; Michaels, *1 Peter*, 208. Grudem, however, claims that no examples of *pneuma* meaning "angelic spirits" have been found without further definition from the context either, see Grudem, "Christ Preaching," 207–8.

27. Kelly, *Epistles*, 154. Italics Kelly.

28. "As it was in the days of Noah, so it will be at the coming of the Son of Man. For in the days before the Flood, people were eating and drinking, marrying and giving in marriage, up to the day Noah entered the ark; and they knew nothing about what would happen until the Flood came and took them all away. That is how it will be at the

human disregard for the impending judgment. Furthermore, the weight of the extra-biblical evidence for human disobedience being the cause of the Flood is substantial. For example, the Sibylline Oracles maintain that Noah exhorted people to repent from their wickedness, but they instead disobeyed and ridiculed him.[29]

Secondly, the "spirits in prison" were said to be disobedient "when God waited patiently" which, as Grudem claims, suggests that God was waiting for them to repent, otherwise there would not be any reason for Peter to mention the patience of God.[30] Neither Old nor New Testaments ever teach the possibility of fallen angels having a chance to repent,[31] yet if Peter is making reference to humans who disobeyed, it would be consistent with what he writes in his second epistle of God's long-suffering to humans, in that "the Lord is not slow in keeping his promise, as some understand slowness. He is patient with you, not wanting anyone to perish, but everyone to come to repentance" (2 Pet. 3:9).

Thirdly, there is extensive Jewish and early Christian tradition about Noah preaching to those around him. In 2 Peter 2:5, he is referred to as a "preacher of righteousness," while Clement writes that "Noah preached repentance and those who obeyed were saved."[32] Thus Grudem contends that since Noah is frequently referred to as a preacher of righteousness to those around him during the building of the ark, this "should at least prompt us to consider the possibility that when Peter speaks of preaching "to spirits in prison who formerly disobeyed . . . during the building of the ark," he is in some way alluding to the preaching activity of Noah, familiar to his readers from Jewish tradition."[33]

---

coming of the Son of Man."

29. Sibylline Oracles, 1:171–2. See Grudem, "Christ Preaching," 216–7, who lists forty-five texts from every strand of Jewish tradition, which is to be compared with three texts that support a tradition of angelic sin at the time of the Flood. He writes, "The overwhelming weight of extra-biblical tradition—as well as the biblical evidence itself—emphasizes human sinners, not angels, as the most likely to be meant by Peter's phrases."

30. Grudem, "Christ Preaching," 217–8. He also states that the word "waited" *apekdechomai* "has the nuance of hopeful or expectant waiting for something to happen." However, it would not be unfeasible to understand the "spirits in prison" who were disobedient as a reference to fallen angels [view E] with the phrase "God waited patiently in the days of Noah" as a reference to the people of Noah's day to repent of their evil ways, especially since, according to some Jewish intertestamental literature, the fallen angels were responsible for the Flood.

31. Though Feinberg, "1 Peter 3:18–20," does allow for the possibility since the Bible does not explicitly teach that fallen angels cannot repent.

32. Lightfoot, "First Clement," ch 7, v.6. See also Sibylline Oracles, 1.128–9; 150–98.

33. Grudem, "Christ Preaching," 219.

Those who would claim that angelic spirits are being referred to [see position E] rely on the unproven assumption that Peter's readers are aware of the use of *pneuma* in 1 Enoch, which refers to "angels who sinned and were consigned to a place of punishment awaiting final judgment,"[34] where Enoch went to the underworld and preached to them.[35] A strong appeal is made to Jewish apocryphal and intertestamental literature where angels are linked to the disobedience that occasioned the Flood, that is, the "sons of God" who married the "daughters of men" (Gen. 6:2) were angels.[36] This identification is also based on linking this text to 2 Peter 2:4 and Jude 6.[37] Once this connection is made, 1 Peter 3:19 is then interpreted as Christ preaching to angels who were disobedient in the days of Noah. Jeremias contends that Christ's going to preach to the spirits in prison the possibility of repentance is "intentionally contrasted with Enoch's going and proclaiming to them that their plea for forgiveness will never be granted."[38] Whilst this view of the "spirits in prison" has much to commend it, especially since there was considerable interest in angels in the Jewish tradition at this time, there are also significant difficulties.

Firstly, there is no certainty that the "sons of God" in Genesis 6:2 are angels.[39] Their being angels is disputed especially in the light of Matthew 22:30 where Jesus stated that angels do not marry.[40] Feinberg correctly as-

34. Dalton, *Christ's Proclamation*, 166–8; Cranfield, "The Interpretation," 370. See 1 Enoch 10; 11–16; 18:13–16.

35. 1 Enoch, chapters 6, 12–16. 1 Enoch apparently embellishes Gen. 6:1–4 (where the sons of God married the daughters of men) which immediately precedes the Noah narrative. According to 1 Enoch, the "Watchers were fallen angels who had abandoned heaven (12.4), slept with human women (15.3), produced children, referred to as 'giants' from whose bodies 'evil spirits' have come. These evil spirits have taught people 'deeds of shame, injustice and sin' (13.2) and will continue to corrupt the earth until 'the day of the great conclusion, until the great age is consummated, until everything is concluded' (16.1) . . . These 'spirits' that came from the bodies of the giants fathered by the Watchers through human women were the cause of the human evil that led to the great Flood during the time of Enoch's grandson, Noah," see Jobes, *1 Peter*, 244.

36. Jubilees, 10:4–5; 1 Enoch, 67:8–13. This would appear to be the most popular modern view, see Donelson, *I & II Peter and Jude*, 112.

37. 2 Pet. 2:4 "For if God did not spare angels when they sinned, but sent them to hell, putting them into gloomy dungeons to be held for judgment"; Jude 6 "And the angels who did not keep their positions of authority but abandoned their own home—these he has kept in darkness, bound with everlasting chains for judgment on the great Day."

38. Cited by Cranfield, "Interpretation," 370.

39. For more information see Grudem, "Christ Preaching," 212, who claims that "the Targums and Rabbinic literature are unanimous in viewing the 'sons of God' as human beings."

40. "At the Resurrection people will neither marry nor be given in marriage; they

serts that "Genesis 6 is another notoriously problematic passage, and resting the exegesis of one problem passage on the exegesis of another problem passage is a very risky hermeneutical procedure."[41] Secondly, neither 2 Peter 2:4 nor Jude 6 explicitly state that the angels were disobedient in the time of Noah. Thirdly, the evidence from Enoch and intertestamental literature is inconclusive.[42] It is impossible to know whether Peter's readers were aware of 1 Enoch and Enoch's descent to the underworld. This view is even more problematic for the Gentile readers of Peter's epistle who might have been ignorant of this tradition. Although Jobes argues that "Peter's allusion to the tradition of the Watchers does not necessarily require a literary knowledge of the book of 1 Enoch" as the tradition might have been more widely known, much in the way that many people today are familiar with the idea of Purgatory, but would not be able to make reference to the religious texts in which the doctrine is stated.[43] Feinberg contends that "appealing to Enoch gives us a clue as to what Peter *could* mean. Only the context of 1 Peter 3 can tell us what it does mean. Arguing that Peter speaks of angels because Enoch does . . . apart from any direct evidence from the context of 1 Peter 3 begs the question."[44]

Some have asked why Peter refers to "spirits" if he has in mind humans? Whilst it is possible that the phrase "spirits in prison" might refer to those imprisoned at the time the preaching took place, it is not necessarily so. It is equally possible to understand the term "spirits in prison" (v. 19) as referring to those who are in Hades now, but who were formerly human beings on earth in the time of Noah. The NASB translates verse 19, "He went and made proclamation to the spirits now in prison, who were once disobedient, when the patience of God kept waiting in the days of Noah, during the construction of the ark." Grudem states, "It is quite natural to speak in terms of a person's present status even when describing a past action which occurred when the person did not have the status. For example, it would be perfectly correct to say, 'Queen Elizabeth was born in 1926,' even though she did not become Queen until long after 1926."[45] Therefore, to understand

---

will be like the angels in heaven."

41. Feinberg, "1 Peter 3:18–20," 323.

42. Feinberg claims that it is "overrated," see Feinberg, "1 Peter 3:18–20," 321, yet Michaels claims that Feinberg's own view "must be judged a failure," Michaels, *1 Peter*, 210.

43. Jobes, *1 Peter*, 245.

44. Feinberg, "1 Peter 3:18–20," 322.

45. Grudem, "Christ Preaching," 209. This is the way that the majority of commentators interpret 4:6. The NIV actually inserts the word "now" to make this explicit, "For this is the reason the gospel was preached even to those who are *now* dead, so that they

"spirits in prison" to mean that Christ preached to those who are now "spirits in prison" (Hades) but who at the time of preaching in Noah's day were human beings living on earth, remains a possibility.[46]

Whilst there is no place for dogmatism in attempting to understand a most difficult passage, those who claim "spirits in prison" refers to human spirits would disqualify viewpoint [E] from being a viable alternative. Conversely, those who maintain that "spirits in prison" refers to angelic spirits would exclude all other views, including [B] which proponents of posthumous salvation often solicit to support their theory.

What did Christ proclaim?

The word "preached" *kēryssō* in 1 Peter 3:19 is to be understood from the immediate context. Feinberg argues, "There is nothing implicit in the meaning of the word which suggests the content of the heralding, but only that proclaiming or heralding is done. Moreover, usage of the word in the NT is inconclusive as to its meaning in 1 Peter 3:19."[47] Reicke proposes five options of what might have been preached: (a) he offered the spirits, at least some, salvation; (b) he urged them to repent; (c) he confirmed their eternal damnation; (d) he proclaimed the secret of the gospel, without any information of their release; (e) he showed them his true glory, thereby putting them to shame.[48] To this list Feinberg adds: (f) he announced the release of Old Testament saints from Hades to be transferred to heaven; (g) if Christ preached at his ascension, then the content was the announcement to the evil spirits of his victory over them.[49]

One's response to what Christ actually proclaimed will be guided by one's answer to the earlier question of who were the "spirits in prison," humans or angels. If it is assumed that the "spirits" were angelic, then the probable message to the evil spirits would be the announcement of his victory over them. This would also link contextually with 3:22 as Donelson asserts, "The imagery of 3:22 and the example of Enoch suggest that Christ does not offer forgiveness but instead announces to the spirits their final defeat and subjugation. Perhaps the victories described in 3:18 and 3:22 provide the content."[50]

---

might be judged according to men in regard to the body, but live according to God in regard to the spirit."

46. Grudem, "Christ Preaching," 210; Feinberg, "1 Peter 3:18–20," 330.

47. Feinberg, "1 Peter 3:18–20," 325.

48. Reicke, *Disobedient Spirits*, 119.

49. Feinberg, "1 Peter 3:18–20," 325–6.

50. Donelson, *I & II Peter*, 112.

However, if one assumes that the "spirits" refer to humans, as do Grudem, Feinberg, and Erickson, then it is to be argued that *kēryssō* could not mean condemnation. Grudem contends that the phrase "when God waited patiently" is linked with those "who disobeyed long ago" (v. 20), suggesting that the preaching to the "spirits in prison" calls for repentance by those who disobeyed, otherwise the mention of God waiting patiently would be irrelevant.[51] Furthermore, Grudem claims that if only a proclamation of condemnation was in view, Peter would need to have said something like "proclaimed condemnation" (*katakrima*) or "proclaimed judgment" (*krisin*) since the suggestion of preaching of repentance would be otherwise understood.[52]

Erickson argues that *kēryssō* could not be taken as the proclamation of bad news or condemnation, as it would be inconsistent with the rest of Jesus' preaching. Whilst there is record of Jesus speaking harshly to the Pharisees, the idea of Jesus "lording it over" those who were already "in prison," is questionable. Furthermore, the message of condemnation does not fit in with the overall context of bearing witness and giving account of one's faith with "gentleness and respect" (v. 15).[53] Feinberg similarly asks, "Were not their imprisonment and eternal damnation reprehension enough? The picture one gets of Christ is a picture of a merciless victor who has no concern for those whom he has defeated. That simply does not square with other 'biblical' portraits of the Lord."[54] However, despite the emotive terminology of "lording it over" and "merciless victor," both the views of Feinberg and Erickson are essentially valid if one concludes that the "spirits in prison" refer to humans, and would therefore disqualify view [C]. Yet, as Donelson argues, if fallen angels/evil spirits are in view, then the proclamation could quite legitimately refer to "their final defeat and subjugation."[55]

View [F], which holds that Christ proclaimed release to Old Testament believers, is an unlikely interpretation as it does not cohere with the immediate context. Apart from this, there is no apparent reason why such

51. Grudem, "Christ Preaching," 224. Though the two phrases need not be linked as it remains a possibility that those who "disobeyed long ago" might refer to the fallen angels/evil spirits, whilst "God waited patiently" is a reference to either God's wait for the ark to be built or for humans to repent. Furthermore, according to Kelly (*Epistles*, 155), "the abode of the dead is nowhere else depicted as a gaol in biblical or extra-canonical literature."

52. Grudem, "Christ Preaching," 224.

53. Erickson, *How Shall*, 169.

54. Feinberg, "1 Peter 3:18–20," 328.

55. Donelson, *I & II Peter*, 112.

a proclamation should be made to those who disobeyed during the time of Noah, rather than to all believers who died pre-Christ.[56]

View [D], which holds that Christ preached the completion of redemption to those who repented just before they died in the Flood, has similar difficulties to [F]. Firstly, this view is based on a mere assumption since there is no such reference to repentance from this group of people in the account the Flood. Secondly, if others in Old Testament times who had repented were saved, why should it be thought that this group is any different? Why should they be the focus of this preaching by Christ and not any other group?

As previously stated, if our passage points towards Christ preaching to fallen angels/evil spirits, then view [E] is to be accepted and all others, including [B] which is used to support posthumous salvation, are to be rejected. If, however, this passage points towards Christ preaching a message of repentance, not condemnation, to humans who disobeyed in the time of Noah, then views [C], [D], [E] and [F] are ruled out. These findings however would be consistent with view [A] (Christ preached through Noah when the ark was being built) and [B] (Christ preached between his death and Resurrection, giving those who disobeyed in Noah's day the opportunity to repent and be saved). Therefore, to decide between view [A] and [B] it is necessary to discover when the preaching took place, as will be discussed in the following section.

WHEN DID CHRIST PREACH?

Assuming that the "spirits" refer to humans,[57] the two main interpretative options concerning at what point Christ preached to the "spirits in prison" are either the time after his death (or Resurrection) or during the time that Noah was building the ark, namely, viewpoint [B] or [A] respectively.

A key issue in answering this dilemma is the reference to the days of Noah who was building an ark. If view [B] is to be accepted, that Christ preached to the disembodied spirits following his death, then an explanation of why those who disobeyed in the days of Noah are singled out, is required. For if Christ is preaching in the underworld, it would be expected that he would preach to all present, not just those who disobeyed in the time of Noah. Beasley-Murray argues that those who lived at this time were mentioned because they were "the wickedest generation of history" and if they were not beyond the limits of God's mercy then this gives evidence of "the universal

56. Grudem, "Christ Preaching," 225.

57. If they refer to angelic spirits, the argument for this passage being a biblical basis for posthumous salvation is lost anyway.

reach of Christ's redeeming work."[58] However, the question of why this group and not the people of Sodom and Gomorrah, for example, still needs to be explained. Erickson suggests that Beasley-Murray has turned a plausible explanation into a probable one, "but with no further evidence than the theory itself."[59] The dilemma of the reference to those who disobeyed in Noah's time is solved if Christ actually preached through Noah in his pre-incarnate state. However, in modern times, this view has fallen out of favor due to Augustine's figurative understanding which caused some commentators to either criticize or dismiss its fanciful "spiritualized" interpretations, such as "prison" referring to the spiritual bondage of people in that day.[60] It is claimed that such use of "prison" was not intended by Peter. Dalton refers to this as "an unreal allegorization foreign to the thought of 1 Peter."[61] The adapted view of Christ preaching in his pre-existent form through Noah, as adopted by Grudem and Feinberg, has withdrawn itself from such whimsical interpretation through emphasizing that such explanations are not essential to this view.

The real acid-test of all positions, not least views [A] and [B], is how well a view fits with the immediate context. Dalton has objected to view [A], claiming that it has no link with the larger context.[62] This criticism itself will be evaluated below. View [B] which proclaims that Christ preached the gospel to the "spirits in prison" sometime after his death does not cohere with the context where Peter is encouraging fellow believers to stand firm and to share their faith even in the midst of persecution. Grudem poignantly states that if Peter "then proceeds to tell them that even the worst of sinners in all history, the generation of the Flood, can be given another chance to repent after they have died, he would then be defeating his purpose in writing: what need would there be for believers to endure suffering now if those who refuse to become Christians now because of the cost involved can repent after death? And what point is there in enduring suffering as a Christian now if there is another chance to be saved after death?"[63] Again, it is necessary for advocates of this view to explain why only sinners in this one ancient generation are given the opportunity for salvation. What about those that had no opportunity in this life to hear the word of God and repent?

58. Beasley-Murray, *Baptism*, 258.

59. Erickson, *How Shall*, 174.

60. Cranfield, "Interpretation," 370, refers to it as a far-fetched position. France, "Exegesis in Practice," doesn't even mention this position in his study on 1 Pet. 3:18–20.

61. Dalton, *Christ's Proclamation*, 44.

62. Dalton, *Christ's Proclamation*, 44.

63. Grudem, "Christ Preaching," 229–30. See also Feinberg, "1 Peter 3:18–20," 332.

It is quite remarkable that in evaluating the evidence for and against views [A] and [B], Grudem, Feinberg, and Erickson claim that view [B] should be ineligible since the concept of having an opportunity of salvation after death is irreconcilable with the teaching of Scripture. All three theologians offer two biblical texts to support their thesis, namely, Luke 16:19–31 and Hebrews 9:27. Both of these texts will be evaluated later in this chapter. Feinberg and Erickson also refer to even more questionable texts of Revelation 20:11–15 and Psalm 49. The manner in which all three proof-text on this subject causes one to ask whether they have made an *a priori* decision against the opportunity of salvation after death and then "automatically" quote the long-established and accepted texts as apparent scriptural proof without further inquiry.[64] The value of such Scriptures will be assessed later in this chapter.

Despite Dalton's contention that view [A] is not linked with the larger context, there is actually evidence of a considerable relationship. Firstly, the immediate context of this passage in 1 Peter 3 is one of Peter encouraging persecuted Christians, informing them that it is better to suffer for what is right than for the wrong reason (v. 17). Peter then draws on Christ as the supreme example of one who suffered unjustly for the right reason (v. 18), but for Christ there was ultimate glory and vindication (v. 22). The challenge to these persecuted Christians is that glory and vindication will also follow suffering, as with Christ. In this context, how then might verses 19–20 fit in? Christ suffered as a righteous individual for the benefit of others. "Just as he was put to death by the hands of others, he will also be raised from the dead by another, the Holy Spirit."[65] Similarly, if Christians will allow themselves to be ill-treated by others, another (God) will make sure that they too will be vindicated as Christ was through his Resurrection and Ascension. It appears that Peter is offering Christ as the supreme example, but then introduces another example, Noah. In this second example, Christ, by the Holy Spirit, went and preached through Noah to the people of his day. The result was that Noah was ridiculed and persecuted, in the same way as the Christians that Peter was writing to in his day. Peter's readers were also aware of the outcome; that is, the persecutors were destroyed in the Flood, whilst Noah was vindicated. Therefore, the themes of suffering followed by glory are observed through the examples of Christ's death, Resurrection and Ascension, and through the story of Noah, which were included by Peter to be an encouragement to

---

64. Feinberg, "1 Peter 3:18–20," 326; Erickson, *How Shall*, 172; Grudem, "Christ Preached," 230.

65. Feinberg, "1 Peter 3:18–20," 335.

persecuted Christians demonstrating to them that in following Christ there will be suffering, but there will also be vindication and glory.

Some might object, claiming that this interpretation is far from being a straightforward understanding of the text, further maintaining that Peter would probably not have conceived of such an idea. In response, one might refer to both Peter's use of Noah as a "preacher of righteousness" (2 Pet. 2:5) and that Peter understood that the "Spirit of Christ" had been active in the Old Testament era in the prophets by "predicting the sufferings of Christ and the glories that would follow" (1 Pet. 1:11).[66] Given Peter's understanding of Christ's pre-incarnate work in the Old Testament prophets, it would not be a huge leap for him to think of Noah, as a preacher of righteousness, in the same light, namely, a man who faithfully declared what the spirit of Christ had given him.[67]

The appeal of View [A] is that it fits in with Peter's aim of encouraging persecuted fellow believers to be faithful witnesses to antagonistic and aggressive unbelievers, for Christ is at work in them as he was in Noah, and like both Christ and Noah, the glory follows the suffering. Of all the views listed, this position contextually emerges as probably the most compatible making most sense of the reference of those who disobeyed in the days of Noah.[68]

As stated earlier, the Petrine passage is regarded by many proponents and opponents of posthumous salvation as a crucial text. As Erickson asserted, for this passage to be used as a scriptural foundation of posthumous salvation one needs to demonstrate that, firstly, the passage teaches that

66. I assume that 1 and 2 Peter were written by the same author.

67. Grudem, "Christ Preaching Through Noah," 230–2. Grudem lists six parallels between the situation of Noah before the Flood and the circumstances of Peter's readers: (i) Noah was in a small minority of believers who were surrounded by hostile unbelievers. Peter's readers were also surrounded by hostile unbelievers who were causing suffering (3:13–14; 4:4); (ii) Noah was a righteous man (Gen. 6:22; 7:5; 2 Pet. 2:5). Peter also exhorts his readers to live righteously in similarly difficult circumstances; (iii) Noah witnessed boldly to the unbelievers of his time, preaching repentance and impending judgment (2 Pet. 2:5, 9). Likewise, Peter encourages his readers not to fear (3:14) but to speak out boldly (3:15–16) even in their suffering (3:16; 4:16); (iv) Christ, though he was in an unseen spiritual realm was preaching through Noah to those around him (3:19–20). Likewise, Peter, by inference, reminds Peter's readers that it was Christ who was working in an unseen spiritual way in their lives also; (v) In the time of Noah, God awaited repentance from unbelievers, but finally brought judgment. Similarly, in Peter's time, God is waiting for repentance from unbelievers (2 Pet. 3:9) but will certainly bring judgment (4:5; 2 Pet. 3:10); (vi) Noah was rescued with a few others (3:20). Likewise, Peter reminds his readers that they too will be saved, even if they are few in number, for Christ has triumphed and they will share in his victory and glory (4:13, 5:10).

68. That said, Donelson offers a strong argument for "an ordered and coherent theological narrative" in 3:18–22, when one adopts view [E]. See, Donelson, I & II Peter, 115, for his summary of the passage.

Christ preached the gospel to those in Hades, during the period between his death and Resurrection, providing them with a genuine opportunity for salvation. Secondly, provided the first step can be proved, it is then necessary to demonstrate that the offer of salvation made by Christ on that occasion is available to all persons who live and die in subsequent generations.[69]

As discussed, the text in question which has been the focus of significant research over many generations is both opaque and controversial, resulting in diverse opinion. Such divergence of opinion has been caused by the varied interpretations on the questions that have been listed earlier in this chapter, namely, who are the "spirits in prison" and what and when Christ preached to those "spirits"? Whilst, due to the space available, only a relatively superficial treatment of the issues has been possible, considerable concerns have been raised over whether this theory is the most contextually credible of options. There is no place for dogmatism over such passages, yet the above discussion provides sufficient uncertainty, even improbability, thus failing Erickson's first test. However, even if the argument for 1 Peter 3 referring to Christ offering salvation to those in the underworld were accepted, Erickson's second test is still to be passed, namely, how does one then prove that this was a guarantee that all people at all time would also have a similar opportunity for salvation beyond the grave, for it might have been a unique situation. Bloesch, for example, does not appear to acknowledge that there is a second test to pass as he moves from the former to the latter seamlessly, stating, "What the descent doctrine affirms is the universality of a first chance, an opportunity for salvation for those who have never heard the gospel in its fullness."[70]

Erickson claims that "the doctrine [posthumous salvation] is based on a series of interpretations of Scriptures and philosophical and other assumptions which, by admission of the proponents of this view, are in many cases at best possibilities, and scant in number."[71] His evaluation rests partly on his assumption that the Petrine passage is fundamental to the success of the concept of posthumous salvation, though in fact, there are other arguments in favor of the concept of probation after death.[72]

Feinberg correctly argues that "if Scripture does teach anything about an underworld, one cannot demonstrate so from 1 Peter 3:18–22. Consequently, whatever one wants to say about biblical teaching concerning the

69. Erickson, *How Shall*, 165–6.

70. Bloesch, "Descent," 314.

71. Erickson, *How Shall*, 175.

72. As will be shown in chapter 4.

intermediate state, he must say it on the basis of some other passage than this one."[73]

Ephesians 4:7-10 — Descended to the lower, earthly regions

Support for the concept of the *Descensus*, apart from the Petrine passage, has been found in Matthew 12:40,[74] Acts 2:27,[75] Romans 10:6-7,[76] John 5:25-29,[77] and Ephesians 4:7-10, which reads:

73. Feinberg, "1 Peter 3:18-20," 336.

74. Matt. 12:40 "For as Jonah was three days and three nights in the belly of a huge fish, so the Son of Man will be three days and three nights in the heart of the earth." Whilst these words of Christ point towards his death and Resurrection, there is no reference to the descent of Christ or what he did during his *triduum*. See also 1 Cor. 15:3-4.

75. Acts 2:27 "because you will not abandon me to the grave, nor will you let your Holy One see decay." Peter, in his Pentecost sermon quotes from Psalm 16:10, which in the KJV reads: "Because thou wilt not leave my soul in hell, neither wilt thou suffer thine Holy One to see corruption," a translation that adds confusion. The word "hell" is the Greek term "Hades" and can mean "grave" or "death," as the NIV translates, which is contextually preferable. The immediate context is that God raised Christ from the dead and that it was impossible for death to keep its hold on him (see v. 24). The main emphasis is therefore about Christ's Resurrection from the grave. It is silent on the *triduum*.

76. Rom. 10:6-7, "But the righteousness that is by faith says: 'Do not say in your heart, "Who will ascend into heaven?" (that is, to bring Christ down) or "Who will descend into the deep?" (that is, to bring Christ up from the dead).'" The context for these verses is Paul's teaching on a righteousness that comes through faith in Christ and not through the law. Paul, rather puzzlingly (so thinks Moo, see Moo, "Romans," 63) quotes from Deuteronomy 30:12-13, a passage where Moses is actually encouraging the Israelites to obey the law. Fitzmyer (*Romans*, 591) suggests that Paul has no intention of quoting this passage, but it is to be compared with the way that people sometimes lift words out of a Shakespeare play with no regard to the original context. The context of Deuteronomy is that understanding, believing, and obeying the law was not too difficult for the Israelites, or beyond their reach, and in quoting this passage, it would appear that Paul is claiming that the righteousness that is by faith is also near and accessible for everyone who responds in faith. That is, one does not need to ascend into a place that is inaccessibly high or inaccessibly low, for Christ is not inaccessible or unreachable, for "the word is near you" (v. 8). Again, we find no clear reference or affirmation to the Descensus. Furthermore, Paul's quotation from Deut. 30 is different from the original in that Deut. 30:13 asks "Who will cross the sea to get it?" Paul asks, "Who will ascend into the deep?" Moo suggests that Paul might be influenced by the wording of Psalm 107:26, in that "sea" and "depths" (or abyss) were often interchanged in the OT and Judaism, see Moo, *Romans*, 64.

77. John 5:25-29, declaring, "I tell you the truth, a time is coming and has now come when the dead will hear the voice of the Son of God and those who hear will live. For as the Father has life in himself, so he has granted the Son to have life in himself. And he has given him authority to judge because he is the Son of Man. Do not be

"But to each one of us grace has been given as Christ apportioned it. This is why it says: 'When he ascended on high, he led
captives in his train and gave gifts to men.' (What does 'he ascended' mean except that he also descended to the lower, earthly
regions? He who descended is the very one who ascended higher
than all the heavens, in order to fill the whole universe.)"

Advocates of posthumous salvation interpret this text as referring to
Jesus descending into Hades and leading a great number out from captivi-
ty.[78] The captives would then be the equivalent of their view of the "spirits
in prison" of 1 Peter 3:19. MacCulloch contends that the "lower, earthly
regions" (NIV) or "lower parts of the earth" (KJV) of verse 9 is referring to
Hades in current beliefs, and that no part of the universe—Hades, Earth,
Heaven—was to be unvisited by Christ.[79] However, as was the case for the
1 Peter 3 passage, there are a variety of viewpoints on the Ephesian passage,
and specifically, for the purpose of this chapter, the question of whether
the *Descensus ad Inferos* (descent to the dead) was behind this text, is
significant.[80]

Most modern commentators are agreed concerning verses 7 and 8.
In verse 7, Paul writes, "To each one of us grace has been given as Christ
apportioned it," which acts as an introduction to the following passage,
emphasizing Christ's grace in bestowing different spiritual gifts (or better,
spiritually gifted persons) that are intended to strengthen and mature God's
people, preparing them "for works of service" (v. 12), so that the body of
Christ might be built up in love.

Paul's words concerning Christ's grace (gifts) is then substantiated by
a quotation from Psalm 68:18, "This is why it says: 'When he ascended on
high, he led captives in his train and gave gifts to men.'"[81] As with verse

---

amazed at this, for a time is coming when all who are in their graves will hear his voice
and come out—those who have done good will rise to live, and those who have done
evil will rise to be condemned." However, Nash responds critically to Fackre's commis-
sioning this text to support posthumous salvation, claiming that Jesus was referring to
the "spiritually" dead hearing the voice of Christ, with John 5:28–29 referring to the
general Resurrection, see Nash, "Restrictivism," 99–100.

78. For example, Fackre, "Divine Perseverance," 85 and MacCulloch, *Harrowing*,
47.

79. MacCulloch, *Harrowing*, 46. This is also implied in Philippians 2:10: "that at
the name of Jesus every knee should bow, in heaven and on earth and under the earth."

80. Due to the limits of space, it is not possible, or probably warranted, to extend all
arguments for the correct view of Eph. 4:7–10, though as with the 1 Pet. 3 Descensus
passage, there are significant arguments against the *Descensus ad inferos* view.

81. The Psalm reads, "When you ascended on high, you led captives in your train;
you *received* gifts from men," which differs from the Eph. 4:8 quotation, which states

7, there is little disagreement on the interpretation of verse 8 amongst commentators. The Psalm 68:18 quotation is understood to refer to the victorious ascent of Christ after his death and Resurrection and his bestowal of gifts to his church.[82]

The exegetical difficulty comes in verses 9 and 10 which comprise a Midrash on the Psalm 68 quotation, which states: "(What does 'he ascended' mean except that he also descended to the lower, earthly regions? He who descended is the very one who ascended higher than all the heavens, in order to fill the whole universe)." In an attempt to resolve the difficulty of these verses, Harris lists two questions that require answering, namely:

- To where did Christ descend?

- When did this descent take place in relation to the ascent mentioned in verse 8?

He further claims that nearly all recent interpreters have regarded the answer to the first question as Christ descending from heaven to earth (i.e., the Incarnation) or from the earth to the grave (i.e., Sheol, the place of the dead).[83] Regarding the second question, Harris further claims that most modern scholars believe that the descent mentioned by Paul in the Midrash of 4:9-10 preceded the ascent of verse 8. Harris, however, follows in the steps of von Soden and T. K. Abbott at the close of the nineteenth century

---

he "*gave* gifts to men." Stott claims that "after every conquest in the ancient world there was invariably both a receiving of tribute and the distributing of a largesse. What conquerors took from their captives, they gave away to their own people. The spoils were divided, the booty was shared." See Stott, *Ephesians*, 157. Martin, declares that the Hebrew psalmist and LXX use "received," though Jewish interpretations (found in Syriac Peshitta and Aramaic Targums) have the verb "to give" and contends that the author is using a current Aramaic paraphrase and changing the meaning from Moses who gave the law, to Christ who gives grace (gifts), see Martin, *Ephesians, Colossians and Philemon*, 50.

82. This subject is previously mentioned in Eph. 1:20-23. The Psalm, in its original context, is a cry to God to vindicate his people as he did in former times, for he went victoriously before his people after the exodus (Ps. 68:7) so that Mount Sinai trembled and the kings were scattered before him (v. 11-14). Then, desiring Mount Zion as his dwelling place he left Sinai for Zion (v. 16-17), ascending the mount, leading captives in his train. Stott claims that this very vivid imagery depicting the transfer of the ark to Zion is compared with Yahweh's triumphant march to his capital. Paul applies this image to Jesus who in his ascension to heaven also led captives in his train, namely the "principalities and powers he had defeated, dethroned and disarmed," Stott, *Ephesians*, 156-7.

83. He further explains that this view of descent to Sheol is "more or less equivalent to the ancient doctrine of the *Descensus ad Inferos*, except that no activity (such as preaching to the imprisoned spirits) is required of Christ during the *triduum*. The descent of Christ into the grave simply affirmed the reality of His death," see Harris "Ascent," 198-214.

and more recently George B. Caird and Andrew T. Lincoln in contending that the descent that is introduced in verses 9–10 was subsequent to the ascent and "represents the return to earth of the ascended, exalted Christ, as the Spirit at Pentecost"[84]

The descent therefore becomes an indirect reference to Christ's coming in the person of the Holy Spirit at Pentecost (Paul had previously associated the exalted Lord and the Holy Spirit in 2 Corinthians 3:17 "Now the Lord is the Spirit, and where the Spirit of the Lord is, there is freedom"). Thus Psalm 68 is fulfilled through, "the present Christ-in-the-Spirit . . . who gave both his Spirit and the gifts of the Spirit to furnish the church with all needful ministries."[85] Stott refers to this view as both "novel" and "ingenious," preferring to believe that the descent is a reference to the Incarnation.

Martin, who sides with Harris, claims that once the adverb "first" (v. 9, KJV) is omitted, as in the best textual readings, the view with the ascent preceding the descent best fits the sequence and refers to the Pentecost event.[86] Harris contends that if Paul's intention, by quoting Psalm 68:18 (v. 19 LXX), was to declare that at Christ's victorious ascent he gave gifts to his church, there would be no need whatsoever to include the Midrash of 4:9–10 which speaks of a descent, since the Psalm quotation refers to gifts being given at the ascent. He argues that "verses 9 and 10 are therefore relegated to the status of a somewhat extraneous comment."[87]

---

84. Harris, "Ascent," 201, who cites: von Soden, *Hand-Kommentar zum Neuen Testament*, 135–6; Abbott, *Epistles*, 115–6; Caird, "Descent of Christ," 2:535–45; Lincoln, *Ephesians*, 242–8. See also, Lincoln, "Old Testament in Ephesians," 18–25.

85. Martin, *Ephesians*, 50. Harris, "Ascent," 214, states, "As far as the believer's present experience is concerned, the exalted Christ and the Spirit of God are one." He points out that this is a functional identity not an ontological one.

86. Martin, *Ephesians*, 50. "Now that he ascended, what is it but that he also descended first into the lower parts of the earth?" KJV v. 9.

87. Harris, "Ascent," 205. Harris presents a viable alternative to the more traditional views, especially by showing the relationship between Targum Psalm 68:19 and Ephesians 4:8. The Targum Psalm 68:19 makes reference to Moses, who ascended Mount Sinai, who captured the words of the Torah and brought them down the mountain, giving the Torah as gifts to the sons of men. If Paul was aware of this targumic tradition encapsulated in Psalm 68, then it might throw light on the meaning of Ephesians 4:9–10, as Moses' descent and the giving of the gift of the Torah would have clearly followed the ascent. The problem with this view is that the Targum Psalms are thought to be written in the post-Christian era, though that difficulty is countered with the belief that Targum Psalm 68 reflects a Jewish tradition far older than the Targum itself, (209–10). Although it is difficult to demonstrate the association of Moses' ascent with Psalm 68 in pre-Christian tradition, the linking of Psalm 68 with the feast of Pentecost, the Jewish feast commemorating the giving of the law, in synagogue liturgy was known at an early date (first or second century BC), see Thackeray, *Septuagint*, 46–54. Stott (*Ephesians*, 157) claims that Paul's use of Psalm 68 as a "reference to the Christian

Lincoln—though advocating the view that the descent was subsequent to the ascent and represents the return to earth of the ascended, exalted Christ, as the Spirit at Pentecost— admits that "the choice between the three views of the descent to which the Midrash refers is a difficult one."[88]

Interestingly, MacCulloch mentions that many of the (early church) Fathers, such as Origen, believed in the transference of souls from Hades to Paradise, though he also states that this view is "problematical and must not be pressed," further asserting that the earlier Fathers, such as Justin Martyr and Irenaeus, actually interpreted the clause in Ephesians 4:8 in different ways "and did not see in it a reference to the release of captives from Hades."[89] Perhaps his words contain both good advice and profound wisdom in recognizing that no particular view is without its problems "and must not be pressed" for at best the Ephesian passage is by no means clear and unambiguous, also remembering that in all the canonical texts, only in 1 Peter is there any suggestion of Christ preaching in the realm of the dead. It would therefore be incorrect for proponents of posthumous salvation to use this passage to support or authenticate their theory.

Matthew 12:32 — Forgiveness in the age to come

> "Anyone who speaks a word against the Son of Man will be forgiven, but anyone who speaks against the Holy Spirit will not be forgiven, either in this age or in the age to come."

Pentecost then makes a remarkable analogy." That is, just as Moses received the Torah and gave it to Israel, so Christ received the Spirit and gave him and his gifts to the church (see 4:11–13). This focus on receiving and giving is also displayed in Acts 2:33, which states, "Exalted to the right hand of God, he has received from the Father the promised Holy Spirit and has poured out what you now see and hear." Harris continues, claiming that it seems "highly probable" that the "giving of the Torah on Mount Sinai had come to be associated with the Feast of Weeks at some time before Paul wrote Ephesians, further claiming that by the time Ephesians was written, it is also highly probable that Psalm 68:19 had come to be interpreted as a reference to Moses' ascent of Sinai to bring down the Torah. A precedent would have thus been established for interpreting Psalm 68:19 in terms of an ascent-descent motif, with the descent inferred from the ascent and related to a subsequent giving of gifts at the Feast of Pentecost," see Harris, "Ascent," 212.

88. Lincoln, "Old Testament in Ephesians," 24. However, while Bloesch claims that the Ephesians 4 passage "seems to indicate the extension of the saving work of reconciliation and redemption to the souls in the nether world of Hades" (Bloesch, "Descent," 313), Bietenhard conversely asserts, "In modern exposition the reference of this passage to the descensus ad inferos ('he descended into hell' in the Apostles' Creed) is almost without exception rejected" (Bietenhard, "Hell," 2:210).

89. MacCulloch, Harrowing, 47–48.

Boyd asks, "Does this not presuppose that there are other sins that may be forgiven 'in the age to come'?" To understand whether this is feasible, one needs to appreciate the immediate context of Jesus' words. In Matthew 12:22, we read that Jesus had just healed a demon-possessed man who was blind and mute which resulted in the man being able to both see and talk. The Pharisees, who were unable to deny Christ's power, questioned its source. They responded by claiming that Jesus could only do this through the power of Beelzebub, the prince of demons. This was not only an accusation that was absurd (vv. 25–29), but they were making a decision against Jesus (v. 30) and against the Holy Spirit by whose authority he was acting (vv. 31–32) and for which they would one day be judged (vv. 33–37).

More immediately, in verses 31–32, Matthew states that every sin and blasphemy will be forgiven, except the blasphemy against the Spirit. In other words, the sin of which the Pharisees were guilty was uniquely serious.[90] This sin essentially declares oneself against God and it is to "call evil good and good evil" (Isa. 5:20).[91] The significance of Jesus' exorcisms was manifestly plain for everyone to see and there was no excuse for attributing the work of the Holy Spirit to Beelzebub. This sin, says Jesus, "will not be forgiven, either in this age or in the age to come" (v. 32).

France asserts that "'this age' and 'the age to come' are Jewish terms which apply primarily to the contrast between this life and the next rather than to successive phases of life on earth . . . In Matthew the term is used especially in the phrase 'the end (or fulfilment) of the *aiōn*' . . . What follows from that 'end of the *aiōn*' is the '*aiōn* to come.'"[92] Ladd similarly asserts that "this idiom views redemptive history not as a series of unending ages, but of two distinct and contrasting periods of time."[93] This present age will come to an end at the *parousia* when the Son of Man will send his angels to separate the wicked from the righteous.[94] Ladd summarizes, "In brief, this age is the period of Satan's activity, the human rebellion, of sin and death; the age to come, introduced by the *parousia* of Christ, will be an age of eternal life

90. France, *Matthew*, 483.

91. The question of why it is less serious to speak against Jesus as the Son of God is not especially relevant to this discussion and is ignored, but see France, *Matthew*, 484, for a fuller treatment.

92. France, *Matthew*, 484.

93. Ladd, "Age, Ages," 19–21.

94. "As Jesus was sitting on the Mount of Olives, the disciples came to him privately. 'Tell us,' they said, 'when will this happen, and what will be the sign of your coming and of the end of the age?'" (Matt. 24:3); ". . . and the enemy who sows them is the devil. The harvest is the end of the age, and the harvesters are angels. As the weeds are pulled up and burned in the fire, so it will be at the end of the age" (Matt. 13:39–40).

and righteousness, when Satan is destroyed and evil swept from the earth."[95]
The question of whether Christ deliberately leaves open the door of opportunity for posthumous salvation in Matthew 12:32 is a pertinent one. It is
fascinating that most commentaries do not attempt an answer, negatively,
positively, or agnostically, to this question. Hendriksen, for example, writes
more than a thousand words in his commentary on verses 31–32, virtually
ignoring the phrase ". . . will not be forgiven, either in this age or in the age
to come." His only comment on this phrase is a denunciation of the concept
of Purgatory.[96]

Frame and Plumptre are two other scholars who offer comment on
this phrase. Frame claims that "Matt. 12:32 does not say that any sins will
be forgiven after death, only that some will *not* be,"[97] which begs the question of why did Jesus emphasize this point in the manner he did? After all,
Jesus might have said, ". . . but anyone who speaks against the Holy Spirit
will not be forgiven," omitting "either in this age or in the age to come."
Plumptre is more receptive to the possibility of postmortem forgiveness.
He writes, "Our Lord's words, it may be noted, clearly imply that some sins
wait for their full forgiveness, the entirely canceling of the past, till the time
of that 'age to come' which shall witness the great and final Advent. Does
this imply that repentance, and therefore pardon, may come in the state
that follows death? We know not, and ask questions that we cannot answer,
but the words at least check the harsh dogmatic answer in the negative. If
one sin only is thus excluded from forgiveness in that 'coming age,' other
sins cannot stand on the same level, and the darkness behind the veil is
lit up with at least a gleam of hope."[98] Despite Plumptre's openness to the
possibility of forgiveness being available postmortem, based on this verse,
it would be highly contentious to consider this Scripture as a sturdy and
sound foundation for this belief.

---

95. Ladd, "Age, Ages," 20. He also emphasizes that the blessings of this future age
have entered into this evil age in that Christians live in two ages; they live bodily in this
present evil age but live spiritually in the age of righteousness and life. The eternal life
that belongs to the age to come is also a present possession.

96. Hendriksen, *Matthew*, 527–30.

97. Frame, "Second Chance," 992. His italic.

98. Plumptre, *Bible Commentary*, 73.

1 Corinthians 15:29 — Baptism for the dead

> "Now if there is no Resurrection, what will those do who are baptized for the dead? If the dead are not raised at all, why are people baptized for them?"

Throughout 1 Corinthians chapter 15, Paul has been trying to convince his readers that there will be a resurrection of the dead and that believers will receive the kind of spiritual body that Christ received. Paul argues that if the dead are not raised then:

- not even Christ has been raised (v. 13).
- their preaching was a waste of time (v. 14).
- the faith of believers is futile (vv. 15, 17).
- believers are false witnesses about God having raised Christ from the dead (v. 15).
- Christians remain in their sins (v. 17).
- believers who have since died are "lost" (v. 18).
- believers are to be pitied as they put up with hardships and persecution for nothing (vv. 19, 30–32).

It is in this context that Paul asks, "Now if there is no resurrection, what will those do who are baptized for the dead? If the dead are not raised at all, why are people baptized for them?" (15:29). Much has been written on this verse through the centuries, with diverse opinions.[99] Fee asserts that whilst one might need to "finally admit ignorance," what is certain is how the text functions in the overall argument.[100]

Fee contends that the normal reading of the text is that some Corinthians were being vicariously baptized on behalf of others who had died, even suggesting that the reason a plethora of opinions exists is due to this verse appearing to support vicarious baptism.[101] Fee's comments are in contrast, and are to be preferred to MacArthur who, whilst claiming that there are many possible interpretations to this difficult verse, states that he can be dogmatic over what the text does not mean, "We can be sure . . . that it does not teach vicarious, or proxy, baptism for the dead, as claimed by the ancient heretics such as Marcion and the Mormon church today."[102] It would appear that MacArthur associates vicarious baptism with salvation since he

---

99. For a 51 page survey of opinion, see Rissi, Mathis, *Die Taufe*, 6–57.

100. Fee, *Corinthians*, 763.

101. Fee, *Corinthians*, 764.

102. MacArthur, *1 Corinthians*, 424–5.

immediately follows by discussing the error of baptismal regeneration. Fee favorably cites Oepke, who contends that "all interpretations which seek to evade vicarious baptism for the dead . . . are misleading."[103] The difficulty of interpreting this text lies in there being no orthodox historical or biblical precedent for such vicarious baptism. The only references to such a practice refer to the heretical Marcionites and a Jewish-Christian heretic named Cerinthus.[104] The second difficulty arises by Paul appealing to a practice which suggests a "'magical' view of sacramentalism of the worst kind, where a religious rite, performed for someone else, can have saving efficacy."[105] Fee is not suggesting that this practice actually had saving efficacy, only that this is how some scholars understood this text, which in turn has caused the upsurge in other explanations being sought. It would appear that Paul is neither approving nor condemning of the practice; he simply shows that such a practice would not be necessary or rational if there is no resurrection of the dead. It is conceivable that Paul did not consider this practice to be as serious a problem as do many interpreters. Fee suggests that maybe 2 Maccabees 12:39–45, in which Judas Maccabeus offers prayer and makes a sin offering for some of his soldiers who had been slain while wearing "sacred tokens of Jamnia," might not have been a vicarious sacrifice for the dead so much as an appeal for God to have mercy on circumcised Jews who at the time of their death were wearing idolatrous amulets. Fee searchingly asks whether the practice of baptism for the dead fell into this general category of "innocence" so that Paul felt no great urgency to correct it.[106]

Rissi, Trumbower, Fee, Barrett, and Bruce all agree that the most logical explanation for the original practice is that some believers were being baptized for those who either were, or were on the way to becoming, Christians when they died but had not been baptized—in later times those who would be called catechumens.[107] Chrysostom reported that this was

---

103. Fee, *Corinthians*, 764, n. 16, which cites Oepke, *TDNT* 1, 542 n. 63. This is also favored by Rissi, *Die Taufe*, 89–92, Trumbower, *Rescue*, 35, Conzelmann, *1 Corinthians*, 275–7.

104 Chrysostom describes this practice among the followers of Marcion (Chambers, "Homily 40"), as cited by Fee, *Corinthians*, 764, n. 17. One might legitimately question Chrysostom as a source for Marcionites, whom he regarded as heretics. Tertullian two hundred years earlier, in *On the Resurrection of the Flesh*, 48.11, admits that some in Corinth were baptized for the dead, but in his later work *Against Marcion*, 5.10, he is careful to reject any reading that gives a legitimacy to vicarious baptism for the dead. See Trumbower, *Rescue*, 37–38. For Cerinthus, see Epiphanius, *Panarion Against 80 Heresies*, 1.28.

105. Fee, *Corinthians*, 764–5.

106. Fee, *Corinthians*, 767, (see esp. n. 32).

107. Rissi, *Die Taufe*, 91; Trumbower, *Rescue*, 39; Fee, *Corinthians*, 767; Barrett,

the practice of the Marcionites in Corinth. That is, if a Marcionite catechumen died before baptism, an already baptized Marcionite would be placed under the couch on which the deceased lay and would answer the baptismal question on behalf of the dead believer. The living person would then be baptized in water, with the deceased gaining spiritual credit. Furthermore, Epiphanius provides an account of the practice of posthumous baptism for dead catechumens, referring to the heretic Cerinthus: "Among them [the Cerinthians] there also exists the tradition of which we have heard, namely that when some of them die before being baptized, others are baptized in place of them in their name, so that when they rise in the resurrection they may not pay the penalty of not having received baptism and become subject to the authority of the one who made the world."[108] If the practices of the Marcionites and first-century Cerinthians are true reflections on a practice that Paul might have been referring to, then 1 Corinthians 15:29 cannot legitimately be used to support posthumous salvation of non-Christians, as the beneficiaries may have been believers before their deaths.

Biblical passages used to oppose posthumous salvation

Proponents of posthumous salvation assert that final destinies are not necessarily sealed at death, but opportunity for salvation is possible beyond death and up until the time of the final judgment. Conversely, opponents of the concept argue that death seals a person's eternal destiny and terminates any hope of salvation for those who have not turned to Christ in their lifetimes. The most important biblical text of all which represents the state of unbelievers after death as fixed, according to Berkhof, is Luke 16:19–31.[109] Erickson also believes that death ends all opportunity for decision for Christ, using this passage as his main evidence.[110] Similarly, Grudem, when assessing the claim that Christ preached to the (human) "spirits in prison" offering them opportunity to turn to Christ, asserts that this could not be true because "the idea of a chance of salvation after death is difficult to reconcile with other parts of the New Testament."[111] The two texts he then quotes are Luke 16:26 and Hebrews 9:27, further commenting that it

---

First Epistle to the Corinthians, 364; Bruce, *1 and 2 Corinthians*, 148–9.

108. Epiphanius, *Panarion*, 28.6.4–28.6.5, as cited by Trumbower, *Rescue*, 38. Epiphanius himself believed that 15:29 referred to those catechumens who were *about* to die ought to be granted a speedy baptism.

109. Berkhof, *Systematic Theology*, 693.

110. Erickson, "Is there," 141. He also lists Ps. 49, Heb. 9:27 and Rev. 20:11–15.

111. Grudem, "Christ Preaching," 230.

is unlikely that Peter would have taught of Christ preaching to the "spirits in prison" offering them salvation (1 Pet. 3:19—4:6), as this would have differed fundamentally from other leaders in the early church.

Feinberg is another example of a scholar whose base line for interpreting the correct meaning of the Petrine passage is that there is no further chance of salvation after death, because "such a notion contradicts the teaching of Scripture."[112] He also interprets the parable of the rich man and Lazarus rather literally, claiming that the "point of the story seems to be that there is a gulf fixed between the blessed and the condemned, and there is no crossing over that gulf."[113] There appears to be an assumption in Grudem, Feinberg, and others, that all one needs to do is quote the traditional proof-text of the rich man and Lazarus and the argument is decided, blindly ignoring that this passage is itself highly contentious and controversial, as was the Petrine text. The following sections question whether the biblical texts that are traditionally used to claim that death ends a person's probation actually substantiate that view.

Luke 16:19–31 — A great chasm

"There was a rich man who was dressed in purple and fine linen and lived in luxury every day. At his gate was laid a beggar named Lazarus, covered with sores and longing to eat what fell from the rich man's table. Even the dogs came and licked his sores. The time came when the beggar died and the angels carried him to Abraham's side.[114] The rich man also died and was buried. In Hades, where he was in torment, he looked up and saw Abraham far away, with Lazarus by his side.[115] So he called to him, 'Father Abraham, have pity on me and send Lazarus to dip the tip of his finger in water and cool my tongue, because I

112. Feinberg, "1 Peter 3:18–20," 326. The Evangelical Alliance Commission on Unity and Truth Among Evangelicals (ACUTE) report (Hilborn, *Nature of Hell*, 10), also claims that Hebrews 9:27 is featured prominently in classical evangelicalism to validate the idea that there is no possible salvation for those who die as unrepentant sinners, though it does admit that there are some evangelicals, more recently, who believe that the text does not preclude a postmortem "second-chance."

113. Feinberg, "1 Peter 3:18–20," 326, n. 43.

114. Or "Abraham's bosom," a term that is not attested to in pre-Christian Jewish literature, though might be a development of the Old Testament idea of sleeping with one's relatives (Gen. 15:15; 1 Kgs. 1:21). The bosom was a place of honor at the banquet and a metaphor for intimacy and security, see Forbes, *God of Old*, 188–9.

115. The apparent proximity might reflect the concept of a twin compartment, one for the righteous and one for the unrighteous (see 1 Enoch 22:8–14).

am in agony in this fire.'[116] But Abraham replied, 'Son, remember that in your lifetime you received your good things, while Lazarus received bad things, but now he is comforted here and you are in agony. And besides all this, between us and you a great chasm has been set in place, so that those who want to go from here to you cannot, nor can anyone cross over from there to us.'[117]

He answered, 'Then I beg you, father, send Lazarus to my family, for I have five brothers. Let him warn them, so that they will not also come to this place of torment.' Abraham replied, 'They have Moses and the Prophets; let them listen to them.' 'No, father Abraham,' he said, 'but if someone from the dead goes to them, they will repent.' He said to him, 'If they do not listen to Moses and the Prophets, they will not be convinced even if someone rises from the dead.'"

The parable of the rich man and Lazarus has been the subject of considerable scholarly debate.[118] Hock, however, argues that although the number of studies is considerable, the "relative lack of vigorous analysis and constant comment over the years has tended to produce a scholarly tradition that is usually stable, uniform, and . . . self-satisfied."[119] Luke alone records this story, the only parable in which Jesus includes a person's name. Lazarus is almost certainly the Greek form of the Hebrew *Eleazar*, mean-

---

116. Hades is the Greek equivalent of Sheol, being used on sixty-one occasions in the LXX for Sheol, a place where the dead existed. Sheol is pictured as a gloomy underworld where the righteous and unrighteous dwell with little distinction. In intertestamental times the concept of Hades developed with separate compartments for the godly and ungodly (especially in pseudepigraphal Enoch). In the New Testament, Hades is mentioned on just ten occasions and translated as "hell" in the KJV which has led to confusion as the Greek word Gehenna, traditionally accepted as a place of eternal punishment, is also translated as "hell." See Buis, "Hades," 7–8. The relationship between Hades and Gehenna is not especially clear. Forbes, *God of Old*, 189, n. 46, cites two scholars who take very different views on the relationship between Hades and Gehenna: Boyd ("Gehenna—According to J. Jeremias," 9–12) who insists that there is no sharp distinction between the two terms in the NT, that Hades and Gehenna are synonymous; and Osei-Bonsu ("The Intermediate State in Luke-Acts," 115–30) who maintains a distinction between the two terms, claiming that Gehenna is the final and eternal place of punishment, with Hades being an intermediate state for all the dead. This is also the view of Jeremias, (see "Hades" 1:148–9); Jeremias, *Parables*, 185.

117. Forbes, *God of Old*, 190, suggests that the chasm is meant to contrast the gate (v. 20) that the rich man could have passed through to assist Lazarus, but did not. Now Lazarus cannot assist him, for the gate has become a great chasm, a chasm dug by the rich man because of the way in which he lived.

118. Kreitzer, "Luke 16:19–31," 139–42.

119. Hock, "Lazarus and Micyllus," 447–63 [447].

ing *God has helped*.[120] The inclusion of a proper name might suggest that Jesus is speaking of someone who is known to his audience, though the etymological consideration of this name is probably deliberate in shedding light on the man's character in the parable. Luke's introduction of "There was a rich man . . ." would be unnatural for a story about known persons.[121] The opening formula is also identical to 16:1 and would indicate that this story is a parable and not an actual historical account.[122]

Background to Luke 16:19–31

The parable makes use of two narrative motifs that are paralleled in other ancient literature, namely, the reversal of fortunes experienced by the rich and poor after death and a dead person's return from the dead with a message for the living.[123] However, according to Hock, the previous scholarly interpretations of this parable are "self-satisfied" in that the assumptions of scholars like Adolf Jülicher, Hugo Gressmann, and Rudolph Bultmann have gone unchallenged for too long, with most recent scholars largely accepting their proposals.[124] For example, Fitzmyer accepts Jülicher's belief that the parable falls into two parts, verses 19–26 and verses 27–31,[125] claiming that either Jesus or the early church added the second part.[126] Likewise, the extra-biblical parallel to this parable, of the Egyptian folktale of Setme and Si-Osiris, has largely been accepted since Gressmann's proposal in 1918.[127]

---

120. Morris, *Luke*, 252–5.

121. Knight, "Rich Man and Lazarus," 277–83.

122. Forbes, *God of Old*, 184. On the genre of this passage, see also Bock, *Luke 9:51—24:53*, 1361–4.

123. Bauckham, *Fate*, 97. The motif of the dead returning to the living is actually refused in the parable. This is a point that will be discussed later.

124. Hock, "Lazarus and Micyllus," 448–50.

125. Fitzmyer, *Luke*, 1126, and Jülicher, *Die Gleichnisreden Jesu*, 2:634. Others who divide the parable into two parts include, Bultmann, *History*, 203; Jeremias, *Parables of Jesus*, 183. For this parable as a unity, see Marshall, *Luke*, 633–4, and Grobel, "Neves," 373–82.

126. Also, Crossan, *Parables*, 65–66, argues that vv. 27–31 is a post-Resurrection application of the parable. The parallels between 16:27–31 and Luke 24:11–12, 25, 41, include motifs of (disbelief), 24:27, 44 (Moses and the Prophets), 24:46 (Resurrection), and 24:47 (repentance) are critical to his case. He claims that these verses are directed against those who refuse to accept Jesus' Resurrection or the witness of the OT to this event.

127. Easton, *Gospel*, 254; Creed, *Gospel*, 209–10; Jeremias, *Parables of Jesus*, 183; Crossan, *Parables*, 67; Marshall, *Luke*, 633; Fitzmyer, *Luke*, 1127. Gressmann was the first to draw attention to this example, see Gressman, *Vom reichen Mann und armen*

Jeremias views this folktale as "essential" for understanding the parable.[128] Bauckham, however, believes that the use of the Egyptian story of Setme and Si-Osiris and the later Jewish derivatives, have since dominated the scholarly discussion on this parable, and advises caution on the possible misuse of such extra-biblical parallels. Hock is similarly critical of the emphasis that scholars have placed on the Egyptian story.[129] Likewise, Forbes claims that the similarities between the Egyptian story and the parable have obscured their differences.[130]

The parable and its possible sources

The story of the rich man and Lazarus only appears once in the New Testament though there are Egyptian, Jewish, and Greek stories with key similarities known. As stated, the dominant story has traditionally been that of Setme and Si-Osiris, which will be the main reference point in discussion on the parable. However, other stories include Bultmann's preference for a Jewish legend as the source for the parable, which according to Hock, has not met with scholarly approval, whilst scholars, such as Kreitzer and Aalen have found parallels to the parable in the Enoch literature, which it is claimed illuminate the Lukan passage.[131] Grensted suggested that 1 Enoch 22 provided the possible background for the Hades imagery contained in the parable.[132]

Hock's preference is that of Lucian's *Gallus* and *Cataplus* to reconstruct the social milieu of the parable, contending that sources from the larger Greco-Roman world need to be considered alongside those with a Palestinian-Jewish milieu.[133] *Cataplus* offers the same plot as the parable in which there is a reversal of fortunes following the deaths of a rich man and a poor man. In *Cataplus*, three souls make the journey to Hades, a philosopher, Micyllus (a poor shoemaker) and Megapenthes (a rich tyrant). The philosopher and Micyllus were found to be upright whilst Megapenthes was deserving punishment. Lucian's stories have a number of direct

---

Lazarus, as cited in Bauckham, *Fate*, 97, and Hock, "Lazarus and Micyllus," 449.

128. Jeremias, *Parables of Jesus*, 185.

129. Hock, "Lazarus and Micyllus," 447–63.

130. Forbes, *God of Old*, 183.

131. Hock, "Lazarus and Micyllus," 450; Kreitzer, "Luke 16:19–31 and 1 Enoch 22," 139–42; Aalen, "St Luke's Gospel and 1 Enoch," 1–13.

132. Grensted, "Use of Enoch," 333–334.

133. Hock includes *Gallus* only because this story involves the character Micyllus, a poor man who also appears in the story of *Cataplus*, or (*Trip to Hades*), who is central to Hock's thesis that Lucian's dialogues are possible sources for the parable.

and indirect incidents that mirror the parable, though his underlying theme is that wealth and morally reprehensible lives are associated. Lucian makes it clear that the wealthy have probably amassed their wealth by unjust or dishonest means, with the aim of living hedonistic and sexually promiscuous lives. Conversely, the poor are depicted as pious since poverty promotes diligence, simple living, and self-control, the antithesis of the things that ruined self-indulgent Megapenthes.[134] This scenario is then transferred into the parable of the rich man and Lazarus as the criterion for their respective judgments, though it is to be argued that Hock's use of the Lucian dialogues to explain the reversal in fortunes is as uncertain as the Egyptian folktales.

Setme and Si-Osiris

The story of Setme and his son Si-Osiris is about an Egyptian in Amente, the realm of the dead, who was allowed to return to earth as the reincarnated son of a childless couple. The child is called Si-Osiris. His work was to deal with an Ethiopian magician who was becoming too powerful for the magicians in Egypt. At the age of twelve, he overcame the Ethiopian magician and then returned to Amente. However, before this, he and his father observed the funerals of a rich man who was buried with great ceremony and a poor man who was buried without ceremony or mourning. The observing father claimed that he would rather have the rich man's lot than the poor man's. The son disagreed, and in order to justify his claim he took his father on a tour of the seven halls of Amente to demonstrate the reversal of fortunes in the afterlife. In Amente there were three classes of the dead: those whose bad deeds outnumber their good deed (like the rich man), those whose good deeds outnumber their bad deeds (like the poor man), and those whose good deeds and bad deeds are equal.[135]

Bar Ma'yan and the Torah scholar

Jeremias proposes that Alexandrian Jews brought the Egyptian story to Palestine where a Jewish version developed, an example of which is found in the Palestinian Talmud.[136] This version tells of a rich tax collector named

134. Hock, "Lazarus and Micyllus," 447–63.

135. Bauckham, *Fate*, 98.

136. Jeremias, *Parables of Jesus*, 183. Gressmann, *Von reichen*, 70–86, draws attention to seven versions of the Jewish story; see also Beare, *Earliest Records*, 182. Conversely, Bauckham, *Fate*, 99, suggests that the story as found in the Palestinian Talmud could have come from versions of the story that existed independently and not via the

Bar Ma'yan and a poor Torah scholar who lived in Ashkelon. The two men died on the same day. The tax collector was buried with ceremony and style, but the poor man's death went unnoticed. A friend of his was troubled by the contrast between the funerals of the two men until he had a dream of the fates of the two men in the afterlife. The rich tax collector is tormented in hell whilst the poor man is in paradise.[137] The impressive funeral of the rich tax collector was his reward for his one good deed in life and the poor man's one sin was punished in life by having a pauper's funeral. The principle is that "the righteous are punished for their few sins in this world, so that in the next world they may enjoy only bliss, whereas the wicked receive in this world the reward for their few good deeds, so that in the next world they may justly receive only punishment."[138]

Evaluation

Bauckham asserts that the Jewish version in the Palestinian Talmud and the Egyptian story are the same, but this cannot be said of the parable. He further contends that if the other stories are to be enlightening for interpreting the parable then both the resemblances and the differences between the stories must be scrutinized. Bauckham lists the following comparisons and contrasts:[139]

- The Egyptian and Jewish stories focus upon the burials of the two men. The contrast is between their *burial* and their state in the afterlife, whilst the parable focuses upon the state of the men in the afterlife compared to their *life* in this world.

- The Egyptian and Jewish stories speak of a revelation of the fate of the two men after death which is given to a character in the story. Conversely the readers or hearers of the parable learn what happens to the rich man and Lazarus after death. The parable goes even further and raises the possibility of revelation of the postmortem fates of the two men, to the rich man's brothers, and then rejects it. The parable relates a different means of revelation to the Jewish and Egyptian stories.

Egyptian story.

137. The torment is pictured as his trying to drink from a river, but being unable to do so, which has a striking comparison with the rich man in the parable who wanted Lazarus to dip the tip of his finger in water to relieve his suffering.

138. Bauckham, *Fate*, 99.

139. Bauckham, *Fate*, 99–101.

- The Egyptian and Jewish stories reveal that the postmortem fate is due to either good deeds outweighing bad ones or vice versa. By contrast, the parable does not refer to either the deeds of the rich man or of Lazarus. The reason for the reversal of fortune is stated clearly in verse 25 "But Abraham replied, 'Son, remember that in your lifetime you received your good things, while Lazarus received bad things, but now he is comforted here and you are in agony.'"

He further asserts that the Jewish and the Egyptian stories may have a similar provenance since they use the two motifs of the great reversal of the two men and the revelation of the fate of the dead to the living in the same way. The parable however uses the two motifs, as suggested above, quite differently. As Bauckham asserts, "it does not tell the same story."[140]

It is quite possible that Jesus would have known about the Jewish story as it circulated within first-century Palestine, or indeed may have known other stories which used these motifs. The important point however is whether these motifs function in Jesus' new story of the rich man and Lazarus. As previously stated, the parallel stories offer enlightenment on the parable through comparing and contrasting the detail. Bauckham asserts that while the stories might be instructive, "it would be a mistake to give them a privileged role in the interpretation of the parable."[141]

Bauckham further argues that the exclusive concentration on the Egyptian story as being the actual source of the parable has had the detrimental effects of (i) fostering the idea that the parable has two distinctive parts (that is, since vv. 19–26 are apparently based on the Egyptian story, it is then assumed that vv. 27–31 "the revelation to the dead motif" has been added later[142]), and of (ii) encouraging the supposition that the criterion for judgment of the rich man and poor man is the same as the Egyptian story.[143] This second point is particularly significant as Luke 16:25 does not make any such comment on the great reversal being due to deeds done while in this world. Abraham's reply to the rich man was "in your lifetime you re-

---

140. Bauckham, *Fate*, 101.

141. Bauckham, *Fate*, 101.

142. Forbes, *God of Old*, 183–4, states that it seems strange that the request for a messenger to be sent back from the dead is thought of as a secondary addition to the parable, which itself was adapted from an Egyptian folktale, when one of the central features of that folktale concerns an envoy being sent from the realm of the dead. Furthermore, such a division breaks up the dialogue between Abraham and the rich man. Finally, vv. 27–31 serves to move the focus away from the afterlife to the earthly situation, enabling the parable to drive home its point regarding the proper use of wealth.

143. That is, the criterion of judgment is based on the good or bad deeds of a person in this life.

ceived your good things, while Lazarus received bad things, but now he is comforted here and you are in agony."

Undoubtedly, some who would struggle with the concept of a rich man suffering because he is rich and a poor man being rewarded because he is poor have been relieved at the interpretation that the Egyptian parallel proposes.[144] Some have assumed that the rich man was condemned because he misused his wealth,[145] or because he acquired it unjustly,[146] or because he neglected to give charitably to the poor man at his gate.[147] Hock claims that this is "virtually the unanimous view of the scholarly tradition," which derives from Lazarus being outside the rich man's gate or from the supposed content of Moses and the Prophets which the brothers were to heed.[148] Likewise, Lazarus is assumed to have not only been penniless but pious.[149] Yet, in actuality, there is no mention of the piety or morality of the two men in the parable. What this parable appears to teach, claims Bauckham, in contrast to the other mentioned ancient writings, is the injustice of one man living in abject poverty and the other in opulence, an injustice that will be put right in the afterlife. He further argues, "To try to base the fate of the two men in the parable on considerations other than these stated facts is to evade the parable's clear-sighted view of the flagrant injustice of the situation it sketches. What is not stated is not relevant."[150]

Such a discovery is indeed shocking and controversial, especially as it would then appear that the eternal destiny of individuals should be determined by whether they are rich or poor. Indeed it would be outrageous if this were a statement about human destiny in the afterlife. However, if Bauckham is correct, this is not a parable about human destiny at all but one whose message addresses the subjects of wealth and poverty. He asserts, "If the theme of eschatological reversal were taken as a literal description of how God's justice will operate after death it would be morally intolerable." Yet, as Bauckham suggests, this parable is not aimed at describing details of the afterlife, but belongs to the popular religious folklore of the poor.[151] That

---

144. Jeremias, *Parables of Jesus*, 185, proposes that Jesus did not need to explain the reversal of fortune of the two men since the Egyptian story was so well known.

145. For example, Plummer, *Critical*, 390; Fitzmyer, *Luke*, 1132.

146. For example, Derrett, *Law in the New Testament*, 90.

147. Fitzmyer, *Luke*, 1128.

148. Hock, "Lazarus and Micyllus," 453–4.

149. For example, Jeremias, *Parables of Jesus*, 185; Marshall, *Luke*, 632.

150. Bauckham, *Fate*, 104.

151. Bauckham, *Fate*, 105.

is, their hope in the justice of God to redress the balances of the injustices they have experienced in this life.

Bauckham's thesis is certainly a step forward in the scholarly discussion on the parable which has been tied too closely to the Egyptian folktale and its Jewish derivatives. Even so, what he appears to miss is that the reversal of fortunes of the two men is not necessarily automatic, for as Forbes points out, Abraham himself was a rich man. Forbes also poignantly states that "to say that reversal is based on the injustice of inequality then raises the obvious question of who is responsible for such injustice."[152] Whilst the parable does not explicitly condemn the rich man, the unmistakable inference is that he had done nothing to alleviate the suffering of a destitute man outside his own gate. Forbes is also correct to assert that if the rich man's morality is not at stake, the repentance motif, introduced in vv. 27–31, is superfluous and pointless.[153]

In Luke 16:27–31, the rich man requests that Lazarus be sent to warn his brothers by revealing the fate of their brother in Hades, declaring that unless they repent and amend their lives they too will be sent to Hades. The motif of the dead returning to reveal aspects of the afterlife to the living would have been familiar in first-century Palestine.[154] However, this request was refused by Abraham, a noteworthy aspect of the parable. Thus, the story "deprives itself of any claim to offer an apocalyptic glimpse of the secrets of the world beyond the grave. It cannot claim eyewitness authority as a literal description of the fate of the dead. It only has the status of parable."[155]

Abraham refuses the rich man his request for Lazarus to visit his five brothers because they already have Moses and the Prophets and they will not be convinced should someone rise from the dead. Moses and the Prophets represent the ideal egalitarian view of equality and justice among the people of God, denouncing the complacent and arrogant rich and bringing God's hope to the poor.[156] The story of the rich man and Lazarus emphasizes material inequality in God's world, and to understand this injustice one only needs to listen to Moses and the Prophets. If these five brothers, like the rich man himself, fail to open their eyes to the stark division between the very rich and desperately poor in society as already revealed through the Hebrew Scriptures, then no revelation of the afterlife will be able to convince them.

152. Forbes, *God of Old*, 192.

153. Forbes, *God of Old*, 193.

154. For example, the story of Jannes and Jambres, where Jannes returns from the underworld to warn his brother of the terrible suffering, urging him to lead a good life rather than share the fate of Jannes, in Pietersma, *Apocryphon*, 119.

155. Bauckham, *Fate*, 117.

156. See Deut. 15:7–14 and Amos 5:7–15; 8:4–7.

Following the tour to the afterlife, this parable brings us back to the reality of rich and poor co-existing in this life, all because they do not listen to Moses and the Prophets. Forbes asserts that this parable "is certainly not a discourse on the afterlife," but "makes some powerful statements about the requirements God places on one's present life." He continues, stating "the radical demands of the kingdom require that wealth be used to alleviate the sufferings of those in need."[157]

Trumbower contends that "the key to posthumous bliss in this story is not whether one is a believer in the saving power of Jesus' death and Resurrection, but rather, whether one is rich or poor."[158] Although there is nothing in this parable that suggests that Lazarus was pious and good, let alone a Christian believer, the inference is that the rich man was selfish by ignoring the material needs of Lazarus who lay by his gate each day. Bauckham is correct to emphasize that verse 25 reveals that the reason for their postmortem fates is simply a reversal of fortunes, though Abraham's warnings in verses 29 and 31 presuppose that there is something that the five brothers can do to alter their fates, something that can be derived from Moses and the Prophets. Thus, Jesus' point is repent and act properly now while you have opportunity.[159]

This story does not deal with conversion to Christianity, for after all, it is not even implied that Lazarus was a Christian, yet he enjoys his posthumous reward. This parable has often been reinterpreted by many to mean that conversion must be attained before death. Hendriksen is an example of such thinking, stating that "the one truth here emphasized is that once a person has died, his soul having been separated from his body, *his condition*, whether blessed or doomed, *is fixed forever*. There is no such thing as a 'second chance.'"[160] Similarly, Bock argues "one message rings clear: once God has rendered judgment, it is permanent. The ethical choices of this life last for eternity. The encounter with Jesus and his teaching has long term implications, bringing either comfort or torment."[161] Yet this is surely to read too much into the text, as there is no mention of encountering Jesus and his teaching, as a basis for one's ultimate comfort or torment, found in

---

157. Forbes, *God of Old*, 195. He further claims that this parable does not condemn wealth *per se*, but graphically illustrates Jesus' teaching about the difficulty of a rich man entering into the kingdom of God (Luke 18:24), though this is not impossible (Luke 19:1—10).

158. Trumbower, *Rescue*, 42.

159. Trumbower, *Rescue*, 42. See also Green, *Gospel of Luke*, 610.

160. Hendriksen, *Luke*, 785. His italics.

161. Bock, *Luke 9:51—24:53*, 1377–9.

this parable. The purpose is essentially ethical, focusing on the manner in which one uses one's wealth to meet the needs of the poor.[162]

Geldenhuys, more astutely asserts, "The Saviour related this parable not in order to satisfy our curiosity about life after death but to emphasize vividly the tremendous seriousness of life on this side of the grave"[163] Similarly, Knight writes, "The appeal of the story is not to satisfy curiosity concerning Hades, Hell, Heaven, 'the intermediate state,' nor any other fascinating esoteric topic related to life beyond death. It is set in a collection of parables that call for careful stewardship of life's opportunities." Both the contemporary readers of Jesus' story and indeed readers of all generations are challenged "not only to be careful stewards of life's goods and opportunities but also to be their brother's and sister's keepers."[164]

For those who still cannot accept that this is a parable solely concerned with wealth, but claim that it contains a message of one's ultimate eternal destiny being fixed by death, other questions remain.[165] Firstly, attention would need to be given to the concept of an "intermediate state" between death and the final judgment and whether this parable truly represents such an intermediate state. For example, why are the two men portrayed as having bodies at this juncture? Secondly, even if the parable is taken to mean that eternal destiny is fixed at death, would it apply to the unevangelized, for the message to the rich man's brothers was that they are without excuse because they already have Moses and the Prophets. Such a statement assumes

---

162. Luke 16 is dominated by two parables on the "Use and Abuse of Riches" (see Nolland, *Luke 9:21—18:34*, 792–833) with Luke 16:1–13 being a positive encouragement to be generous with one's money and possessions, and Luke 16:19–31, being a negative example, as observed in the rich man's response to Lazarus. In vv. 14–15 Luke rebukes the Pharisees, who he claimed "loved money" and were the immediate focus of Jesus' teaching.

163. Geldenhuys, *Luke*, 427.

164. Knight, "Luke 16:19–31," 281–2.

165. Wenham, (*Parables*, 17) asserts that it is an over-simplification, if not an arbitrary theory, to suggest that Jesus' parables only have one main point. This theory, he claims, has resulted in "artificial and distorted interpretations." Fee and Douglas (*How to Read*, 125) make a similar point by stating that in some cases (e.g. the parable of the Wicked Tenants, Mark 12:1–11; Matt. 21:33–44; Luke 20:9–18) the "parable may approach something very close to allegory, where many of the details in the story are intended to represent something else." The parable of Lazarus and the rich man, is not a one-point parable as it makes several related points, namely: a warning to the rich about neglecting the poor, a warning against a sign-seeking which masks disobedience, an affirmation of the role of the Law and Prophets which expresses the will of God, and the announcement of the standards of the kingdom of God (see Wenham, *Parables*, 149–50). Though to suggest, as does Bock (*Luke 9:51—24:53*, 1377–9) that it also contains a message of one's ultimate eternal destiny being fixed by death would be to read into the parable a concept foreign to its context.

that they were Jews who had God's revelation by way of the Hebrew Scriptures. Therefore, would this be relevant to the unevangelized who do not have Moses and the Prophets? Thirdly, does this teach that poverty equals piety and, conversely, that wealth equals wickedness, for to suggest that the final destinies of the rich man and Lazarus are decided by their response to Christ is to read into the text what is simply not there?[166] Fourthly, will there be contact between those in eternal bliss and those in torment, for such a scenario would certainly suppress and subdue the joyous reverence of the righteous? Caird correctly stated, that "it was not the intention of Jesus to propagate a strict doctrine of rewards and punishments . . . or to give a topographical guide to the afterworld."[167]

Given the above understanding on a controversial and misunderstood biblical passage, one must conclude that the use of this parable as a defense of the concept of death being a point beyond which no opportunity for salvation exists must be refuted and refused.

Hebrews 9:27–28 — Death then judgment

> "Just as man is destined to die once, and after that to face judgment, so Christ was sacrificed once to take away the sins of many people; and he will appear a second time, not to bear sin, but to bring salvation to those who are waiting for him."

As previously discussed, Hebrews 9:27 is often quoted as a proof-text to disqualify the belief of there being any opportunity for salvation beyond death.[168] Erickson emphasizes that it "seems to assume an invariable transition from death to judgment, with no mention of any additional opportunities for acceptance" of Christ.[169] Likewise Packer, in a *Christianity Today* article entitled *Can the Dead be Converted?*, answers in the negative to a direct question of whether there is opportunity for salvation beyond death based on this verse, though he quickly moves away from the question asked and focuses his reasoning on "God's prevenient grace."[170] He argues that

---

166. Bock, *Luke 9:51—24:53*, 1377–9; Hendriksen, *Luke*, 785. Bock asserts "the image is strong and suggests that how we respond in this life is decisive for where we reside in the next, a key point that some find hard to accept" (see also n. 28, 1373).

167. Caird, *Saint Luke*, 191. See also Wenham, *Parables*, 144–5.

168. Wright, *Radical*, 98; Berkhof, *Systematic Theology*, 693; Erickson, "Is there," 142; Grudem, "Christ Preaching," 230; Feinberg, "1 Peter 3:18–20," 326, n. 43; Frame, "Second Chance," 992; Packer, "Can the Dead," 82. Grudem, *Systematic Theology*, 822–3.

169. Erickson, "Is there," 142.

170. Packer, "Can the Dead," 82, answers a question posed by Paul Gavitt.

coming to Christ is not like choosing a preferred dish from a menu, for in salvation there is a "sense of inevitability about it" which arises from "the pressure of the gospel truth that feels too certain to be denied, plus the sense of God's presence forcing one to face the reality of Jesus Christ, plus the realization that without him, one is lost . . . and desperately needing to be changed." Packer continues by asserting that all this is generated by God's prevenient grace in making the first move and that there is no commitment to Christ without "this convicting divine action." He further adds that "Scripture says nothing of prevenient grace triggering post-mortem conversions, and that being so, we should conclude that the unbeliever's lack of desire for Christ and the Father and heaven remains unchanged."[171] He concludes by asserting that for God to extend the offer of salvation by even 30 seconds beyond the moment of death would be pointless for nothing would come of it.

Packer's response to the question is inadequate. Firstly, he does not explain how Hebrews 9:27 is actually supposed to teach against postmortem opportunity. He merely states, that "the unrepeatable reality of physical death leads directly to reaping what we sowed in this world." Proponents of posthumous salvation would challenge this position, asking when after death is the judgment? Field states, "Two thousand years nearly have come and gone since these words were written: has judgment come?"[172] He argues that the end of human probation is not death but the final judgment. He further claims, "We have neglected the eschatology of Scripture, and made death the judgment and death the coming of Christ."[173] Secondly, Packer's introduction of prevenient grace into his answer might indeed argue against a theological position that rests heavily on human decision as opposed to the work and agency of the Trinity, but it does not answer the question of why prevenient grace is only possible this side of the grave. Whilst one can agree with his assertion that "Scripture says nothing of prevenient grace triggering post-mortem conversions," one can also argue that Scripture does not argue against this concept either. In fact, one might argue that the prevenient grace of a Divine Being who is described as Love (1 John 4:8, 16) would continue to reach to those who remained unchanged whilst on earth. One is also left confused by Packer's assertion that should God extend the offer of salvation beyond the moment of death that nothing would come of it. But again Packer is unclear why he feels that this is so.

171. All above quotes from Packer, "Can the Dead," 82.
172. Field, "Andover Theory," 469.
173. Field, "Andover Theory," 469.

The context of 9:27 is the unique sacrifice of Christ. The author explains that in Old Testament times, the tabernacle furnishings required cleansing and consecration by animal blood but these things were mere earthly copies of the heavenly realities which they represent. The blood of animals can only make a person ceremonially clean but cannot truly cleanse a person from sin. This can only come through the blood of Christ, who has become the mediator of the new covenant. Christ's sacrifice was unlike the animal sacrifices of the Old Testament in that he did not need to offer himself again and again. Rather, he has "appeared once for all" (v. 26) to do away with sin by the sacrifice of himself. The author then introduces verses 27–28, "Just as man is destined to die once, and after that to face judgment, so Christ was sacrificed once to take away the sins of many people; and he will appear a second time, not to bear sin, but to bring salvation to those who are waiting for him." The point of this verse is to illustrate the once-for-all aspect of the work of Christ, as opposed to the unfinished nature of the Old Testament sacrificial system, and is not a reference to personal eschatology.[174] Whilst arguments from silence are always uncertain, it is nevertheless of interest that biblical commentaries do not choose to use this verse in the manner that it is often quoted in contemporary evangelicalism, and make no reference to this verse as referring to death being the end of human probation.[175] The writer of Hebrews uses this reference to show that human death is a once-for-all occurrence as a consequence of sin, so too Christ died once-for-all to take away the sins of many people. The phrase "and after that to face judgment" is often interpreted to mean immediately after death humans experience judgment, thereby ruling out the opportunity of postmortem salvation. Boyd, however, contends that this "reads too much into the text." He continues, "While this verse certainly rules out reincarnation, it does not rule out the possibility of intermediate events between death and judgment."[176] He also reminds us that most evangelicals agree that there are other events between death and judgment, such as, Christ's return and the bodily Resurrection, and the postmortem view merely adds one more event or process, namely, the evangelization of the previously unevangelized. This

174. Popular usage of this text appears to fall foul of Fee and Stuart's basic hermeneutical rule of "a text cannot mean what it never could have meant to its author or his readers." See Fee and Stuart, *How to Read*, 60. It is improbable that the writer of Hebrews would have placed a teaching on personal eschatology in this passage on Christ's once-for-all sacrifice.

175. The following cross-section of biblical commentaries were observed: Brown, *Message of Hebrews*, 168–76; MacArthur, *Hebrews*, 242–3; Barclay, *Letter to the Hebrews*, 109–11; Stedman, *Hebrews*, 99–102; Hewitt, *Hebrews*, 153–4; Evans, *Hebrews*, 153–71; Wiersbe, *Hebrews*, 107–8; Lane, *Hebrews*, 114–28; Bruce, *Hebrews*, 227–33.

176. Boyd, *Across*, 188.

passage offers no timescale as to how long after death that judgment comes, thereby failing to link death with loss of opportunity, which is commonly taught in evangelical circles.

2 Corinthians 5:10 — Judgment for 'things done while in the body'

> "For we must all appear before the judgment seat of Christ, that each one may receive what is due to him for the things done while in the body, whether good or bad."

This Scripture is cited to indicate that one's conduct in life (not after death) is what determines the final award at the judgment.[177] "For" (*gar*) indicates that the requirement to appear before the judgment seat of Christ is the motivation for believers to live lives that are pleasing to the Lord (see v. 9). In this section, starting at 4:16, Paul's focus is believers, not unbelievers.[178] The "judgment seat" (*bema*) in Corinth had two primary functions in the civic life of the city. Firstly, it was used as the platform for public speeches and, secondly, as the place for judicial verdicts.[179] Some at Corinth might even have remembered Paul himself who stood accused before the Roman Governor Gallio facing accusation from Jewish antagonists (Acts 18:12–17). However, Paul's concern is not with the judgment seat of Gallio, but that of Christ.

Paul's imagery of a future eschatological revelation and judgment, in receiving back one's due, "for the things done while in the body, whether good or bad," is to be linked with one's determination to please the Lord (v. 9).[180] This position of judgment by works was held in tension with Paul's justification by faith, for in this passage we find both Paul's confidence for those who are "in Christ," who were forgiven (v. 19) and righteous (v. 21) as well as being assured that they have a "building from God" (v. 1), and Paul's teaching that all believers will "appear before the judgment seat of Christ."[181] "The sure prospect of the judgment seat reminds the Corinthians—and all

---

177. For example, see Grudem, *Systematic Theology*, 823, 1143–4. The parable of the sheep and goats is often quoted for the same reason in that the blessing or condemnation granted on the Day of Judgment depends upon how one has conducted his/her life on earth, Matt. 25:41–46. See also Matt. 7:22–23; 10:32–33; Luke 12:47–48; Gal. 6:7–8.

178. Barnett, *Second Epistle to the Corinthians*, 273.

179. Hubbard, "2 Corinthians," 221. Jesus himself stood before the *bema* of Pilate, see Matt. 27:19 and John 19:13.

180. Barnett, *Second Epistle to the Corinthians*, 275, n. 47.

181. See also 1 Cor. 3:10–15.

believers—that while they are righteous in Christ by faith alone, the faith that justifies is to be expressed by love and obedience . . . and by pleasing the Lord."[182] Barnett proposes the possibility "that some at Corinth held to a superspirituality associated with an overrealized eschatology leading to a less than earnest approach to their responsibilities during the present age" which caused Paul to remind them of their coming judgment. He further contends that one's confidence of being "with the Lord" (v. 8) is to be held in tension with the "fear of the Lord" (v. 11).[183]

Since this text is quite patently referring to a believers' judgment of works, those who claim that it disproves posthumous salvation by providing evidence that one's conduct or decisions in life, not in the afterlife, are what really matters, are claiming far more than this verse permits. This verse has no bearing to those who have not heard the gospel during their lives.

Conclusion

Christ's descent to Hades and the concept of his preaching the gospel there, whilst not implausible or impossible, as we have observed from the Descensus passages, is an interpretation that remains doubtful at best. Whilst there is no room for dogmatism in attempting to understand and interpret passages like 1 Peter 3:18—4:6, which are particularly opaque and unclear, considerable concern has been raised in this chapter over the contextual credibility of such Scriptures to offer support to posthumous salvation. The claim that posthumous salvation is not explicitly taught in the Bible is to be viewed as essentially correct, despite what some of its advocates might maintain.[184] Erickson is also correct in warning advocates that it is unwise to rest this concept on such an obscure passage as 1 Peter 3:18—4:6, though he is wrong in believing that this passage is the foundation for posthumous salvation, which is a major misconception amongst the critics of this view.[185] A further area of ambivalence and uncertainty for many scholars is the inclusion of the "descended into hell" clause in the Apostles' Creed,

---

182. Barnett, *Second Epistle to the Corinthians*, 277.

183. Barnett, *Second Epistle to the Corinthians*, 277.

184. For example, Fackre, "Divine Perseverance," 71–95.

185. Erickson, "Is there," 144. He states, "It is strange to rest a doctrine about the eternal destiny of humans on such an obscure passage. The doctrine is based on a series on interpretations of Scriptures and philosophical and other assumptions which, by the admission of the proponents of this view, are in many cases at best possibilities, and which are scant in number."

which is correctly regarded by some as a late intruder with dubious origins and uncertain scriptural foundations.[186]

The criticism of the concept of posthumous salvation not being explicitly taught in the Bible is not as damning as one might suppose, for it would be more accurate to state that the concept of posthumous salvation is neither confirmed nor disqualified by the Bible's teaching. As has been observed in this chapter, the often quoted biblical "proof-texts" such as Luke 16:19–31 and Hebrews 9:27 which apparently support the concept of death being the end of one's probation, with there being no opportunity for repentance and salvation in the afterlife, do not confirm this position in the manner that popular evangelicalism often suggests. Otherwise careful scholars like Feinberg, Grudem, and Erickson all quote the above proof-texts, blindly ignoring that their interpretation of such Scriptures is equally contentious and controversial as the interpretation of the Descensus passages by scholars advocating posthumous salvation. In reality, the use of Scriptures such as Luke 16:19–31 and Hebrews 9:27 as biblical evidence for death being the point beyond which no opportunity for salvation exists must be refuted and refused. Furthermore, it might be argued that a number of the church's central doctrines, such as the Trinity and the hypostatic union of the human and divine natures of Christ in one person, are not explicitly taught in the Scriptures either, which could lead some, more forceful proponents of posthumous salvation, to assert that their belief in posthumous salvation is as viable and valid as a Trinitarian orthodoxy.

Pinnock admits, "Although the scriptural evidence for post-mortem encounter is not abundant, its scantiness is relativized by the strength of the theological argument for it. A post-mortem encounter with Jesus actually makes very good sense."[187] Pinnock's opinion will be evaluated in chapter 4 when the theological arguments for and against posthumous salvation will be assessed.

186. For example, Grudem, "He did not," 103. See Appendix B.
187. Pinnock, *Wideness*, 169.

4

Theological Evaluation of Posthumous Salvation

Introduction

In chapter 3, biblical passages, which purportedly supported or undermined the concept of posthumous salvation, were evaluated. It was concluded that whilst there is no room for dogmatism in attempting to understand such passages—given that some are particularly opaque—the claim that posthumous salvation is not explicitly taught in the Bible was found to be essentially correct. However, this was to be balanced by the counterclaim that this view is not necessarily at variance with biblical doctrine. Biblical passages and verses that have been traditionally used by advocates and critics of posthumous salvation proved to be inconclusive and uncertain at best, with the Scriptures neither unambiguously confirming nor refuting the concept of postmortem opportunity for salvation. Pinnock acknowledges that although the scriptural evidence for this concept is not abundant, its strength lies in its theological argument, which is the main focus of this chapter.[1]

In chapter 1, the twin theological axioms of particularity and universality were laid as foundational for this research, and are, for the purpose of this book, understood to be established. In this chapter, a significant area of theological inquiry will be considered as a test case, having a direct bearing on whether the concept of posthumous salvation is an acceptable belief for evangelicalism. That is, the doctrine of God's attributes will be evaluated in order to discern what the Bible teaches about God that, in turn, will shed light upon the question of the possibility of postmortem opportunity for

---

1. Pinnock, *Wideness*, 169. Similarly, Parry & Partridge, *Universal Salvation?* xxix, also insist that the "broader theological debate is often more determinative" than specific texts about hell or universal salvation (the focus of their book) in evaluating the claims of the related doctrine of universalism.

salvation. Discussion will center essentially on the impartiality and eternity of the love of God and divine justice in a way that maintains the unity (or simplicity) of God's attributes. Traditionally, God's mercy and justice have been viewed as distinct, if not contrary or conflicting, characteristics within the being of God; a view that stretches back to Augustine.[2] That is, God, as a righteous and just judge, needed to punish sin, but as a loving father he desired to offer mercy and forgiveness and permit his children to escape punishment. Thus, Atonement was required that would appease the wrath of God and satisfy his justice, thereby putting an end to his "conflict of heart." In essence, Christ died so that God might be merciful to sinners without doing violence to his own sense of justice.[3]

This discussion will extend to include, for example, soteriology, eschatology, Christology, pneumatology, anthropology, and the doctrine of the Atonement, though any ventures into these disciplines will be limited to the extent that they connect to the subjects of the love and justice of God and the question of the possibility of posthumous salvation. The temptation to focus on certain aspects of eschatology in this chapter, such as the intermediate state and views on mortality/immortality of humans, will be resisted. I will accept that there exists a variety of views on life after death and prior to the judgment, such as those that Erickson lists: soul sleep, Purgatory, immediate Resurrection, and intermediate state.[4] For the purpose of this chapter, the question of the merits of each view is largely superfluous, as the essential element is whether a postmortem Christ-encounter exists which potentially provides an opportunity for repentance, irrespective of it being at the time of death, the time in between death and judgment, often referred to as the intermediate state, or at judgment and beyond.

Furthermore, belief in conditional immortality would not make the possibility of a postmortem encounter with Christ redundant, on the condition that God will allow the unbeliever to pass out of existence following a postmortem encounter with himself, or at least, raise the unbeliever at the Resurrection, before the person then passes out of existence. The only form of annihilationism that would not permit this is *pure mortalism* (a form of annihilationism that contends that human life is so closely tied to the physical being, that when the body dies, the person ceases to exist) which is the belief of some sectarian groups such as the Socinians and Christadelphians.[5]

2. Outler, Albert C., translator. "Enchiridion," Chapter XXV.

3. Talbott, "Punishment," 151–68.

4. Erickson, *Christian Theology*, 1181–9.

5. For more information on this view which is not popular in Christianity, see Warfield, "Annihilationism," 447–50, and Erickson, *Christian Theology*, 1244–7. See also Hilborn, *Nature of Hell*, 73.

Doctrine of God

As previously claimed, the concept of posthumous salvation is not decided within the arena of biblical exegesis, which is largely inconclusive on the issue, but in the area of theological debate. Johnson asserts that "no one does presuppositionless exegesis of Scripture" and that there are "always larger theological issues to be taken into account before one can pronounce that 'this is the teaching of the Bible' on a given subject."[6] In this section, the question of whether God's attributes, or nature, are able to throw any light on the possibility of God's grace extending beyond the grave, is to be explored. Whilst space does not permit an exhaustive examination of all of God's attributes, the attributes of God's love and justice, and their relationship to each other, will be evaluated because of the clear relationship of such characteristics to the topic. Many wider hope theologians, like Pinnock and Brow, view the love of God as at the core of God's being, with other of God's attributes being viewed as less fundamental to his essential nature. They state, "It is wrong to imagine divine wrath as an attribute of God like his mercy, as though God had competing and even conflicting attributes that led him sometimes to forgive and other times to condemn."[7] They also strongly argue that there are not "two gods with two divine wills—one longing to save and the other needing to condemn," rather, that God's wrath is subordinate to his love, as is implied in Exodus 34:6 "The Lord, the Lord, a God merciful and gracious, slow to anger, and abounding in steadfast love and faithfulness," (ESV) which shows that it is his love, not his wrath, that is everlasting. However, others, like Grudem, disagree, stating that "when Scripture speaks about God's attributes it never singles out one attribute of God as more important than the rest."[8] At face value, these views appear to be polarized, yet this might not be so, as it is arguable whether wrath is a permanent attribute of God at all, but should rather be understood as a reaction of God to sin. That is, God's wrath arises as a result of injured love. Thus, God's righteousness and holiness would be his attributes, and core to his nature, which would cause a holy anger against all that is unrighteous and unholy. That is, as Travis argues, if there were no sin, there would be no wrath.[9]

---

6. Johnson, "Wideness," 78.

7. Pinnock and Brow, *Unbounded Love*, 67.

8. Grudem, *Systematic Theology*, 178.

9. Travis, *Christ*, 70.

Before exploring what the Scriptures teach about the love and justice of God, it is important to understand something of the relationship of God's attributes to each other.

Divine simplicity

Thomas Talbott, who advocates Christian universalism, objects vehemently against a "schizophrenic" view of God which contests his mercy against his justice and vice versa.[10] Talbott provides autobiographical reflections of his spiritual journey into universalism in the first part of his book *The Inescapable Love of God*.[11] Following a conservative upbringing, Talbott's faith was challenged by an atheistic professor, which led to a crisis of faith. His thesis is built upon love being God's essential nature insisting that the Scriptures do not even hint at God's mercy allowing something that his justice would not, or that his justice should demand something that his mercy does not. Daniel Strange supports Talbott's view, adding that the doctrine of divine simplicity would help guard against this error.[12] Grudem defines divine simplicity as God not being divided into parts and agrees with Strange that it would be incorrect to speak of a "fundamental attribute" that "is more central than any other attribute."[13] Grudem prefers to speak of God's unity rather than simplicity due to the word *simple* being understood as easy to understand or unintelligent. Keathley defines the simplicity of God as there being "no division, tension, or conflict within God. God is never in a quandary or has conflicting desires."[14] He lists four options regarding God's will and salvation: (1) Universalism—God wills that all will be saved; (2) Double predestination— God wills that only the elect will be saved, he does not desire the salvation of the reprobate; (3) God has two wills—a revealed will and a hidden will; (4) God has two wills—an antecedent will and a consequent will, meaning that God desires all to be saved (antecedent) but consequently wills that faith is a condition to salvation. Only those who be-

10. Talbott, "Pauline Interpretation," 32. "Schizophrenic" is Talbott's description.

11. Talbott, *Inescapable*, 1–39.

12. Strange, "Calvinist Response," 145–68. Divine simplicity is characteristic of Classical Theism and shall for the purpose of this chapter be accepted. Divine simplicity teaches that God is without parts and that his being is identical to his attributes. That is, God does not have goodness, but simply is goodness. The philosophical, and often complex, arguments, both for and against divine simplicity, and the challenges of Plantinga who contests Aquinas's theory, are beyond the scope of this book. However, for an introduction into this subject, see, Davies, *Introduction*, 158–80, (chapter 8).

13. Grudem, *Systematic Theology*, 177; Strange, "Calvinist Response," 155.

14. Keathley, "Salvation," 3–22. (see p. 4, n. 2).

lieve will then be saved. Keathley provides a brief overview of the strengths and weaknesses of each view, stating that those who emphasize the simplicity of God generally argue for options (1) or (2), that God only has one will. Furthermore, Frame asserts that "God cannot be God without his goodness, his wisdom, and his eternity . . . None of his attributes can be removed from him, and no new attribute can be added to him . . . None of his attributes exists without the others . . . each is qualified by the others."[15] Grudem similarly emphasizes that with reference to John's description of God as love (1 John 4:8) and light (1 John 1:5), there is no suggestion that part of God is love and part is light, or that God is partly love and partly light, rather, "it is *God himself* who is light, and it is *God himself* who is also love."[16]

Grudem further argues that the unity of God should caution us against singling out one attribute of God as more important than another.[17] Similarly, Erickson, who would not be classed as a proponent of the wider hope views of salvation, recommends that we begin with the assumption that God is an integrated being whose divine attributes are harmonious; thus God's justice is *loving* justice and God's love is a *just* love, even though Erickson affirms that there is indeed some basis for viewing love as the basic attribute of God.[18] Undoubtedly Erickson is correct here, as Christ, out of love came to save the world, not to condemn it, or to demonstrate his wrath. The divine objective for the Incarnation and Atonement was love, not wrath. As previously mentioned, God's wrath is injured love.[19]

This assumption of God's attributes being harmonious will be accepted as a reasonable postulation in the following discussion on divine love and justice. Erickson perceptively suggests that the reason these attributes sometimes appear to conflict is the result of defining them in isolation to each other.[20] That is, when love is detached from justice, there is danger of sentimentality and when justice is estranged from love there is the risk of arbitrariness. Undoubtedly, the greatest example of God's love and justice working together is to be found in the sacrificial death of Christ, as traditionally understood. God's justice requires that a payment be made for the penalty of sin, whilst God's love desires humans to be reconciled to him.

---

15. Frame, *Doctrine of God*, 226.

16. Grudem, *Systematic Theology*, 178. His italics.

17. Grudem, *Systematic Theology*, 179. Furthermore, one needs to be aware of the danger of *Sachkritik* (the criticism and rejection of one part of Scripture on the basis of another), see Marshall, "Evangelical Approach," 79–85.

18. He quotes 1 John 4:8, 16; 2 Corinthians 13:11; John 14:31; and Matthew 3:17 as a basis for his views.

19. Erickson, *Christian Theology*, 318.

20. Erickson, *Christian Theology*, 324.

In Christ's death, Atonement was made and both the love and the justice of God were met. God is both righteous and loving, and has himself given what he demands.[21]

One's view of God's nature is absolutely imperative to the way in which one's theological framework is constructed, life is lived, and ministry is conducted.[22] It is, therefore, important to recognize this connection between God's attributes and his acts, for God's acts are outflows of his nature. This could also be argued the other way around, by saying that God's attributes are often revealed in his actions—ranging from Christ praying for his persecutors from the cross to some of the seemingly harsher passages of the Old Testament which condone, even command, the mass slaughter of nations. Yet, the question of whether these visions of God can be complementary, or are indeed contradictory, is beyond the scope of this chapter. However, for the purpose of this work, I accept that Jesus is the full and final revelation of God and I choose to interpret all other biblical portraits of God through the lens of Christ. This is a view also adopted by Keith Ward in, *The Word of God: The Bible after modern scholarship*, who maintains that Jesus' life and teaching is the "normative divine revelation of moral goodness, and the key to interpreting all particular texts in the Bible."[23] Sharon Baker similarly refers to "The Jesus Lens" through which she interprets the more difficult passages of Scripture.[24] In the context of our inquiry, one needs to establish what the Bible teaches concerning the nature of God in order to evaluate the possibility of postmortem opportunity for salvation. Especially important is the question of whether God's love would allow him to make such an offer, or whether his other attributes in some way constrain or veto his love.[25]

The Love of God

The overarching theme of the Bible is that of God, a loving Creator, unceasingly pursuing humankind to bring it into a relationship with himself. However, according to Carson, "what the Bible says about the love of God is much richer and more complex than the reductionistic appeal to God's

21. Erickson, *Christian Theology*, 325.

22. Erickson, *Christian Theology*, 290, provides examples of distorted understandings of God, where God is viewed as a "celestial policeman" or as a "kindly grandfather" figure.

23. Ward, *Word of God*, 99.

24. Baker, *Razing Hell*, 59–65.

25. Dodd, *Johannine Epistles*, 110, contends, "To say, 'God is love' implies that all His activity is loving activity. If He creates, He creates in love; if He rules, He rules in love; if He judges, He judges in love."

love sometimes found in pluralist literature and in popular polemic." Carson then lists at least four ways in which he believes love is understood in the Bible.[26]

The Bible defines God as love (in 1 John 4:8, 16), a love that is firstly expressed within the Trinity, but is also extended to mankind. Jesus explained to Nicodemus that, "God so loved the world that he gave his one and only Son, that whoever believes in him shall not perish but have eternal life" (John 3:16). Paul wrote similarly that, "God demonstrates his own love for us in this: While we were still sinners, Christ died for us" (Rom. 5:8). John likewise asserts, "This is love, not that we loved God, but that he loved us and sent his Son as an atoning sacrifice for our sins" (1 John 4:10). Peter also affirms God's love to the world, a love that desires that none should perish, but that everyone should come to repentance.[27]

Carson challenges texts used by wider hope theologians (namely 1 Tim. 2:3–4, 1 John 2:2; 2 Pet. 3:9; Titus 2:11) to provide evidence that God loves everyone with a redeeming love. He plausibly shows that 1 John 2:2 and Titus 2:11 cannot bear the weight that is being made to rest on them, suggesting that they mean "all without distinction" rather than "all without exemption." That is, God died for blacks as well as whites, women as well as men, for the educated as well as the ignorant, for Arabs as well as for Jews.[28] He further suggests that the clause "God our Savior, who wants all men to be saved..." (1 Tim. 2:3–4) does not logically end in "hard" inclusivism, for many Arminians would also believe in that statement, yet adopt the restrictivist view that a conscious decision for Christ is required in this life. Carson is correct in this, though chooses not to discuss the implications of this view, namely, that such a theological stance assumes that the unevangelized are held culpable because of the inability of others who refused to tell them of Christ.

God's loving initiative is most gloriously observed firstly in the Incarnation and then in the Atonement of Christ. Associated with the view of God's unmerited and unconditional love for humanity is the question of the extent of the Atonement. Advocates of posthumous salvation favor the belief of unlimited or universal atonement, recognizing that Christ died for the whole world and not for a specific group of people, the elect, as those from a Reformed or Calvinistic tradition would believe. Given their understanding of the nature and extent of God's love, proponents of posthumous salvation believe that God's love perseveres beyond death into the afterlife,

---

26. Carson, *Gagging*, 238.

27. 2 Peter 3:9.

28. See Carson, *Gagging*, 287–9.

especially for those who have not had adequate opportunity to make a faith response to Christ during their earthly lives.[29]

Carson is highly critical of some wider hope theologians who, according to his understanding, misunderstand what the Bible says about the love of God. Pinnock is typical of those berated by Carson, when he asserts, "If God really loves the whole world and desires everyone to be saved, it follows logically that everyone must have access to salvation."[30] Carson warns of the danger of taking one strand of the theme of the love of God and "spinning it" in such a manner that it contradicts other biblical evidence. He further contends that "one of the most important hermeneutical constraints one should adopt in order to avoid such reductionism is this: Permit the various attributes and characteristics of God to function in your theology only in the ways in which they function in Scripture" and to "never permit them to function in your theology in such a way that the primary data, the data of Scripture, are contradicted."[31] This is indeed good advice and helpful in one's evaluation of the writings of any theologian, including Carson himself, whose Reformed theology on occasion appears to act as an interpretive grid for his understanding of Scripture. For example, Carson claims that the major thesis of Sanders's book, *No Other Name*, is profoundly flawed by theological reductionism and offensive caricature of the exclusivist position. The same allegation might be targeted at Carson himself, who is not only occasionally vitriolic against the views of "hard" inclusivists, like Pinnock and Sanders, but who also might be accused of reductionistic tendencies in evaluating their view "as some lifeless philosophic idea" and missing their concern for both the unevangelized and for God who is sometimes portrayed as arbitrary.[32]

Does God love impartially?

For some, at least, the answer to "Does God love impartially?" is "No." For instance, Strange, from a Calvinistic perspective, argues that "God does not have to love all of humanity (and eventually save them) for him to be love."[33] His rationale is based on the self-sufficiency of God's love within the Trinity which means that he is not dependent on anything outside of himself. That

29. For a fuller discussion on this, see chapter 2: "*Destinies are not determined at death*," p. 32.

30. See Carson, *Gagging*, 285; Pinnock, *Wideness*, 157.

31. Carson, *Gagging*, 286.

32. *Gagging*, 285–91, 291.

33. Strange, "Calvinist Response," 157.

is, if God had not created anything at all, he would still be love. MacDonald argues that the concept of God not having to love all of humanity is non-sense, for once God creates other persons, his being "love" will mean that he can do no other than love them as this is intrinsic to his nature.[34] However, the next step in Strange's logic is that the decrees of creation and redemp-tion are not necessary, because if they were, God would be constrained by them. He states, "God's freedom to create or not to create can also apply to redemption."[35] However, whilst Strange is correct to assert that God is love, a love that is independent of his creation, his point about God not having to redeem his creation, is questionable as it would be akin to parents bringing a child into the world whom they subsequently ignore and neglect, claim-ing that they are not to be constrained by some requirement to love their child. Strange deploys a further argument in support of his claim, that is, if God needed to exercise mercy, then "'mercy' would not be mercy." In this respect, he argues, mercy is quite different from justice, in that God has to exercise justice, but not mercy. Whilst admitting that God is perfectly free to exercise his saving mercy on all, should he desire, he believes that this is an untenable position "both for the doctrine of God and a true understanding of mercy,"[36] though he does not offer any reason why such a position should be "untenable."

Carson refers to the doctrine of God's love as a "difficult doctrine" in a book entitled *Difficult Doctrine of the Love of God*. He argues that God's love is a difficult doctrine because of the manner that the Scriptures speak of God's love in a variety of ways, some with regard to salvation and some not, some focusing on eternal issues, others on temporal. Further still, some texts are universal, whilst others are particular.[37] Strange similarly cites that Calvinistic thought embraces a threefold typology, namely, intra-trinitarian love, common grace (which restrains sin and God's wrath and includes God's gracious provision for all his creatures through divine providence, in that it is "common" to all and universal in its reach), and special grace. Special grace is understood as the grace by which God redeems and is "bestowed only upon those whom God elects to eternal life through faith in his Son."[38] Strange asserts that the Bible overwhelmingly supports the claim that God "has set his affection on particular individuals, or the church in a way that

34. MacDonald, *Evangelical Universalist*, 103, n. 57.

35. Strange, "Calvinist Response," 156.

36. Strange, "Calvinist Response," 157–8,

37. Carson, *Gagging*, 239–42, e.g., God loves the world providentially, ruling over it with mercy (Matt. 5:45); God loves the world with salvific intent (John 3:16); God loves the elect (Deut. 7:7–9; 10:14–15; Mal. 1:2–3; Rom. 9:10–13).

38. Hughes, "Grace," 479–82.

he has not done with others."[39] However, one might respond by asserting that the division between common and special grace is merely a theological and man-made construct which is called to serve a particular theological viewpoint. Henry, similarly to Strange, and in response to those who claim that election-love is discriminatory, argues that all love is preferential or it would not be love.[40] This is a rather extraordinary statement which ignores the possibility that God's love might indeed be universal and extend to all, leaving none cast aside or discriminated against. Strange pithily states that "*in his common grace* God loves all in some way and *in his saving grace . . .* God loves some in all ways."[41] However, it is possible that semantics can sometimes camouflage a defective theology, even when solemnly held.

Against this Calvinistic backdrop, Talbott argues that if God discriminates against specific individuals (the non-elect) in the matter of salvation, humankind need not get animated about lesser forms of discrimination. That is, compared to the discrimination on the most important matter of all, salvation, all other forms of discrimination, sexual, racial etc., would be viewed as lesser.[42] He affirms that God loves all people equally and it is against his nature to show partiality.

Talbott illustrates the logical absurdity of exclusivism by claiming that if he loves his daughter as himself, and as commanded by God, then God could not possibly love him without loving his daughter also, for he is not some isolated monad whose interests are distinct from his loved ones. That is, should God do less for his daughter, he would do less than his best for him. Furthermore, Talbott claims that as long as he loves his daughter, he could neither love God nor worship him unless he believed that God loved his daughter as well. The concept of loving his daughter and loving a God, who might not redemptively love his daughter, he regards as logically absurd. That is, if he truly loves his daughter and desires the best for her, whilst God does not, then (a) his will is not in conformity with God's, (b) he could not consistently approve of God's attitude towards his daughter, and (c) neither could he be grateful to God for the harm that he is doing to his daughter. He claims that it is a logical impossibility to obey both commands, to love others as himself (including his own daughter) and to love God, unless God loves his daughter.[43] John Piper's reaction is quite different to Talbott,

---

39. Strange, "Calvinist Response," 160. He chides Thomas Talbott for fusing together God's special and common grace.

40. Henry, "Is It Fair?" 253–4.

41. Strange, "Calvinist Response," 161. Italics his.

42. Talbott, *Inescapable*, 11–12.

43. See Talbott, *Inescapable*, 138–41.

for when Talbott challenges Piper how he would react to the knowledge that God had not elected one of his sons, he replies, "But I am not ignorant that God may not have chosen my sons for his sons. And, though I think I would give my life for their salvation, if they should be lost to me, I would not rail against the Almighty. He is God. I am but a man. The Potter has absolute rights over the clay. Mine is to bow before his unimpeachable character and believe that the Judge of all the earth has ever and always will do right."[44] Though Piper's frankness and honesty is impressive, he appears to be conceding Talbott's main point, in that Reformed theology teaches God might not love our children as much as we do.

Talbott argues, "If God is love, if love is a part of his very essence, then he cannot act in unloving ways towards anyone, even his enemies."[45] On the basis of this truth Jesus instructed his disciples to love their enemies, and in doing so they would "be perfect" even as their "heavenly Father is perfect" (Matt. 5:43–48).

With a measure of incredulity, Talbott seeks to understand how proponents of limited election might understand and interpret the "God is love" statements in 1 John 4:8 and 16. He provides three examples of the methodology used, namely, to ignore the texts that speak of God's love, to deal with such texts inconsistently, and to engage in a "seemingly intentional kind of subterfuge," which he regards as the most serious difficulty.[46] I shall follow Talbott's argument against the proponents of limited election, offering comment and observation.

Firstly, a number of proponents of limited election simply disregard the texts referred to. Amazingly, Berkhof wrote an entire Systematic Theology without citing either text. Similarly, John Calvin did not regard them as significant enough to include in his *Institutes of Christian Religion*, which Talbott rightly thinks is "truly astonishing" as there are over 1500 pages in Calvin's monumental work. He further notes that in the Westminster Press edition, the index of Bible references alone is 39 pages of small print, with 3 columns per page, yet there is not a single mention of either Johannine declaration.[47]

Secondly, Talbott claims that other advocates of limited election are sometimes inconsistent. He quotes Jonathan Edwards referring to God as infinite, overflowing, inexhaustible, unchangeable, and the eternal source

44. Piper, "How Does," 13.

45. Talbott, *Inescapable*, 108.

46. Talbott, *Inescapable*, 109–18.

47. Talbott, *Inescapable*, 109.

of love.[48] However, when Edwards refers to the damned, he writes, "In hell God manifests his being and perfections only in hatred and wrath, and hatred without love."[49] One is indeed left wondering how Edwards managed to reconcile both statements. Talbott, temptingly, questions what one might think if Edwards had in one place referred to God's *righteousness* as inexhaustible, infinite, unchangeable, and so forth, but then asserted that he acts to some people *without righteousness*. Such inconsistency would be, and is, bewildering at best.

Thirdly, Talbott claims that some engage in "a seemingly intentional kind of subterfuge." The target of Talbott's censure is Packer's book *Knowing God*. On the subject of God's love, Packer commences two successive sections in his book, with the following assertions:

- "'God is love' is not the complete truth about God so far as the Bible is concerned."[50]

- "'God is love' is the complete truth about God so far as the Christian is concerned."[51]

Talbott argues that from the above statements it would appear that either the Bible or the Christian is mistaken about the assertion that "God is love." Indeed, Talbott questions whether Packer intends saying that the Christian's standpoint is at odds with the Bible. However, underlying the apparent vagueness of Packer's statements is the belief that God does not love all human beings, a belief that he understandably chooses to communicate in ambiguous rather than in explicit language.

Calvin is equally confusing in his commentary of the Johannine epistles when he refers to the statement *God is love* (1 John 4:8, 16). He writes, "But the meaning of the Apostle is simply this—that as God is the fountain of love, this effect flows from him, and is diffused wherever the knowledge of him comes, as he had at the beginning called him light, because there is nothing dark in him, but on the contrary he illuminates all things by his brightness. *Here then he does not speak of the essence of God, but only what he is found to be by us*"[52] [i.e., the elect].

Talbott argues persuasively that Calvin having explained that God is the very source (fountain) of love, he then appears, without further explanation, to contradict himself by declaring that love is not the essence or nature of God, but only as the elect perceive him. This, essentially, is what Packer

---

48. Edwards, "Charity," 369, cited in Talbott, *Inescapable*, 110.

49. Edwards, *Works*, 390.

50. Packer, *Knowing*, 132.

51. Packer, *Knowing*, 135.

52. Calvin, *Catholic Epistles*, 239. Italics mine.

appears to be communicating in his statement, "'God is love' is the complete truth about God so far as the Christian is concerned,"[53] although one wonders what Packer might understand by *complete* truth. One would also ask whether Calvin and Packer would use the same exegesis for the statements of "God is light" (1 John 1:5) and "God is Spirit" (John 4:24) by claiming that these statements are not about God's essence, but are the believer's understanding of God. Talbott is correct to assert that, "in Johannine theology at least, God is love in exactly the same sense that he is spirit and is light; that is, it is as impossible for God not to love someone as it is for him to exhibit darkness rather than light."[54]

Talbott further reveals the logical inconsistency of Packer through comparing the statement *God is love* with the statement *God is holy and righteous*. He argues that although the latter statement does not articulate the complete truth about God, it does express a truth about God's nature. If this statement is true, then it would be logically impossible for God to act in any way that is unholy or unrighteous. The same logic would apply for the statement that *God is love*, for if this expresses a truth about the nature of God, then surely it would be impossible for the person of God to fail to love someone, or to act in a way that is unloving. This would be incompatible with the statement *God is love*.[55] MacDonald adds, "If God is love, then *all* God's actions must be compatible with his love. This means that his holiness is loving, his justice is loving, and his wrath is loving."[56] He continues by asking, "How could God be love if he draws a line at death and says, 'Beyond this point I will look for the lost sheep no more; and even if they try to return, I shall turn them away'?"[57]

A scriptural passage often used to support the limited election of God is found in Paul's words of Romans 9:1–23.[58] Piper, in response to Talbott, writes, "What stops him [God] from saving some is, in fact, ultimately his own sovereign will. In order that the purpose of God according to election might remain he loved Jacob and hated Esau (Rom. 9:12, 13). Therefore, I also accept the inference that there are people who are not the objects of God's electing love."[59] Whilst a detailed exegesis of this passage is beyond

---

53. Packer, *Knowing*, 135.

54. Talbott, *Inescapable*, 116.

55. Talbott, *Inescapable*, 113.

56. MacDonald, *Evangelical Universalist*, 103–4.

57. MacDonald, *Evangelical Universalist*, 104.

58. See, for example, Piper, *Justification of God: an exegetical and theological study of Romans 9:1–23*.

59. Piper, "How Does," 10.

the scope and space of this chapter, it is noteworthy that not all scholars understand the doctrine of election in the traditional manner of being good news for some but not for others.[60] For example, according to Barth, election is God's decision in eternity to elect himself to be God of his people and his election of humankind is incorporated into the election of his Son. Jesus is not only the eternal Son, but also the representative human being who uniquely represents humankind universally. Christ is the elect human being in order that all might be elect in him, but he is also the reprobate, and in order to deliver humankind he has borne the judgment of God at Calvary. Nigel Wright calls for a rethinking of election, contending that the proper arena for understanding the doctrine is not eternity but history, with God choosing to work out his purposes in his own free way, through whomever he chooses, however unworthy they might be.[61] Therefore, such statements as "Jacob I loved, but Esau I hated" (Rom. 9:13, see also Mal. 1:2–3) refer to a historical fact that God, for his own reasons, chose to work out his purposes through Jacob, not Esau. This Scripture, therefore, would not refer to some eternal election and reprobation of Jacob and Esau, or anyone else. Brunner concurs by contending that Paul is not speaking of a double decree of God to damnation and everlasting life. Rather, Paul is referring to "God's freedom to cut across natural ties," and also to the history of redemption which runs through Jacob and not Esau being God's free act. Brunner asserts that "there is no word here regarding the bliss or wretchedness of Jacob or Esau."[62]

Wright continues by emphasizing that the "purpose of divine predestination is to elect peoples and persons *for a missionary work, not for exclusive privilege.*"[63] The nation of Israel is an example of what Wright is claiming, that is, they were called by God to be a missionary light to the Gentiles, rather than to rest in a position of privileged status. Wright also speaks of election as an essentially personal activity, not about magisterial decrees promulgated in eternity, and further argues that attention needs to be given to the concept of eternity, as "the concept of past eternity is questionable, since for God there is surely no past eternity but only and always the sovereign freedom over time and eternity."[64] Talbott similarly asserts that "the election of an individual inevitably reaches beyond the elected person to incorporate . . . the community in which the person lives."[65] Abraham could

---

60. Barth, *Church Dogmatics*, 318–9. See also McCormack, "Grace," 93.

61. Wright, *Radical*, 37–43.

62. Brunner, *Romans*, 85.

63. Wright, *Radical*, 38. Italics his.

64. Wright, *Radical*, 38–39.

65. Talbott, *Inescapable*, 120.

be viewed as such an example, for God's promise was that "all peoples on earth will be blessed through you" (Abraham).[66]

Even if this is correct, it is necessary to ask why Paul attributes to God a hatred for Esau? Talbott suggests that this is an anthropomorphism which implies nothing more than "Esau lost—and was destined to lose—in a struggle that he wanted, or thought he wanted to win."[67] In understanding what Paul meant by hatred, one needs to first consider Jesus' statement that "if anyone comes to me and does not hate his father and mother, his wife and children, his brothers and sisters—yes, even his own life—he cannot be my disciple" (Luke 14:26). Jesus' remark was a typical hyperbole found elsewhere in his sayings,[68] meaning that someone must love Jesus as a priority.[69] This could not mean a literal hatred or it would contradict his other sayings, such as the command to love one's enemies (see Matt. 5:44; Luke 6:27, 35).[70] Paul undoubtedly uses "hatred" in a similar hyperbolic manner, showing that as far as God's purposes of election were concerned, it was Jacob not Esau, who was to be God's special instrument in redemption history. Taken this way, the election of Isaac and Jacob in no way implies the ultimate rejection of Ishmael and Esau. In fact, in the struggle between the twins for the birthright, Jacob would win, not because he deserved to win, but because of God's purpose in election, through which means God extends his mercy to all, including Esau. Talbott further argues that one needs to interpret the seeming severity of God's actions (in Rom. 9) in the light of the conclusion to the argument (Rom. 11:32), "For God has bound all men over in disobedience so that he may have mercy on them all."[71]

Often associated with the doctrine of limited or unconditional election is that of limited or particular atonement which claims that Christ's sacrificial death is for the benefit of the elect and not for all people.[72] Reformed theologians believe that when Christ died on the cross, his death paid the price only for those who would ultimately be saved (the elect) and not for the entire human race. That is, they believe that the Atonement of Christ

---

66. See Gen. 12:3; cf. Gal. 3:8.

67. Talbott, *Inescapable*, 122. Bruce, *Romans*, 193, suggests that the context indicates that the nations of Israel and Edom, rather than the individuals of Jacob and Esau, are in view.

68. Other such examples would be found in Matthew 5:21–26; 27–30; 38–42; 7:3–5.

69. Even that a person's love for family would seem like hatred in comparison to their love for Jesus, See Strauss, "Luke," 444–5.

70. See Stott, *Romans*, 267, who views the antithesis as a "Hebrew idiom for preference."

71. Talbott, "Pauline Interpretation," 37–39.

72. For an excellent defense of universal atonement, see Marshall, "For All," 322–46.

is *sufficient* for all sin, but *efficient* only for the sin of the elect. Conversely, Arminian theologians would argue against this view, claiming that if Atonement is limited then the free offer of grace, and God's love, is also limited. Reformed theologians, like Strange, contend that if Christ's death actually made Atonement for the sins of all people, then there is no penalty left for anyone to pay, and it necessarily follows that all people, without exception, will be saved. Thus, God would not condemn anyone to eternal punishment whose sins are already atoned for, as that would demand a double payment, and would be unjust.[73] Such a view, can lead into the "Reformed" universalism of Talbott. Crisp recognizes this and affirms that "it is both coherent and plausible to claim that someone could be both a traditional Augustinian and a universalist."[74]

The problem that traditional Augustinianism faces is that of arbitrariness. That is, if God could have created a world where all humans were elect and where all sin was dealt with in Christ, why didn't he? According to Augustinianism, God elects some in order to display his mercy and grace and reprobates others in order to display his wrath and justice. For God, it is claimed, not to exercise both his grace and his justice would be an affront to God's honor. For example, Jonathan Edwards claimed that a failure by God to display grace and mercy as well as wrath and justice would be a failure to display the fullness of God's character and his own glory.[75] Similarly, Bray states, "If the non-elect have no hope of salvation and God does not want them to suffer unduly, why were they ever created in the first place? Their existence must serve some purpose, and once that is admitted the view that their eternal punishment glorifies the justice of God seems perfectly logical."[76] Yet, even within the Augustinian mind-set, why would it not be possible for God to elect one more person? Crisp states, "All that this argument for the exemplification of divine justice requires is that at least one person be in hell, so that at least one person is punished for their sin in order that divine justice be displayed and divine holiness vindicated." He further reveals that Augustinians often appeal to the inscrutability or mysteriousness of the divine will, and that although to humans God's will might appear arbitrary, this does not make it so.[77]

---

73. See Grudem, *Systematic Theology*, 594–5; Strange, "Calvinist Response," 160–1.

74. Crisp, "Augustinian Universalism," 127.

75. Edwards, "End of Creation in Ethical Writings," 530, as cited in Crisp, "Augustinian Universalism," 130–1.

76. Bray, "Hell," 23.

77. Crisp, "Augustinian Universalism," 132–3.

Crisp demonstrates that there is no good reason why the "restricted elect" view is necessary to advance God's justice and glory. He argues that Augustinian universalism is compatible with the theological principles that are held by those who believe in a restricted elect position namely:

1. God decrees to create and elect humans. In the case of traditional Augustinianism, God elects *some* but not all persons, but in the Augustinian universalism concept described by Crisp, God elects *all* persons.

2. God decrees that the mechanism by which the sin of all humans is atoned for is the death of Christ.

3. The sin and guilt accruing to all sinful humans is transferred to Christ, who is punished on their account on the cross.[78]

Should God elect all humans (1), then all will be saved, thus avoiding the pitfall of arbitrariness to which the traditional view is vulnerable, yet essentially keeping intact Augustinian theology.

Does God love eternally?

Talbott asserts that "there is no suggestion anywhere in Scripture . . . that God's forgiveness has a built-in time limit or that the judgement associated with the *parousia* eliminates every possibility of repentance in the future."[79] Rather, Jesus compared himself to the good shepherd who pursues the one sheep that is lost "*until he finds it*" (Luke 15:4, my italics). This picture portrays Jesus persistently pursuing the sinner until the point of repentance. Similarly, Jesus likens himself to the woman who lost a silver coin. She sweeps the house and searches carefully "*until she finds it*" (Luke 15:8, my italics). The lesson is, when that which was lost is found, there is great rejoicing, as there will be great rejoicing in heaven over the one sinner who repents. The third example that Jesus provides in Luke 15, is that of the parable of the lost, or prodigal, son (Luke 15:11–31) which is perhaps the most poignant of all, clearly portraying the prodigal's father as illustrative of Father God whose broken heart was healed when he saw his son in the distance—"But while he was still a long way off, his father saw him and was filled with compassion for him; he ran to his son, threw his arms around him and kissed him" (Luke 15:20). As with the parables of the lost sheep and the lost coin, a celebration ensued as the son who was lost is now found (v. 32). Whilst none of the above passages explicitly teach of postmortem opportunity, they do portray Christ as a Savior who will not be deflected

78. Crisp, "Augustinian Universalism," 135.

79. Talbott, "Reply to my Critics," 255.

from his mission to the lost, but will continue seeking until he finds. In the absence of any explicit "biblical" understanding on this subject, one is left to assume that such persistence might continue beyond the grave.

Advocates of posthumous salvation typically contend that Christ is the "Hound of Heaven" who pursues his creation to the end and to suggest that death is the boundary of God's loving intent for his creation actually places a boundary upon his love—a boundary that, some propose, is artificial and unfounded.[80] For example, Boyd asks, "Why should we assume that death is an insurmountable obstacle for the Lord when his most definitive act involved defeating the one who had the power of death and overcoming the grave?"[81] It is also argued that God has not changed from love to hate simply because one has died, or that God should forbid anyone who had not loved him before death to do so after death.[82]

Furthermore, Jesus portrayed God as a good Father, infinitely superior in character and morality to any human father. Jesus states, "Which of you, if his son asks for bread, will give him a stone? Or if he asks for a fish, will give him a snake? If you, then, though you are evil, know how to give good gifts to your children, *how much more* will your Father in heaven give good gifts to those who ask him!"[83] Gulley and Mulholland reveal how being parents helped them glimpse the heart of God and that their first few minutes of fatherhood taught them more about love than years of theological study, as they passionately desired to guard, guide, and bless their children.[84] Whilst no human being would ever claim to be the perfect parent, many would give their lives for their children and do anything and everything within their power to save their children from harm or destruction. If God is, as Jesus declared, the perfect parent, would he not also do everything within his power to bring salvation to his children, including the offer of salvation beyond the arena of this life, if that was required?

Some might accuse such a view of God as overly sentimental, a "benignly doting father who carries a photograph of you in his wallet" kind of portrayal, but this is often an overreaction to the traditional view being challenged. It is doubtful whether any advocate of posthumous salvation would support such an over-romantic view of God. To promote the love of God is not to demean his justice or discipline, for what good parent would

---

80. See, for example, Fackre, "Divine Perseverance," 71–95, who actually prefers the term Divine Perseverance for posthumous salvation.

81. Boyd, *Across*, 186.

82. Boyd, *Across*, 186; Pinnock, *Wideness*, 171.

83. Matthew 7:9–11. My italics.

84. Gulley & Mulholland, *If Grace is True*, 58.

excuse the bad behavior or conduct of their child, or, would just say "yes" to every request from their child, or indeed, would withhold discipline that was required? Even so, ultimately, the punitive or disciplinary actions of good parents have the objective of their child's ultimate good. It would therefore, surely, be unimaginable for God, who is infinitely good, to do any less than a human parent by closing the door to any who would see the error of their ways, or wish to acknowledge the Lordship of Christ, beyond the span of this life. It is to be accepted that the sentimental concept of a benignly doting father who turns a blind eye to the conduct of his children is clearly unbiblical and problematic, but, it can be argued, so is the concept of a dualistic God who, as McLaren so poignantly states, is sometimes portrayed as suffering from "borderline personality disorder or some worse sociopathic diagnosis." McLaren, a leading figure in the so-called Emerging Church, writing for a populist readership, caricatures the way that God is sometimes portrayed in contemporary Christianity: "God loves you and has a wonderful plan for your life, and if you don't love God back and cooperate with God's plans in exactly the prescribed way, God will torture you with unimaginable abuse, forever."[85]

In the words of Fackre, "Because Christ really is Life, death has no hold on him. His ministry cannot be constrained by our 'No trespassing' signs."[86] Such sentiment appears to mirror the words of St. Paul who writes of God's love as indestructible and unyielding, "For I am convinced that *neither death* nor life, neither angels nor demons, neither the present nor the future, nor any powers, neither height nor depth, nor anything else in all creation, *will be able to separate us from the love of God* that is in Christ Jesus our Lord" (Rom. 8:38–39).

The justice of God

As previously contended, if God is love, then all of God's attributes and actions must be compatible with his love, which means that his holiness is loving, his justice is loving, and his wrath is loving. The antithesis is also obviously true, in that God's love, holiness, and wrath is just.[87] Erickson defines God's justice as his fair administration of his law, not showing favoritism or partiality.[88] Thus his "justice is loving justice and love is just love." Furthermore, Erickson is probably correct in asserting that the rea-

85. McLaren, *Last Word*, xii.

86. Fackre, "Scandals," 32–52, [51].

87. MacDonald, *Evangelical Universalist*, 103–4.

88. Erickson, *Christian Theology*, 315.

son divine love and justice conflict is because these attributes are defined in isolation from one another.[89] Therefore, an attempt will be made in this section to understand how God's justice and love are to be understood as complementary, rather than contradictory, truths about the nature of God. This present section on the justice of God will be further divided into two subsections, namely, "justice as retribution" and "justice as restoration." The latter will be presented as a possible alternative to the more traditional position of divine justice being essentially punitive.

Justice as retribution

Traditionally, sin is defined as an affront to God's glory.[90] For example, Bavinck states that eternal punishment is necessary due to the sinfulness of sin and the integrity of the justice of God. He asserts that "sin is not a weakness, a lack . . . [or] imperfection, but in origin and essence it is lawlessness (*anomia*), a violation of the law, rebellion and hostility against God, the negation of his justice, his authority, even his existence."[91] Strange adds that God is angry with sin, for "it represents a negation of his being and must be exposed and attacked, God cannot be or seen to be morally indifferent to sin."[92] This understanding of sin provides the theological backdrop to the concept of divine retribution, which means that sinners must pay the penalty for their sin. Divine retribution is, therefore, not remedial, restorative, nor discretionary,[93] for in the retributive model of justice, God has no choice but to punish sin, with hell being the place where God's wrath is dispensed against sinners who have disobeyed his law.[94]

According to this view, sin is to be punished infinitely, as it is claimed that a sin committed against an infinite God constitutes an infinite punishment.[95] That is, the punishment must fit the crime. Strange asserts, "Pun-

89. Erickson, *Christian Theology*, 324.

90. See Rom. 1:21–25; 3:23; and Fernando, *Crucial Questions*, 99–104. See also Ps. 53:4.

91. Bavinck, *Last Things*, 151.

92. Strange, "Calvinist Response," 150.

93. Hilborn, *Nature of Hell*, 68–76, lists five positions on the doctrine of hell, namely, eternal conscious physical and spiritual torment; eternal conscious spiritual torment; eternal separation from God; conditional immortality; annihilationism.

94. This is what Crisp refers to as the "strong justice claim," in that God's justice does not *permit* forgiveness, in contrast to the weaker view which maintains that God's justice does not *require* forgiveness. This stronger view holds that a person's sin *must* be punished and cannot remain unpunished, see Crisp, "Divine Retribution," 36–37.

95. Original (or inherited) sin is often introduced into this conversation, where it is

ishment in hell is not about making people better but is about retribution 'imposed because wrong is wrong and God is against it.'"[96] Essentially, it is taught that sinners are punished infinitely in hell "because they deserve it, because justice is served in this way."[97] Anselm originally argued that since God is infinitely great, any sin against him will incur an infinite demerit.[98] However, Adams emphasizes that the social background to Anselm's argument is of a feudal society where the seriousness of a crime is evaluated by both the offence and the social status of the victim and carries little weight today as the social status of a victim would no longer be considered.[99] Many

---

claimed that, apart from their own actual sin, a person is guilty and deserving of God's wrath due to Adam's sin. Talbott is logically correct to claim that original sin compounds the difficulty of the retributivist theory of punishment, for, if people have a depraved or corrupt nature, and are subject to evil impulses not of their own making, then God has less to forgive, not more. He argues that one of the most important intuitions of the retributivist theory is that a person is neither responsible nor justly punished for the sins of another. See Talbott, *Inescapable*, 151–3. Crisp, "Divine Retribution," 46–47, responds by quoting Jonathan Edwards's view that there is a double guilt associated with sin—that which has been accrued by Adam, but also that which has been accrued through an individual's actual sin. See footnote 34, page 47.

96. Strange, "Calvinist Response," 151, citing Donnelly, *Heaven and Hell*, 19. The kind of punishment meted out in hell is not essential to the focus of this book, though for a variety of views on this subject, see Crockett, *Four Views on Hell*, which presents four views (literal physical punishment, metaphorical view, conditional immortality, and Purgatory).

97. MacDonald, *Evangelical Universalist*, 11.

98. Anselm, "Cur Deus Homo," I:XXI; Aquinas, T. "Venial Sin," art.4, arg. 2.

99. Adams, "Hell and the Justice of God," 433–47. Crisp, "Divine Retribution," 36–53, however, defends the Anselmian view by declaring that crimes committed against humans are more serious than crimes committed against animals. Thus to recognize the ontological difference between humans and animals that makes crimes against humans more legally responsible to punishment and paves the way to support the view that God is ontologically infinitely greater than humans, so that crimes against him would deserve greater (infinite) punishment. However, what Crisp overlooks is that not all crimes are infinitely bad. MacDonald, *Evangelical Universalist*, 12, challenges Crisp's position by a simple illustration: suppose John has 10 units of honor. Imagine that Philip ignores John in public whilst Simon spits in John's face. Both have offended his honor, but the amount of demerit is surely not 10 units in both cases. The nature of their crimes plays a key role in their punishment. He is, I believe, correct to assert that "It does not necessarily follow from the claim that God has infinite honour that *any* crime against him is infinitely bad. This is because the gravity of an offense is determined not merely by the status of the offended party but also by the nature of the offense." Talbott, *Inescapable*, 154–5, adds, the Anselmian concept of every sin being infinitely serious and deserving the same penalty as every other sin, namely everlasting torment, undermines an idea central to the retributivist theory that punishments can be graded in hell. Talbott's assertion is rebutted by Crisp (see "Divine Retribution," 38), who, logically, though unconvincingly, claims that it is feasible to believe that just because all sinners might be punished infinitely, it does not, of necessity, mean that they

find a serious problem of proportionality in the divine retribution view-point and ask "what finite human sin could possibly warrant an eternal punishment?"[100] It is also argued that such a theory would be contrary to God's own law of "an eye for an eye and a tooth for a tooth" (Lev. 24:17–20; Deut. 19:21). Talbott correctly states that this law was instituted "for the purpose of eliminating excessive punishment, such as capital punishment in exchange for a tooth."[101]

According to the retributivist view, God is duty-bound by his own righteousness to punish wrongdoers for their sin, thereby upholding his own moral order. It is held that though God is loving and merciful, he cannot simply forgive sin as divine justice demands satisfaction. Thus the "genius of the cross is that it allows God to satisfy the demands of retributive justice by inflicting the penalty of sin on Christ, while at the same time satisfying his mercy by conferring forgiveness on sinners."[102] The doctrine of penal substitution, which developed out of Anselm's "satisfaction theory," contends that God passed the penalty of condemnation, that the law demanded, on to a substitute. Such notions of legal satisfaction and substitutionary punishment have exercised a dominant influence on Western theology, especially since the time of the Reformation. Marshall is especially critical of the theory of penal substitution, claiming that the "identification of divine righteousness with God's vindictive or punitive justice has had a complex and often distorting effect on Christian thinking about justice."[103]

Marshall argues that, firstly, Paul does not understand the Atonement as a matter of penal substitution as *conventionally understood*,[104] and secondly, that penal substitution gives primacy in the work of Christ to retributive features of divine justice, thereby inheriting all the defects of retributive theories of justice.[105] Discussion on the doctrine of penal substitution has

---

are punished equally. He gives the example of two sinners, Trevor and Gary. Both are consigned to hell forever and therefore suffer infinite punishment in hell, but Trevor is punished just one hour a day compared to Gary's punishment of twelve hours each day.

100. Talbott, *Inescapable*, 150.

101. Talbott, *Inescapable*, 149.

102. Marshall, *Beyond Retribution*, 44.

103. Marshall, *Beyond Retribution*, 44, 60, effectively challenges the view, held by some scholars, like Packer & Morris (see Packer, *What Did the Cross Achieve?*, and Morris, *The Cross in the New Testament*, 382–8), that penal substitution is basic to how Paul understands the Atonement.

104. Italics Marshall, *Beyond Retribution*, 61. For Marshall's argument, see pp. 60–68, where he claims that even though there are elements of sacrifice, substitution, wrath and penalty in Paul's reflections on the cross, he doesn't put them together in a thorough theory of penal substitution.

105. Marshall, *Beyond Retribution*, 65.

been given fresh impetus in recent years following the publication of *The Lost Message of Jesus* in which Steve Chalke and Alan Mann provoked an evangelical outcry by stating, now infamously, that "the cross isn't a form of cosmic child abuse—a vengeful Father, punishing his Son for an offence he has not even committed."[106] Marshall's hypothesis is that early Christians understood justice as a power that "heals, restores and reconciles" rather than that which "hurts, punishes and kills."[107] He criticizes the penal substitution theory for the following reasons:

1. There is a tendency to conceive of justice in abstract, legal terms more than personal or relational terms.

2. The penal model portrays atonement as a forensic transaction between God the Father and God the Son, acting as virtually independent subjects, rather than as a healing of relationships between humanity and God, and where God takes the initiative and personally bears the cost of doing so.[108]

3. God's own freedom is constrained, as it would appear that God cannot forgive until the punishment demanded by the law, is exacted. In this, Marshall explains, "The law becomes the supreme principle, and punishment becomes a necessity imposed on God by a superior rule." Though it might be argued that God places himself under such an imposition and that the "superior rule" is God's chosen way.[109]

4. Punishment is invested with too much efficacy, and sin with too little. That is, sin is thought of as a "debt incurred against God which the punishment imposed on Christ serves to discharge." Marshall claims that Paul takes sin more seriously than a "moral debt on the pages of a divine ledger" and depicts sin as an "alien power that distorts personality, corrupts relationships, and enslaves the human will." He contends that it is unclear how punishment can affect the kind of comprehensive

---

106. Chalke & Mann, *Lost Message*, 182. According to Wright, Chalke and Mann were misunderstood by challenging the caricature of penal substitution rather than the doctrine itself, see Wright, *Cross and the Caricature*. Chalke's and Mann's book was the catalyst for a Joint Evangelical Alliance-London School of Theology Atonement Symposium (6–8 July 2005) where scholars debated the nuances of this position. For further study, see, Jeffrey and Sachs, *Pierced for Our Transgressions*; Beilby and Eddy, (eds.), *Nature of the Atonement*.

107. Marshall, *Beyond Retribution*, 33.

108. Marshall, *Beyond Retribution*, 66.

109. Marshall, *Beyond Retribution*, 66.

deliverance from the power of sin and renewal of relationship with God which Paul ascribes to the atoning work of Christ.[110]

5. If God cannot tolerate sin, as penal advocates maintain, then why should God appear more concerned with exacting retribution than rooting out the causes and effects of sin in the lives of sinners? Essentially, why shouldn't a restorative remedy, instead of a retributive one, satisfy God's justice?[111]

Marshall's claim is that Paul does not view justice merely in terms of legal or "forensic" retribution, but that he employs a more Jewish concept of covenant justice, where the emphasis is upon covenant faithfulness, liberation, and restoration. This will be critiqued later in this chapter, though a thorough evaluation of the nuances of the penal theory is neither necessary, nor possible, for the purposes of this book.

Not all scholars who hold a retributivist theology maintain that punishment is imposed by God upon sinners against their will and as a just penalty for their sin. Reitan, for example, distinguishes between the traditional, or classical, understanding of the doctrine of hell and a progressive view. The traditional view, as described above, asserts that the sufferings of the damned are imposed by God, whereas, the progressive understanding holds that the sufferings are "those that necessarily attend the state of alienation from God" and are due to their entirely free choices of rejecting God. That is, while God could overrule a person's free-will choices, he chooses not to do so out of respect for the person's freedom.[112]

From our prior understanding of God's nature, that God's love is always just and his justice always loving, one is confronted with the significant difficulties of the traditional retributivist view which teaches that God imposes his retribution upon the damned. Such action could not be viewed as a justice that is loving; rather, it would be a form of justice that is devoid of love and incompatible with the nature of God.[113] Furthermore, if it is believed that God can, and does, forgive sinners in this age without being unjust, it is not clear why his justice should prevent him from forgiving people postmortem.[114]

The progressive view moves towards solving this dilemma, claiming that the demands of God's justice are no longer an impediment to salvation

---

110. Marshall, *Beyond Retribution*, 67.

111. Marshall, *Beyond Retribution*, 67.

112. Reitan, "Human Freedom," 126. See also Walls, *Hell: The Logic of Damnation*, especially chapter 5.

113. See Walls, "Philosophical Critique," 105–24.

114. See Parry & Partridge, *Universal Salvation?* xxviii.

for anyone, as they have been met through Christ's death. Hell is then viewed not as being forced upon people by a wrathful God, but is the result of their decision to remain alienated from God. C. S. Lewis, who spoke of the doors of hell as being locked from the inside, would have been an advocate of the progressive viewpoint.[115] Others that would embrace this progressive view would include, for example, Bloesch who allows for the concept of people being transferred from hell to heaven, with hell being thought of as "a sanatorium of sick souls presided over by Jesus." For Bloesch, hell is not a place of everlasting punishment; rather it is exclusion from communion with God and "part of God's loving plan." He writes, "We do not wish to build fences around God's grace, however, and we do not preclude that some in hell might finally be translated into heaven. The gates of the holy city are depicted as being open day and night (Isa. 60:11; Rev. 21:25), and this means that access to the throne of grace is possible continuously. The gates of hell are locked, but they are locked only from within." Bloesch asserts "that none will be lost, who do not obstinately to the end and in the end refuse God."[116]

Davis similarly contends that the inhabitants of hell "are in hell because they choose to be in hell; no one is sent to hell against his or her will."[117] He argues that hell is a place of separation, not from God, but from the blessings of a communion with God, claiming that to be a citizen of hell is to be largely miserable for one lives apart from love, joy, peace, and light. His position views God's justice as having been met through Christ, with God offering salvation to all without partiality. Some choose to remain alienated from God, but this is to be viewed as their doing rather than God's imposition.

Reitan insists that if Christ's Atonement only atones for the sins of some, but not all, then "this would seem to derogate from the power and significance of Christ's death on the cross."[118] Wesley, in his day, even more forcibly, pronounced that the kind of love that advocates of limited atonement ascribe to God is such "as makes your blood run cold."[119] Reichenbach poignantly asks, "If he [God] can show irresistible grace to all without harming his omnipotence and goodness, why then does he not?"[120]

---

115. Lewis, *Problem*, 115.

116. Bloesch, *Essentials*, 2:225–7. However, one needs great care in using the symbolism of Revelation to rest the case for posthumous salvation.

117. Davis, "Universalism," 179.

118. Reitan, "Human Freedom," 127.

119. Outler, *John Wesley*, 447.

120. Reichenbach, "Freedom," 290.

Similarly, Pinnock states that hell is "more of a matter of self-destruc-tion, the logical result of final rejection of God. God does not choose hell for people—they choose it."[121] He claims that hell exists for sinners who, though forgiven, continually reject their acceptance by God. That is, "God invited them to his supper, but they declined the invitation." Hell exists because divine love can be refused. In this, Pinnock separates himself from univer-salism by maintaining that God will take "no" for an answer.[122] However, the hell that Pinnock envisages is not one of eternal suffering, but of ultimate destruction, preferring the theory of conditional immortality which holds that humans are created mortal, not immortal.[123] This, he considers, is a more just view of hell as no crime could deserve such eternal punishment, nor would any purpose be served by such unending torture. He also claims that conditional immortality paints a better metaphysical picture, not leav-ing heaven and hell to exist alongside each other for eternity with such stark dualism.[124] Thus, everlasting life is a gift received through faith and not a natural capacity. The biblical images of destruction and ruin are then under-stood as the termination of existence rather than eternal suffering. It would appear that although Pinnock and Lewis agree on a person's ultimate fate being their own doing, rather than God imposing some judgment, Lewis and Pinnock would disagree on the concept of conditional immortality. Lewis interprets hell as where self-centered lives go on forever.[125]

Though the conditional immortality view of scholars, like Pinnock, provides a more cogent model for understanding the justice of God, as it removes the concept of a merciless God who inflicts eternal punishment upon his creation, this concept is only partially helpful as a model for un-derstanding God's justice. Whilst "destruction" replaces "eternal torment," one might still ask whether such "justice" is coherent and compatible with God's love. The language used in describing the "eternal punishment" view is sometimes uncompromising. For example, Stott states, "I find the concept intolerable and do not understand how people can live with it without either

121. Pinnock, *Unbounded Love*, 88.

122. It is outside the scope of this book to argue whether Pinnock is correct in his assertion, but for the opposing point of view see Talbott, *Inescapable*, chapter 11, 181–99.

123. It would appear that the view of conditional immortality can be held in tension with either the classical or progressive view of hell. That is, one might believe that God imposes punishment for sin because he is angry with sinners, or, that sinners are merely reaping the penalty for their own choices.

124. Pinnock, *Unbounded Love*, 93.

125. Pinnock, *Unbounded Love*, 90.

cauterizing their feelings or cracking under the strain."[126] Likewise, Wenham contends that the traditional doctrine of hell speaks of "sadism, not justice. It is a doctrine which I do not know how to preach without negating the loveliness and glory of God. From the days of Tertullian it has been the emphasis of fanatics. It is a doctrine that makes the Inquisition look reasonable. It all seems a flight from reality and common sense."[127]

Robinson argues that love and justice should not be viewed as two parallel attributes which represent different aspects of God's nature, and justice should not be a substitute for love when love has failed. Rather, God's justice is an expression of love's working. Thus, God's love is neither sentimental nor arbitrary and vindictive, asserting that if judgment were God's last word, it would indicate the failure of love.[128] Pinnock similarly states, "The purpose of judgment is mercy. If God had his way, all his judgments would be penultimate."[129]

Proponents of posthumous salvation argue that a God who is just would not condemn those who did not have the opportunity to hear the gospel and believe without first discerning their response to him and the gospel. They strongly oppose the views of restrictivists who believe that the only way of salvation is for people to make a conscious decision for Christ who has been presented to them in this life. Those that believe in "grace beyond the grave" claim that such a view held by restrictivists is unfair and unjust since it is not the fault of someone being born in the wrong place and at the wrong time where s/he cannot hear the gospel. Restrictivists respond to this objection claiming that care needs to be taken before concluding that God is unfair as the standard of justice and holiness is God's own character and it would be presumptuous for the clay to criticize the potter.[130] Carson provides an example of restrictivist misunderstanding, or misrepresentation, in accusing Pinnock, Sanders, and "hard" inclusivists of tragically distorting the love of God. He claims that they have somehow turned the love of God, which is undeserved, unmerited, and lavish, into God being blameworthy for not trying harder to save souls. He states that "what starts

---

126. Edwards & Stott, *Essentials*, 314. Edwards referred to the God presented in the classical view of hell as the "Eternal Torturer" which encouraged this response from Stott. See also Marshall, "New Testament," 60, who believes that the view of endless, conscious suffering is irreconcilable with the love of God.

127. Wenham, *Facing Hell*, 254.

128. Robinson, *In the End*, 114–7.

129. Pinnock, *Unbounded Love*, 70.

130. See Boyd, *Across*, 182.

off as a defense of the love of God quickly turns into an indictment of God." This, I believe, is a distortion of the views of Sanders and Pinnock.[131]

Care does indeed need to be taken in concluding that God is unfair and it is perfectly acceptable to contend that God's own character is the standard of justice and holiness. However, no advocate of posthumous salvation or any of the other wider hope views claims that God is unfair. Rather, he *would be* unfair if he condemned those who had no opportunity to respond positively to the gospel, which is indeed a reason to question the validity of the restrictivists' ideology. Also, since all proponents of the wider hope views fervently disagree with the claims of restrictivism, which they view as an aberration on the character of God, and passionately believe in God's justice and fairness, the allegation directed at them of their claim that God is unfair proves to be invalid.

Furthermore, it can be argued that God has provided humans with a true understanding of what justice means through using human analogy in the Scriptures. For example, Jesus speaks of God as being impartial and who expects his children to follow his example. "But I tell you: Love your enemies and pray for those who persecute you, that you may be sons of your Father in heaven. He causes his sun to rise on the evil and the good, and sends rain on the righteous and the unrighteous . . . Be perfect, therefore, as your heavenly Father is perfect" (Matt. 5:44–45, 48). To suggest that God's standard of justice is somehow of a different kind to what we perceive justice to be, or to think that the word "justice" means something different when referring to God than when demanded from us, is untenable. It makes language so elastic that it no longer means anything. At the heart of biblical ethics lies the conviction that the standard for human behavior is the character and activity of God. For example, the writer of 1 Peter encourages believers to follow the model of God's holiness: "But just as he who called you is holy, so be holy in all you do; for it is written: 'Be holy, because I am holy'" (1:15). Similarly, on other occasions, believers are called to imitate God's mercy (Matt. 5:7, see also Matt. 9:13; 12:7; Luke 10:37); offer forgiveness to others (Matt. 6:14); act with generosity (2 Cor. 8:9); walk in humility (Phil. 2:6–11); practice servanthood (Mark 10:45); be peacemakers (Matt. 5:9; Eph. 2:14–22); and love others (John 13:34; Eph. 5:2).

As demonstrated in this section, the traditional retributivist view of justice has serious deficiencies, not least in its inability to address the issue of a "schizophrenic" view of God which contests his mercy against his justice.[132] Moreover, the God whom believers are called to imitate might be

---

131. See Carson, *Gagging*, 289–90.

132. Talbott, "Pauline Interpretation," 32.

thought of as ultimately vindictive, not forgiving. In the next section, an alternative model which understands justice as restorative will be evaluated.

Justice as restoration

In this section, divine justice will be further examined in an attempt to discover whether it is better understood in terms of restoration, rather than retribution, and whether this model of divine justice is not only robustly biblical, but more theologically viable, resulting in divine justice and love being compatible and complementary characteristics of God, rather than contradictory or competing aspects in God's nature. This section will concentrate on five areas: firstly, an assessment of how the gospel writers considered Jesus' life and ministry as a demonstration of divine justice; secondly, how Paul understood and portrayed divine justice; thirdly, how divine justice is best viewed as a "righting of wrongs"; fourthly, why forgiveness is an appropriate response to sin, by God; fifthly, in the light of a restorative model of justice how one understands the clearly retributive elements and language in the Bible.

JUSTICE AND JESUS

The central theme of Jesus' ministry, as recorded by the Synoptic writers, the declaration and establishment of God's kingdom on earth (e.g., Matt. 3:2; Mark 1:14–15), was, as Hays asserts, an announcement of "the radical restoration of God's justice, setting things right but bringing judgment and destruction to those who resist God's will."[133] Jesus called his followers to "seek first his kingdom and his righteousness" (Matt. 6:33) and to pray that God's kingdom should come and his "will be done on earth as in heaven" (Matt. 6:9–10), which was elucidated and demonstrated through Jesus' teaching and life as recorded in the gospels. This restoration of God's justice was to be pursued through making God's agenda one's own, and by serving the least and the lost, liberating the oppressed, and feeding the poor, as well as caring for the victims of injustice.[134]

Whilst the extent of how Jesus declared and practiced "the radical restoration of God's justice" is well beyond the scope of this short section,

133. Hays, *Moral Vision*, 163. This kingdom message coincided with the Jewish hope that centered on the revelation of divine power to vindicate Israel's trust in God, to chastise the oppressor and liberate the abused and exploited, and to make Israel the center of peace and justice, see Haughey, "Jesus as the Justice of God," 267.

134. See Luke 4:18–19; 6:20–36; 10:25–37 as examples.

Jesus' teaching on forgiveness and non-retaliation which have a bearing on the question of a restorative, rather than retributive, justice will be cited.

Firstly, Jesus discarded the current practice of his day of limited forgiveness and taught his disciples to forgive without limit as recorded in Matthew's Gospel, "Then Peter came to Jesus and asked, 'Lord, how many times shall I forgive my brother when he sins against me? Up to seven times?' Jesus answered, 'I tell you, not seven times but seventy seven times.'"[135] Rabbis of the time taught that people should be prepared to forgive repeat offenders up to three times. Peter suspecting that Jesus would expect more than other teachers, doubles the number and adds one more. Jesus in answering "seventy seven times" was not offering a literal limit to forgiveness, but to rule out any calculation in offering forgiveness to others. The standard of divine justice of God's kingdom demands unlimited forgiveness. In Luke's version of this saying (17:3–4), the offender's repentance is referred to as a basis for forgiveness, even so, the emphasis lies on the gratuitous and uncalculating nature of forgiveness. This is a teaching that Jesus himself put into practice on the cross as he prayed for his persecutors, "Father, forgive them, for they do not know what they are doing" (Luke 23:34), which is indicative of how Christ might act towards sinful humans at the Judgment. It would be difficult to believe that Christ himself would not act in accordance with his own precept when he fulfils his role as Judge. For if Jesus could treat his persecutors and enemies with such overwhelming forgiveness, could he not exercise the same attitude at the *eschaton*, especially towards those who, through no fault of their own, might not have heard the gospel?

Secondly, Jesus places great significance on one's readiness to forgive others, making it a condition for one's own forgiveness by God. The Lord's Prayer links the human and divine aspects of forgiveness, "Forgive us our debts, as we also have forgiven our debtors"[136] and, in Matthew's account, is almost immediately reinforced by, "For if you forgive men when they sin against you, your heavenly Father will also forgive you. But if you do not forgive men their sins, your Father will not forgive your sins."[137] It would be wrong to understand these verses to teach that somehow God's forgiveness is earned or merited by our forgiving attitude. Rather, it is the gift of God's forgiveness which constrains human forgiveness. For example, in Luke 7:47–48 where Jesus said to Simon the Pharisee, concerning the woman who anointed his feet with perfume, "Therefore, I tell you, her sins have been forgiven—for she loved much. But he who has been forgiven little

---

135. Matthew 18:21–22. Alternative reading in footnote: 'seventy times seven.'
136. Matt. 6:12 and Luke 11:4.
137. Matt. 6:14–15. See also Mark 11:25 and Luke 6:37.

loves little." Her passionate response was out of a profound sense of gratitude to Christ for his forgiveness. Jesus showed that for a follower of Christ,
forgiveness is not an optional extra but an obligation, and a demonstration
of the values of the kingdom of God.

In association with Christ's teaching on forgiveness, is his teaching
and example on non-retaliatory love. As 1 Peter 2:23 declares, "When they
hurled their insults at him, he did not retaliate; when he suffered, he made
no threats. Instead, he entrusted himself to him who judges justly," thus
providing an example for his followers. On one occasion, Jesus chastised
James and John for wanting to call fire down from heaven on a Samaritan
village that had not welcomed messengers that Jesus had sent ahead (Luke
9:51–56). He also reprimanded Peter for his violent reaction, of cutting off
the ear of the servant of the high priest with a sword, when the mob came
to arrest Jesus in Gethsemane. Jesus instructed to "Put your sword back in
its place . . . for all who draw the sword will die by the sword" (Matt. 26:52).

Furthermore, at face value, Jesus' teaching appeared to reject the established interpretation of the law of retaliation (*lex talionis*) of an "eye for
an eye" in preference of "turning the other cheek" (Matt. 5:38–42).[138] The
lex talionis was never intended to endorse revenge, which was specifically
forbidden in the law (Lev. 19:18; Deut. 32:35). The *lex* served the purposes
of (i) limiting the destructive aspects of revenge—that is, only an eye for an
eye and no more; (ii) providing an equitable basis for making restitution or
providing compensation in personal injury cases.[139] Marshall claims that
the *lex talionis* was understood in a sense of moral vindication, not literal
physical retribution, and its influence lay in its rhetorical power aimed at
emphasizing that penalties for an offence bore both moral equivalency and
material proportionality.[140] In the light of this, it is unlikely that Jesus would
have been especially perturbed by the *lex talionis* which would have played
an important and justifiable role in the administration of Jewish justice. It is
more likely that Jesus was inviting his hearers to learn to respond to wrongdoing in ways that transcended the principle of equivalence found in the *lex
talionis*. That is, "for Jesus equivalent recompense is not the heart of justice
or the supreme principle of morality. There is something more fundamental

138. The *lex talionis* is found on three occasions in the Mosaic law—Exodus 21:20–
25; Leviticus 24:19–22; Deuteronomy 19:18–21.

139. See Marshall, *Beyond*, 80–84, who provides a fascinating account of how the
lex was administered in Hebrew culture, listing reasons why the *lex* was not applied
literally except in the case of certain capital offences.

140. See Marshall, *Beyond*, 82–84; Kidner, "Retribution," 5; Fisher, "Exploration,"
584–7, [585].

to achieving true justice than justifiable revenge."[141] Rather than repudiating or abolishing the Old Testament commandment, Jesus is rendering it redundant for his followers who are called to surpass the righteousness/justice of the Pharisees and the teachers of the law.[142]

Following the "eye for an eye" principle cited in Matthew 5:38, Jesus provided four tangible illustrations, that is,

- "Do not resist an evil person. If someone strikes you on the right cheek, turn to him the other also" (v. 39).

- "If someone wants to sue you and take your tunic, let him have your cloak as well" (v. 40).

- "If someone forces you to go one mile, go with him two miles" (v. 41).

- "Give to the one who asks you, and do not turn away from the one who wants to borrow from you" (v. 42).

In verse 39, Jesus is commanding one to forego the legal right to seek judicial damages against the wrongdoer.[143] There is a division of opinion on whether the strike on the right cheek is a back-handed slap as a calculated insult, or a closed-fist punch, which would normally have contact with the left side of the victim's face, assuming a right-handed assailant.[144] Either way, Jesus encourages his followers not to seek legal vindication but to absorb the assault.

In verse 40, this is an illustration of someone being sued. The tunic was the undergarment, whilst the cloak was an outer garment, which according to the law could not be held as security by a creditor for more than one day.[145] Again, Jesus is commanding that the wronged party should not appeal to his/her rights, but should take the initiative, possibly as a means of facilitating reconciliation.

In verse 41, it was the Roman custom for a soldier to command someone from a vassal people to provide forced labor. If one mile designates the limit of one's legal obligation, then Jesus is exhorting the victim, not to respond by grasping on to their legal obligation, but to be generous, even to their enemy.

In verse 42, the concept of giving to those in need follows closely to "going the second mile," by showing an open-handed generosity of spirit,

141. Marshall, *Beyond*, 85.

142. See Matthew 5:18–20.

143. Guelich, *Sermon*, 25, 219–20.

144. See Zerbe, *Non-Retaliation*, 180–4, for the insult view, and Hays, *Moral*, 325–6, for the physical attack view.

145. See Exodus 22:25–26; Deuteronomy 24:10–13; cf. Amos 2:8.

rather than a tight-fisted and hard-hearted abiding by the legal obligations. Marshall contests, "Rather than perceiving human relationships as
controlled by legal rights and tit-for-tat equivalence, which in turn presup-
poses that sinful self-centeredness is the ruling principle, Jesus calls for
relationships in which sin and self are no longer the controlling factors."[146]
Immediately following the passage on the outworking of the *lex talionis*
(Matt. 5:38–43), Matthew includes Jesus' teaching on loving and blessing
one's enemies (5:43–48). The reason that Jesus gives for such magnanimous
goodwill towards one's enemies is because that is what God is like, and
followers of Christ need to follow his example, "But I tell you: Love your
enemies and pray for those who persecute you, that you may be sons of your
Father in heaven. He causes his sun to rise on the evil and the good, and
sends rain on the righteous and the unrighteous . . . Be perfect, therefore,
as your heavenly Father is perfect" (Matt. 5:44–45, 48). This clearly links
the morality of Christian disciples to the nature of God himself in that God
does not respond to his enemies merely by the law of equivalence, but places
the restoration of relationships above the principles of strict legal justice.[147]

Restorative justice, which centers on forgiveness and non-retaliation
cannot be charged with minimizing sin, as it takes the reality of evil as seriously as a form of justice that emphasizes retribution.[148] As discussed above,
Jesus' teaching and example on forgiveness and non-retaliation favors the
restorative, rather than the retributive, model of justice.

JUSTICE AND PAUL

Among the multiplicity of ways that Paul explicates Christ's work on the
cross, the metaphor of justice is extensively used. Marshall contends that
modern readers of the New Testament seldom realize how often "justice"
language appears due to the way in which English translations render key
Greek terms (the *dik*—stem), sometimes as "right" terms (right, righteous,
righteousness) and sometimes "just" terms (just, justify, justification). Furthermore, he claims, due to this linguistic peculiarity, that "English-speaking
readers sense little obvious connection between the 'right' language of the

---

146. Marshall, *Beyond*, 88–89.

147. John Piper unconvincingly attempts to sidestep the obvious implication of this
verse by emphasizing the distinction between special grace and common grace. He
asserts, "It is questionable that we are commanded to love in a way which God fails to
love. We are never commanded to dispense electing love. We are not given the assign-
ment of ultimately determining anyone's destiny. We are commanded to show kindness
and patience." Piper, "How Does a Sovereign God Love?" n.p.

148. See Marshall, *Beyond*, 94.

New Testament and the concept of justice." He rightly states that, in English, this problem is further compounded with "righteousness" having a sense of ethical purity or religious piety, whilst "justice" refers to public fairness and equality of rights. That is, "righteousness" belongs to the moral realm and "justice" belongs to the public, legal realm. The "right" word group is semantically loaded and embraces a wide range of applications (including, forensic, socio-political, ethical, and religious). Marshall, claims that neither "righteousness" nor "justice" are adequate translations which contain the idea of well-being, wholeness, and peace.[149]

Paul's letter to Romans identifies the gospel with the righteousness of God, which is the central theme of the letter.[150] The phrase "the righteousness of God" appears in Romans on eight occasions (Rom. 1:17; 3:5, 21, 22, 25, 26; 6:13; 10:3). This is to be compared with this same phrase only appearing twice in other Pauline writings (2 Cor. 5:21 and Phil. 3:9), and three times elsewhere in the NT (Matt. 6:33; Jas. 1:20; 2 Pet. 1:1). In all, there are sixty-three occurrences of "right" terminology.[151] Romans, therefore, as Gunton maintains, could be rightly described as "a treatise on the justice of God" and a logical place to gain a New Testament understanding of divine justice.[152]

According to Marshall, the gospel, as depicted in Romans, is a manifestation of God's justice, which includes the forensic character of justification, though not exclusively. The forensic character of justification refers to the essentially legal concept of a person's legal standing before God, whereby God the righteous judge passes a verdict of acquittal and pardon on a believer due to the vicarious work of Christ. Marshall asserts, "For when the forensic dimension is reduced to rendering a not-guilty verdict in the court of heaven, it fails patently to comprehend the scope of Paul's theology of salvation."[153] McGrath also argues that Paul's interpreters have unwittingly brought to the text an especially Western notion of retributive justice

149. Marshall, *Beyond*, 35–37. Knight "Is 'Righteous' Right?" 1–10, contends that the English word righteousness is a wholly inept translation of the corresponding biblical, especially Hebrew, terms, when applied to God, because it "conjures up a vision of an unattractive, self-righteous individual who knows how to blow his own horn" (9).

150. Rom. 1:16–17 "I am not ashamed of the gospel, because it is the power of God for the salvation of everyone who believes: first for the Jew, then for the Gentile. For in the gospel a righteousness from God is revealed, a righteousness that is by faith from first to last, just as it is written: 'The righteous will live by faith.'"

151. *Dikaoisunē* (righteousness, justice) the most used with 33 occurrences and *dikaioō* (to justify, rectify) used 15 times, see Marshall, *Beyond*, 38, for full listings. See also Dunn, *Theology of Paul*, 341, n. 25.

152. Gunton, *Actuality*, 102.

153. Marshall, *Beyond*, 43.

rather than a Hebraic concept of covenant justice based on relationship.[154] According to Gunton, many of the early Latin Fathers were lawyers, and were predisposed to express the relationship between humans and God in legal terminology.[155]

Furthermore, Dunn argues that it is imperative to appreciate that Paul's understanding of "righteousness" is to be determined more by its Hebrew background than its Greek premise. This is particularly evident when Paul insists that "a righteousness from God, apart from law, has been made known, to which the Law and the Prophets testify" (3:21). According to Dunn, in the Greek worldview, "righteousness" is a concept or benchmark against which the person and person's actions can be measured. In contrast, in Hebrew thought, "righteousness" is more relational.[156] That is, righteousness is essentially the fulfilment of the demands of a relationship, whether with God or people. For this reason, "righteousness" is often spoken of within the covenant relationship between Israel and Yahweh. Thus, to be righteous meant that Israel was to remain faithful to the law of Yahweh and "to treat fellow members of the covenant community with justice." Conversely, to be unrighteous is to "act in ways that break covenant."[157] According to Marshall, the central concern of biblical law was the creation of *shalom*, a state of soundness or "all-rightness" within the covenant community, for which the law provided a pattern. Marshall states that certain laws were considered to be just, not because they corresponded to some abstract ethical norm, but because they sustained shalom within the community.[158] Therefore, covenant justice could be understood as support and assistance for the poor and oppressed. As Isaiah states, "Take your evil deeds out of my sight! Stop doing wrong, learn to do right! Seek justice, encourage the oppressed. Defend the cause of the fatherless, plead the case of the widow."[159]

Moreover, Yahweh's righteousness consists of his obligation of faithfulness towards his covenant people, delivering and saving them in times of need and war, despite Israel's failure.[160] For Israel, divine justice was not

154. McGrath, "The Righteousness of God," 63–78, as cited by Marshall, *Beyond*, 43. Morgan, *Romans*, 144, goes as far as saying that "the explosion of judicial metaphors in western theology . . . fuelled readings of Romans which Paul would scarcely have acknowledged." See also, Dunn, *Theology of Paul*, 341.

155. Gunton, *Actuality*, 85.

156. Dunn, *Theology of Paul*, 341.

157. See Marshall, *Beyond*, 47–48.

158. Marshall, *Beyond*, 48.

159. Isa. 1:16–17; see also Mic. 6:8; Pss. 146:7–10; 119:153–9.

160. Particularly in the Psalms (e.g., Pss. 51:14; 65:5; 71:15) and second Isaiah (Isa. 46:13; 51:5–8; 62:1–2).

some abstract theological adage, but it was a truth they learned of God through the experience of God's actions in rescuing and blessing Israel. Marshall asserts that "righteousness" language in the Hebrew Bible is *action* language. That is, a king is said to be righteous when he acts to bring about justice and fairness in the covenant community, faithfully intervening to save those who cannot save themselves.[161] This is a reason why God's righteousness is characteristically associated in the Old Testament with God's love, generosity, liberation, and forgiveness, with justice and mercy being understood as complementary, not contradictory, truths. Mercy, like justice, is a covenant term, meaning to act compassionately to those in the covenant community who are in need, thereby bringing about justice for them. In one sense, such mercy is undeserved, since the covenant people are persistently faithless, but in another sense, such mercy can be expected as God is faithful to his covenant.[162]

The concept of God's righteousness is not entirely without a punitive dimension, particularly on the occasion when Israel had forsaken the covenant. But even here, God's justice is depicted as a disciplinary means to an end to bring about his righteous purposes, whether liberation of the afflicted or purification of the disobedient. Donahue claims "Yahweh's justice is saving justice where punishment of the sinner is an integral part of restoration."[163]

God's saving justice was questioned at the time of the Exile as it appeared that God had abandoned Israel to her enemies. Therefore, in exilic and post-exilic writings, especially Deutero-Isaiah, God's righteousness becomes the basis of an eschatological hope where God would justify and vindicate Israel's trust.[164] In this respect, God's righteousness is virtually synonymous with the salvation of his people from their enemies.[165] Stephen Mott concurs, stating that "justice in the Bible is an intervening power."[166]

---

161. Marshall, *Beyond*, 50.

162. See Marshall, *Beyond*, 50–51, n. 44. See also Isa. 30:18 "Yet the LORD longs to be gracious to you; he rises to show you compassion. For the LORD is a God of justice. Blessed are all who wait for him!" which provides an example of divine justice and gracious compassion being virtually synonymous.

163. Donahue, "Biblical," in Haughey, (ed.), *In The Faith*, 68–112, as quoted by Marshall, *Beyond*, 52. See also, von Rad, *Old Testament Theology*, 377, and Koch, "Doctrine of Retribution," in Crenshaw, (ed.), *Theodicy in the Old Testament*, 57–87. For example, Exod. 9:27; Pss. 7:12–17; 9:5–8; 75:3; Isa. 5:6–7, 15–16; 10:2, 18, 22; 28:14, 17–18, 22; Lam. 1:18; Mic. 7:9–10; Neh. 9:33; 2 Chron. 12:6. See also, Travis, *Christ*, 14–17.

164. E.g., Pss. 31:1; 35:23–24; 51:14; 65:5; 71:2, 15; 98:2; 143:11; Isa. 41:2; 42:6; 45:8, 21; 46:13; 51:5–6, 8; 62:1–2; 63:1, 7; Ezek. 9:6–13; Neh. 9:6–37.

165. See Olley, "Righteousness," 309–13.

166. Mott, "Partiality," 25.

That is, a restorative justice that makes things right by restoring *shalom* and not primarily about "status."

In returning to Paul's use of righteousness/justice language in Romans, he declares that the gospel is "the power of God for the salvation of everyone who believes" (Rom. 1:16), and in doing so, develops his doctrine of justifying righteousness from the Jewish tradition, portraying "God's righteousness as God's unswerving covenant-faithfulness manifested in the act of eschatological deliverance to restore justice to the world."[167] That is, Paul understands the death and Resurrection of Christ as the act of eschatological deliverance, proving God's faithfulness to his covenant obligation, and a vindication of his justice. The justice of God is disclosed in the gospel because:[168]

1. God treated the sinfulness of Israel with deadly seriousness and impartiality, consigning Israel to the same plight of subjection to his wrath as other nations.

2. This has not necessitated God to renege on his covenant promises to Israel, as God has eradicated sin definitively, restoring Israel to full covenantal relationship with himself through the action of Christ.[169]

3. God's justice is also demonstrated through making the benefits of Christ's atoning work available, by faith, to the Gentiles as well as to the Jews.

The Atonement is therefore a comprehensive, all-embracing, act of justice that restores all who believe into full covenant relationship, Gentiles as well as Jews. According to Brinsmead, to justify a person then means "to secure justice for him," or "to champion someone's cause," which is what God has achieved for all people, through Christ.[170] Likewise, Yoder argues, "We should understand justification not as punishing justice but as shalom justice—justification is liberation from sin in order that things may be right."[171]

---

167. Marshall, *Beyond*, 54.

168. See Marshall, *Beyond*, 54–59, for his more comprehensive argument.

169. Christ is the "sacrifice of atonement" (Rom. 3:25). Israel proved to be faithless (Rom. 3:3) but Christ remained faithful (3:22).

170. Brinsmead, "Justification," 16.

171. Yoder, *Shalom*, 65, as cited by Marshall, *Beyond*, 59.

JUSTICE AS "THE RIGHTING OF WRONGS"

Some restrictivists claim that life is not fair in any respect as some are born into great wealth and others into poverty, some are born healthy, others experience persistent sickness, some are born with intelligence and others not so.[172] Whilst it is permissible to state that "life is unfair" in the present, it would be objectionable to suggest that this unfairness continues and is indeed ratified by God in eternity. Pinnock claims that, "Liberation theology, for all its errors, has rightly called attention to divine judgment as the righting of historical wrongs. The millions who have been trampled down and victimized throughout their earthly lives, not because of their sins but by the sins of others, will be recompensed and vindicated on that day. Victims will be delivered and judgment will be visited on oppressors. Dives, who disregarded the poor man at his gate, will be in torment, while beggar Lazarus will go to Abraham's bosom (Luke 16:19–31). God's judgment means that wrongs will be put right, and justice will be done when God comes to judge the earth."[173]

The inference of much popular eschatology is that the poor, disenfranchised, and exploited, many of whom, who through no fault of their own, are unable to call upon Jesus, will be rejected by God, whilst allowing their oppressors to succeed in their evil deeds. The result is that those who experience only suffering in this life could potentially experience more, and worse, suffering in the next life. That is, instead of experiencing compensation they will experience divine condemnation—"out of the frying pan into the fire." As Pinnock so succinctly asserts, "Popular eschatology simply does not add up."[174] Carson claims that Pinnock turns the storyline of the Bible from mankind as being guilty rebels into "pity the perpetrator."[175] It is doubtful that this is what Pinnock is suggesting. The storyline of the Bible might equally be cast as God's justice being established in the world he has created, where the exploited and abused, as well as the oppressor and abuser, receive divine justice.

Wright contends that the word "judgment" has negative overtones for many people, yet the testimony of Scripture is that "God's coming judgment is a good thing, something to be celebrated, longed for, yearned over. It causes people to shout for joy, and indeed the trees of the field to clap their

---

172. Boyd, *Across*, 182. Boyd refers to the "life is unfair" argument without providing any references of those who argue this way, though the tone of this kind of comment is usual amongst restrictivist theologians.

173. Pinnock, *Wideness*, 151.

174. Pinnock, *Wideness*, 152.

175. Carson, *Gagging*, 290.

hands. In a world of systematic injustice, bullying, violence, arrogance, and oppression, the thought that there might be a coming day when the wicked are firmly put in their place and the poor and the weak are given their due is the best news there can be. Faced with a world in rebellion, a world full of exploitation and wickedness, a good God *must* be a God of judgment."[176] Wright further contends that there must be a judgment whereby God sovereignly declares "*this* is good and to be upheld and vindicated, and *that* is evil and to be condemned."[177]

Moltmann asserts that only after Constantine was Judgment interpreted as a "divine criminal tribunal" where perpetrators of crimes were tried. He claims that prior to this, the Last Judgment was cherished by the victims of injustice as a hope that divine justice would triumph over the oppressors.[178] He further asserts that to correct "this aberration means Christianizing the idea of judgment" and once again understanding the Judge and his judgment as a Liberator who is concerned with his victims.[179] He argues this point forcibly, stating that all sins and injustices of "this murderous and suffering world will be condemned and annihilated" by God, whilst the oppressors themselves will liberated and saved through transformation into what God had created them to be.[180]

Ward argues that the good news of the gospel is sometimes substituted for the bad news that the vast majority of people, unless they have embraced a specific set of beliefs, will be rejected by God.[181] Yet, ironically, it was Jesus who claimed to be this world's judge, announcing that "the Father judges no one, but has entrusted all judgment to the Son," (John 5:22),[182] and that he, as Judge, had "not come to judge the world, but to save it," (John 12:47) also declaring that "God did not send his Son into the world to condemn the world, but to save the world through him" (John 3:17). Moltmann questions, if "Jesus is the judge, can he judge according to any other righteousness than the law which he himself manifested—the law of love for our enemies, and the acceptance of the poor, the sick, and sinners? Can the righteous-

---

176. Wright, *Surprised*, 150.

177. Wright, *Surprised*, 191. Italics his. Wright lists four options of this final judgment, namely, the traditional view of everlasting retribution, the universalist view of salvation for all, the conditionalist view of the impenitent ceasing to exist, and Wright's own theory of those who have continuously rejected the divine promptings who cease to become human or bear the divine image, and pass beyond both hope and pity (193–5).

178. Moltmann, *Coming*, 235.

179. Moltmann, "Destructive Judgment is a Godless Picture." n. p.

180. Moltmann, *Coming*, 255.

181. Ward, *What the Bible*, 129–30.

182. See also Acts 10:42; 17:31; 2 Cor. 5:10; 2 Tim. 4:1.

ness of which the Last Judgment serves be any righteousness other than the righteousness of God which creates justice and redeems?"[183] Moltmann is correct to remind us that when one thinks about divine judgment, it is imperative to associate that judgment with the Christ who shapes one's ideas of God. He contends that "in the crucified Christ we recognize the Judge of the final Judgment, who himself has become the one condemned, for the accused, in their stead and for their benefit. So at the Last Judgment we expect on the Judgment seat the one who was crucified for the reconciliation of the world, and no other judge." Indeed, the coming Judge is none other than the one who came to seek that which was lost and forgive those who crucified him. It will not do to posit the idea that Christ came in love on his earthly mission, but will next time come in wrath, thereby creating an unbiblical dualism. There is no reason to assume that God's justice towards sinners at the Last Judgment will be of a different kind to the justice demonstrated by Christ on earth.[184]

God's judgment being understood as a righting of historical wrongs and as God's redressing the balance in a world of exploitation and wickedness enables the justice of God and the love of God to be complementary, rather than contradictory, truths about the nature of God. Pinnock asks, "What then does it mean to say that God is our Judge?" He answers his own question by stating that it does not concern some internal struggle in God of whether to save or reject. Rather, it "brings his judgment to bear on sin in the work of triumphing over it." He reminds us that the Judge is our Savior, the one who comes to our rescue and deliverance.[185]

JUSTICE AND FORGIVENESS

The retributivist theory of sin which deserves an eternal punishment, because, as Anselm contended, it is an offence against an infinite God, fails to realize that punishment, whether finite or infinite, will not satisfy the demands of justice fully. Punishment, of any sort, cannot make amends for, or cancel, any crime.[186] Fiddes argues, "What justice demands is not payment but repentance; it is finally 'satisfied' not by any penalty in itself but by

183. Moltmann, *Coming*, 236.

184. Moltmann, *Coming*, 250.

185. Pinnock, *Unbounded*, 73.

186. This applies equally to views other than eternal punishment, such as conditional immortality/annihilationism.

the change of heart to which the penalty is intended to lead."[187] This appears to be a fundamental weakness in the retributivist theory.

Marshall, similarly, asserts that "God's justice can be ultimately vindicated not by retribution but only by reconciling forgiveness, for only thus are things made right."[188] Talbott also proposes that the answer to this dilemma is forgiveness.[189] He asks, "What *sort of thing* would satisfy justice *to the full* in the event that one should do something morally wrong? The answer, it seems to me, is obvious: If one could somehow make amends for the wrong action, that is, undo any harm done, repair any damage, in a way that would make up for, or cancel out, the bad consequences of the action (in one's own life as well as in the life of others), one would satisfy justice *to the full*" (original italics).[190] He goes as far as to say that all sinners deserve God's forgiveness, not because they have earned it, but because it is their right as his children. He contends that such forgiveness has nothing to do with merit; rather, sinners are entitled to God's forgiveness in the manner a newborn baby is entitled to parental care. Although at face value this statement appears quite scandalous, his rationale appears to be quite biblical.[191] That is, since God has forgiven us, he has commanded us to forgive others—we have an obligation to forgive and no right not to forgive. He further contends that God has given such a command to forgive unconditionally because forgiveness is always the right and proper response to sin. Crisp is correct to deduce that Talbott has arrived at his conviction that justice *requires* forgiveness from his understanding that the divine moral nature is simple. Crisp further maintains that Talbott's claim that divine "justice will be altogether merciful even as his mercy is altogether just" does not reflect the doctrine of divine simplicity as it has been traditionally articulated.[192]

---

187. Fiddes, *Past Event*, 104.

188. Marshall, *Beyond*, 128.

189. Talbott, *Inescapable*, 157.

190. Talbott, "Punishment," 161.

191. Though this is challenged by Crisp ("Divine Retribution," 48) who claims that it doesn't seem "a straightforward reading of Scripture" to yield "an unequivocal argument in favor of this view." Crisp (p. 48, n. 39) cites Psalms 5:5 and 11:5–6 as the two main texts which apparently support his opposition to Talbott's view. It might be argued that the literary genre of the Psalms does not permit such proof-texting any more than the claim that Psalm 137:8–9 might be used in support of infanticide. Crisp does refer to other texts which he claims both support and challenge Talbott, concluding that there are two sorts of data in Scripture on this issue, both of which appear to have biblical support.

192. See Crisp, "Divine Retribution," 48; Talbott, "Punishment," 164. Crisp contends that for theologians like Augustine, Anselm, and Aquinas, the simplicity of the being of God means that God is "just and benevolent at one and the same time. But

Talbott's proposal is demonstrated through an analogy of the relationship between a father and daughter. He presents a hypothetical case of a teenage daughter of a televangelist being arrested for drink-driving. He surmises: suppose this daughter is heartbroken and repentant and desires to do all she can to make amends, and begs her father's forgiveness, but he refuses. After all, she has disgraced the family and he informs her that he does not wish to see her again. Talbott states that the father has not acted justly as, in his opinion, he has not discharged one of his obligations as a father. In fact, his own sin, in refusing to forgive his daughter, appears to be worse than his daughter's sin. In this case, he claims, it would seem "quite natural to say that the father *owes* it to his daughter to forgive her and that his daughter *deserves* his forgiveness."[193] Thus, Talbott adds, "given the simplicity of God's moral nature, he forgives not only because he is merciful, but because he is faithful and just as well (see 1 John 1:9)."[194]

Talbott continues this illustration with the scenario of, on this occasion, the daughter not being particularly repentant. He suggests that maybe she is going through a particularly rebellious stage, more desirous of the approval of her teenage friends than her parents, and becomes quite obnoxious and defiant. Given this scenario, he again asks whether the father has an obligation to forgive her. Rightly, he again asserts that despite any of the father's personal imperfections or frustrations with his daughter, he is obliged to forgive her. Any appropriate punishment should not be an indication of an unforgiving attitude, rather a sign that he cares for her as a loving parent. If a human father, despite undoubted personal imperfections and struggles, could act forgivingly, then a God who is devoid of such limitations would most definitely discharge such "fatherly" obligations as Creator. This understanding of divine justice requiring forgiveness accords well with the New Testament analogy of God as a loving parent. According to Reformed theology, God opposes sin enough to punish sinners in a region of his creation known as hell, thus keeping it alive for eternity, rather than destroying sin altogether by means of forgiveness. Whilst no analogy can answer every potential question, Talbott's proposal helps move the discussion in the direction where God's love is just and his justice is loving. Moltmann asks, "Does God as their creator, go with all his created beings into life, death and Resurrection—or does God as judge stand over

since they do not construe justice as perfect in forgiveness, deeming instead that it is perfect in retribution, they do not maintain that justice requires forgiveness in every instance." It would appear that Talbott's understanding of divine simplicity is not only in no way inferior to theirs, but actually appears more straightforward.

193. Talbott, *Inescapable*, 162. Italics his.

194. Talbott, *Inescapable*, 163.

and against those he has created, detached and uninvolved, to pardon or condemn? How can the God who loves what he has created condemn not just what is evil, destructive and godless in created beings but also these created beings themselves?"[195]

In John 21, a scenario is presented that might enable one to understand, even more clearly, how the love and justice of God might work together. Peter, as Christ had prophesied, had denied the Lord three times. Peter was heartbroken over his sin, made even more repulsive by Peter's boast that though other disciples might deny Jesus, he would not. In this final chapter of John, Peter is confronted by the Lord who reinstates Peter to his role and ministry amongst the disciples. In this meeting, Jesus asked Peter on three occasions, "Do you love me?" (vv. 15–17) which possibly corresponds to the three occasions that Peter denied the Lord. This was a question that was, it appears, for Peter's benefit, not the Lord's, and was an example of tough love in operation, for this question hurt Peter (v. 17). However, it would appear that the words of Christ were not intended to crush or condemn him, rather they were intended to help Peter learn from, and move on from, his mistake, and become useful to Christ once again.

Paul refers to a "godly sorrow" that brought repentance (2 Cor. 7:10), which would be an apt description of what Peter experienced at this meeting. One might assume that the judgment that Peter experienced at this "reinstatement" meeting was exceptionally sorrowful, especially as he would have looked into the eyes of Jesus, acknowledging his own weakness and sin in denying Christ previously. Whilst this meeting with Christ took place in history, one might ask whether the essence of Christ's meeting with Peter might model how Christ, the Judge, will act at the Judgment to come. It would not be unfeasible to believe that the Judgment might also involve such a combination of love, forgiveness, and justice, where guilty sinners are requested to meet with the risen Lord, and are invited to respond to his question of "Do you love me?" One might also imagine that at that moment every word or action that has dishonored Christ is brought to remembrance, causing much personal shame and sadness in the presence of the incomparable glory of Christ. If this is the way that God's justice might be meted out on the Judgment, it would be no soft option, for there could not be a more awesome or terrifying judgment than the stark realization of one's sin against God, and of one's selfishness towards others. Such an encounter would be comparable to Isaiah's terrifying experience of the awesome majesty and holiness of God which caused him to cry out, "Woe to me . . . I am

---

195. Moltmann, *Coming*, 236.

ruined! For I am a man of unclean lips, and I live among a people of unclean lips, and my eyes have seen the King, the Lord Almighty" (Isa. 6:5).

Indeed, though such a proposition might be thought to extend beyond the explicit teaching of Scripture, it is proposed that it is no less theologically plausible than other models. But if true, it would meet the requirements of both God's love and justice. For a sinner to be confronted by Christ, the Judge, becoming fully conscious of his sin and acknowledging the price paid for his forgiveness, would be the most awesome example of a "just love" and a "loving justice" imaginable. The question of whether, at this point, it would be possible for anyone to resist God's forgiveness, if such an offer of reconciliation were available, is a fascinating thought, but, sadly, beyond the scope of this book.[196] Rob Bell, in his heavily criticized and controversial book, *Love Wins*, agrees that these "are tensions we are free to leave fully intact. We don't need to resolve them or answer them because we can't, and so we simply respect them."[197]

Some might ask, what of the mass murderer who has inflicted genocide upon a people group, or a child rapist, or even a gossip and slanderer who has blackened the character of some innocent person? Whilst God would have redressed the balances for the victims, is it not possible to believe that the oppressors be given the ability to see their sin for what it was, and how it damaged others, and then given the opportunity to repent of every action that brought harm? This coincides with the views of Moltmann, Wright, Pinnock, Ward et al. quoted above, who view God's justice in terms of the victim and the historical "righting of wrongs." Moltmann contends that whilst "the victims of sin and violence are supported, healed, and brought to life by God's righteousness . . . the perpetrators of sin and violence will experience a rectifying transformative justice. They will change by being redeemed together with their victims. The crucified Christ who encounters them together with their victims will save them. They will 'die off' in their atrocities to be 'reborn' to a new life." He supports the view that divine justice is not about the division of humans into the redeemed and the damned, but the victory of "God's great day of reconciliation on earth."[198] Again, such a scenario would be an example of how God's love and justice could coincide and complement each other. If such opportunity were offered for reconciliation, then as stated above, this would not be a soft option, but a powerful and poignant example of God's justice and love working together.

196. For further study on this issue, see Walls, "Philosophical," 105–24; Reitan, "Human Freedom," 125–44; Talbott, "Reply," 247–66; Cook, "Is Universalism?" 395–409; Gray, "Post-Mortem Evangelism," 141–50.

197. Bell, *Love Wins*, 115.

198. Moltmann, "Destructive," n.p., see also Moltmann, *Coming*, 255.

Following apartheid in South Africa, where many atrocities were committed, black against white and white against black, the Truth and Reconciliation Commission, chaired by Archbishop Desmond Tutu, offered amnesty, from civil and criminal prosecution, to those who were willing to take part through confessing their sins, sometimes horrendous acts of violence and murder, and requesting the nation's, or individual's, forgiveness. This was viewed as necessary for the new day of racial equality in the nation of South Africa.[199] Whilst there is general agreement that the Truth and Reconciliation Commission both prevented more bloodshed and inspired similar efforts in other countries, not everyone was enthusiastic over its achievements.[200] Ward, however, refers positively to this model of "restorative justice" maintaining that unlike the retributivist model, which is a backward-looking theory of only taking into account the gravity of the crime for which a penalty will be paid, restorative justice aims at justice for the victim and the restoration of the perpetrator.[201] He rightly maintains that in human affairs this is often an unattainable ideal as the wrongdoer would need to realize the gravity of their offence, show remorse, and seek to make amends for their actions in whatever way is possible. Furthermore, victims would need to accept the efforts made by an offender as sincere and genuine.

Whilst the ideal of "restorative justice" might not always come about in this life, due to hardness of heart or lack of opportunity, Ward suggests that the age to come might provide opportunity and duration for such restoration to take place in which the offender could come to realize the effects of his sin upon his victim and have a genuine change of heart. He rightly

---

199. Tutu writes in his memoir, *No Future Without Forgiveness*, 54–55, that the reconciliation process was inspired by the concept of restorative justice found in the word *ubuntu*, from the Nguni group of languages, which defines the "very essence of being human." Danaher "Towards a Paschal Theology of Restorative Justice," 361, states that although the word *ubuntu* is impossible to translate accurately, it refers to an anthropology that "defines personhood not in terms of autonomy or independence, but in terms of interdependence achieved when we are in harmonious relation to other persons." Tutu writes, "in the spirit of *ubuntu* the central concern is the healing of the breaches, the redressing of imbalances, the restoration of broken relationships, a seeking to rehabilitate both the victim and the perpetrator, who should be given the opportunity to be reintegrated into the community he has injured by his offense," 54–55. See also Battle, *Reconciliation: The Ubuntu Theology of Desmond Tutu*.

200. See Gruchy, *Reconciliation*, 10–13. Islamic scholar Dr. Fared Esack stated that the TRC "put a political bandage over the apartheid era so that we can limp into the new South Africa," in Chapman and Spong (eds.), *Religion and Reconciliation*, 243.

201. Ward, *Word of God*, 139. Ward allows for an element of retribution as "the offender must truly feel the gravity of his offence, and must suffer a deprivation of good because of the offence."

says that life is often too short for it to happen. Besides, it is not always possible, as a murderer would not have opportunity to be reconciled to his victim. Ward claims that such "a change of heart would always be possible (in the afterlife), especially if God stands ready to help and guide." Ward further suggests that such a state might be called "punishment" but not of a purely retributive kind. It would be the "burning fire" of selfish desires and an "outer darkness" of a life without love and compassion, and maybe the deep anguish from the memories that one has of the hurts caused to others during their lives. Ward falls short of a universalistic outcome by suggesting that people might not accept the offer of release because their own obstinate wills refuse divine help. In that sense, it is not God who sends them to hell, but "they choose hell, a state in which hatred, malevolence and unbridled passion rule unchecked, for themselves."[202]

Pannenberg astutely asks, "What, then, is the advantage of Christians at the future judgment?"[203] In answering his own question, he emphasizes the benefit is of one knowing the standard for participation in eternal salvation as well as the standard of judgment. In Christ, who died on the cross for our deliverance, Christians have already received justification and pardon at the hands of the future judge, and with this confidence they move on towards judgment.[204] Pannenberg's view appears to be in line with the confidence of St. Paul, who confesses, "I know whom I have believed, and am convinced that he is able to guard what I have entrusted to him for that day" (2 Tim. 1:12).

Opponents of the concept of restorative justice might claim that such is merely the superimposing of western values of justice onto God. Though Marshall and McGrath would claim the reverse. That is, the retributive concept of justice is a western import to Scripture.[205] Heschel argues that God's concern for justice is not based on what humans believe, but is motivated by God's justice which God has instilled within the human heart.[206] Brown concurs, claiming that "concern for justice is not a trait we project out of our own experience onto God; rather, concern for justice is a divine trait with which God endows us, so that to the degree that we embody justice, God takes form within us."[207] Therefore, the reason that people are deeply discomforted and disturbed by acts that they consider unjust is conceivably

202. Ward, *Word*, 140.

203. Pannenberg, *Systematic Theology*, 616.

204. Pannenberg, *Systematic Theology*, 616–7.

205. Marshall, *Beyond*, 43; and McGrath, "Righteousness," 63–78.

206. Heschel, *Prophets*, 271–2. See also Burrow, "Love," 405–6.

207. Brown, "Some are Guilty," 126.

due to God's imprint in those he has created in his own image and as a part of our moral nature.[208]

JUSTICE AND DIVINE WRATH

The major part of this chapter has focused upon understanding the way in which God's love and justice might be viewed as complementary characteristics within the being of God, thus supporting a justice which is restorative rather than retributive. This emphasis, therefore, necessitates some explanation of the recurring theme of punishment in the New Testament. That is, does the biblical teaching on divine vengeance and wrath somehow invalidate the concept of a justice that is restorative? The aim of this section is merely to recognize the tension of restorative justice and biblical teaching of divine wrath/vengeance and offer some thoughts on understanding this apparent conflict. To explore this question would require a major research project in its own right.[209]

Marshall classifies the New Testament material on the subject of punishment by distinguishing between divine punishment (penalties imposed by God for wrongdoing) and human punishment (penalties inflicted by human agents). Human punishment can be further divided into punishments administered within the community of faith and those that function within wider society.[210] For the purposes of this study, the issues of divine punishment and human punishment imposed by the Church, on God's behalf, are of most relevance.

Firstly, within the context of the church, wrongdoers were reprimanded by personal rebuke, more overt censure, and even temporary expulsion from the church community.[211] Particularly intriguing are the 1 Corinthians 5:1–8 and 1 Timothy 1:19–20 passages, commanding that those being punished are to be handed over to Satan.[212] Whilst these passages are no-

---

208. See Burrow, "Love," 406.

209. For a scholarly evaluation of this subject see Travis, *Christ and the Judgement of God*.

210. Marshall, *Beyond*, 146. He correctly asserts that such distinctions are, however, not absolute, for God's punishments might operate through human channels (Rom. 13:4; cf. Acts 5:1–11; 1 Cor. 11:30), while human punishment may entail the ceremonial handing over of sinners to God, or Satan, for discipline (1 Cor. 5:5; 1 Tim. 1:20).

211. Personal rebuke: Rom. 15:14; Col. 3:16; 1 Thess. 5:14; 2 Thess. 3:14, 15; Titus 3:10, 11. More overt censure: Matt. 18:15; 2 Cor. 2:6; Eph. 5:11; 1 Tim. 5:20; 2 Tim. 4:2; Titus 1:9, 13; 2:15. Temporary expulsion: Matt. 18:17; 1 Cor. 5:11, 13; 2 Thess. 3:14; 2 Tim. 3:1–5; Titus 3:10.

212. 1 Cor. 5:5 "Hand this man over to Satan, so that the sinful nature may be

toriously difficult to interpret, especially as to what is meant by the phrases "sinful nature may be destroyed" and "his spirit saved on the day of the Lord," it would nevertheless be correct to state that Paul was concerned for the offender, whom he wished to bring to restoration through the penalty of excommunication, as well as safeguard the purity of the church at Corinth.[213] The purpose of such punishment, especially in the Corinthian passage, is not vindictive, but a withdrawal of God's protective hand, with the expectation of future repentance and restoration to the church community.

Secondly, the New Testament does cite examples of divine judgment which are temporal or historical, but most references are eschatological.[214] This emphasis can create a tension between the command to non-retaliation and love of one's enemies, as discussed earlier, and the consignment of one's adversaries to divine judgment. For example, Paul pronounces a curse on his opponents in Galatia (Gal. 1:8–9) and Corinth (1 Cor. 16:22) and confers eschatological condemnation on those who undermine his apostolic ministry (2 Cor. 11:13–15). Both concepts, of non-retaliation and divine judgment, are found together in Romans 12:19–20: "Do not take revenge, my friends, but leave room for God's wrath, for it is written: 'It is mine to avenge; I will repay,' says the Lord."

There are two ways in which to interpret these words: to claim that retaliation is not relinquished in principle, but "simply remitted to a higher court. Revenge is still contemplated but given over to God to execute,"[215] or to agree with Ward who claims that it is a fundamental misunderstanding to suppose that though violence is prohibited in this age, that it will be acceptable in the next. However, Miroslav Volf argues that the Christian "practice of nonviolence requires belief in divine vengeance." That is, genuine forgiveness must first exclude before it can embrace. He offers the scenario of someone delivering a lecture on the Christian attitude to violence in a war zone, where among the listeners are people whose cities and villages have been plundered and burned to the ground, whose daughters and sisters have been raped and whose fathers and brothers have had their throats slit. He further argues that given such a scenario the encouragement

---

destroyed and his spirit saved on the day of the Lord," and 1 Tim. 1:20 ". . .Hymenaeus and Alexander, whom I have handed over to Satan to be taught not to blaspheme."

213. See Fee, *God's Empowering Presence*, 324–7; South, "Critique," 539–561.

214. Temporal judgments are often depicted as reformative or educative, where God is using trials to discipline his children (e.g., Heb. 12:5–11; 1 Cor. 11:29–32), though there are occasions when the purposes of such judgment seems to be more destructive than restorative (e.g., Acts 5:1–11, the account of Ananias and Sapphira; Acts 12:18–23, the striking down of Herod Agrippa because of his failure to give glory to God).

215. Marshall, *Beyond*, 168.

of non-violence would require a robust belief in divine vengeance. That is, even though the Christian might refrain from revenge, s/he would be comforted to know that God exercises perfect justice. Whilst Volf is essentially correct in his line of reasoning, divine vengeance, or like-for-like punishment, might not be the only way God might bring his justice to bear.[216] Keith Ward cites Friedrich Nietzsche who referred to this desire for delayed revenge as *resentissement*, the belief that even though we might need to suffer persecution now, God will take revenge in the end. Ward maintains that the true Christian perception is that the cross of Christ is God's last word on violence, and that the God disclosed in Jesus is not a punitive avenger.[217]

To place these verses (19–20) in the context of Romans 12:14–21, where Paul encourages believers to love, feed, bless, pray for, and do good to their enemies, might not suggest that Paul is simply instructing believers to be generous to their opponents in the present, whilst relishing prospects of divine revenge in the future. If this is correct, then to "leave room for God's wrath" (v. 19) might be understood within the context of God's own orientation of gratuitous grace towards his enemies, which would aim at their ultimate transformation and restoration. Thus, believers are called to love, pray for, and bless their adversaries, not simply as an interim measure before the Day of Judgment, but as an expression of the nature of God himself.

Travis claims that the notion of God's wrath has been frequently under discussion for the last 150 years.[218] The major areas of discussion have been:[219]

1. Whether "wrath" (*orgē*) was primarily present (realized) or future (at the final judgment).[220]

2. Whether Paul regards "wrath" as personal or impersonal.[221]

---

216. Volf, *Exclusion*, 304.

217. Ward, *Rethinking*, 41–42. See Neitzsche, *Anti-Christ*, section 24.

218. Travis, *Christ*, 54, claims that Ritschl, *De Ira Dei*, may be taken as the starting point of this discussion, see n. 1.

219. See Travis, *Christ*, 54.

220. For "realized" see 1 Thess. 2:16; Rom. 1:18–32. For "future" see 1 Thess. 5:9; Rom. 2:5, 8.

221. Dodd, *Romans*, 23, classically argued that Paul retains the idea that wrath is the inevitable process of cause and effect and not God's attitude to man. Hanson also adopts this view in *The Wrath of the Lamb*, 69. Travis, among others, is critical of Dodd's position of wrath being seen as impersonal. See Travis, *Christ*, 55; see also Fernando, *Crucial*, 108–12 who cites Rom. 1:18; 2:5, 6; 3:5,6; 9:22 as examples of divine wrath being personal.

3. Whether "wrath" is a feeling (*affectus*) in God, or an action (*effectus*)—
that is, God's action in judging sin.[222]

However, Travis's own question, although distinct, is connected to
these three areas. He asks whether divine wrath involves retributive punishment or if it is a way of saying that "God allows people's wrong choices to
reap their consequences."[223] He explores this question through the use of
wrath in Paul's letters (e.g., 1 Thess. 1:9–10; 2:14–16; 5:9; Rom. 1:18–32;
chapters 2–5; 9:22–23; 12:19–21; 13:4–5), concluding that wrath is essentially a relational term which leads to the judgment of those who reject his
love.[224] Fiddes makes the distinction between "intrinsic" and "extrinsic"
punishment, with the latter being externally inflicted by God and the former
arising as a consequence from one's deeds.[225] Travis concludes by claiming
that when the relational aspect of wrath is understood it demonstrates that
wrath is neither impersonal nor retributive, rather a breakdown in personal
relationship with God. He offers two further clarifications concerning divine wrath, namely, that wrath is not a permanent attribute of God as it
is only contingent upon sin. That is, if there were no sin there would be
no wrath. Ashmon also claims that God's wrath is "neither irrational nor a
part of his eternal nature, unlike gods of other religions." He refers to divine
wrath as God's "alien work" as distinct from his "proper work" which is his
eternal love and mercy.[226] Similarly, Tillich tells of Martin Luther's reference to wrath, anger, and punishment as God's "strange work" while mercy,
tenderness, and forgiveness was "the proper work of love."[227]

Secondly, Travis states that wrath is not intended to be God's final
word.[228] Fernando, however, in *Crucial Questions about Hell*, argues that
wrath and love are to be placed on an "equal-footing as being intrinsic
to God's nature."[229] The basis of his claim rests on Christ who cleared the
temple, denounced the cities of Korazin and Bethsaida, and spoke harshly
to the Pharisees, as well as Paul's use of "wrath" in Romans.[230] Through these
examples, Fernando falls short of proving that love and wrath should be on

222. Tasker, *Biblical Doctrine*, 17, argues that God's wrath is both *affectus* and *effectus*, in that God's judgment on sin arises out of his opposition towards iniquity.

223. Travis, *Christ*, 54.

224. For Travis's argument see 53–70.

225. Fiddes, *Past Event*, 88–96.

226. Ashmon, "Wrath," 351.

227. Tillich, *Love*, 49–50.

228. Travis, *Christ*, 70.

229. Fernando, *Crucial*, 111.

230. See Matt. 21:12–17; 11:20–24; 23:1–39; Rom. 1:18; 2:5, 6; 3:5, 6; 9:22.

equal footing, or that wrath is fundamental to God's nature, though they do demonstrate that wrath is God's (Christ's) reaction to sin. Fernando, based on his belief in the equality of divine love and wrath, then proceeds to claim that "when wrath is given its place as equally a part of God's nature, we can accommodate the belief that the God who saves some eternally also punishes others eternally."[231]

Fernando does appear to present a straw man argument against those who, he claims, remove or ignore divine wrath from their theology. In a subsection of his *Crucial Questions About Hell*, entitled *The results of removing wrath from theology* (113), he criticizes universalist, Nels Ferre, who through claiming the superiority of love, believes all will be eventually saved.[232] It is to be argued, however, that one might take the subject of divine wrath seriously, as indeed Fernando does, yet without coming to his conclusion of the equality of divine wrath and love, or that wrath should be viewed as a permanent quality of God.

Most New Testament references to wrath are found in the Pauline epistles and Revelation, with occasional references elsewhere.[233] The most extensive reflection on divine wrath is found in Paul's letter to the Romans, with Romans 1:18–32 the most focused teaching of all. Hanson considers this passage "a handbook to the working of wrath."[234] Paul writes of God's wrath as being revealed from heaven "against all the godlessness and wickedness of men" (1:18). This wrath was exerted by means of God giving the ungodly and wicked over to their sexual impurity and shameful lusts and depraved minds (vv. 24, 26, 28). In other words, God's wrath was experienced by the ungodly who "suppress the truth by their wickedness" (1:18) through the calculated retraction of his protective influence and control, rather than some direct punitive intervention. Marshall suggests that God's wrath "works itself out through everyday sociological, psychological, and physiological expressions of human decadence and depravity."[235] Thus, God's wrath is experienced as a consequence of one's own choices in life.

Landes asserts that the notion of divine wrath informs us that God is not merely aware of human sins, but is actively motivated to counter them. His wrath, therefore, affirms that God is not indifferent to, or unaffected by, people's violation of the divine will, and demonstrates that God takes

231. Fernando, *Crucial*, 113.

232. Ferre, Nels, *Evil*, 118–9.

233. Mark 14:36; Luke 14:21; 21:23; Matt. 18:34; 22:7; John 3:36; Heb. 3:11; 4:3; James 1:19–20.

234. Romans 1:18; 2:5, 8; 3:5; 4:15; 5:9; 9:22; 12:19; 13:4 (see also 1 Thess. 1:10; 2:16; 5:9; Col. 3:6; Eph. 5:6). Hanson, *Wrath*, 83.

235. Marshall, *Beyond*, 173.

human sin with "utmost seriousness, sympathizes with the victims of human cruelty, and is moved to work for the liberation of those suffering from all types of human oppression."[236] A love which has no anger against the evil doer, or no penalty for evil doing, is immoral and contemptible.[237] Heschel similarly speaks against those who might reject the idea of divine wrath as being "moved by a soft religiosity." That is, even though they believe that God might indeed be "displeased with spousal and child abuse, anti-Semitic, racist, sexist, and heterosexist behavior" they maintain that there is no reason to fear divine wrath.[238] Cone, writing in apartheid America in 1969, makes this point strongly by focusing on the racist behavior of whites, "As long as whites can be sure that God is on their side, there is potentially no limit to their violence against anyone who threatens the American racist way of life."[239] Burrow, in a similar vein, asserts: "If God is love, but does not get pissed off at racism and those who perpetrate it, why should I worship such a God? For it makes no sense to me that this God could really care about me and my people."[240] Heschel rightly claims that "divine anger is not the antithesis of love, but its counterpart, a help to justice as demanded by true love."[241] It would simply make no sense to say that God is angry with injustice and allow that injustice to go unpunished. A God who only loves, but remains passive toward systematic injustice and the violation of others would not be the God revealed in the Bible. Landes similarly stresses that "without wrath, the divine love is in danger of degenerating into sentimentality. It is wrath that keeps the divine love from being viewed as complacent and indulgent." He further argues that "God's wrath is aimed at bringing about change, reversal, and renewal in God's human creatures."[242]

---

236. Landes, "Some Biblical," 10–11. See also Heschel, *Prophets*, 284, who asserts that God's anger demonstrates that God is not indifferent to evil.

237. See Burrow, "Love," 403, who cites Bowne, *Principles*, 110.

238. Heschel, *Prophets*, 296–7.

239. Cone, *Black Theology*, 75.

240. Burrow, "Love," 397.

241. Heschel, *Prophets*, 297.

242. Landes, "Reflections," 11.

The language used in the New Testament to describe final judgment includes: wrath,[243] vengeance,[244] repayment,[245] torment,[246] being "cut to pieces,"[247] and destruction and death,[248] yet it is important to recognize that such figurative, parabolic language is being used in an attempt to describe realities which lie outside human experience, some of which are mutually exclusive, such as fire[249] and darkness.[250] Similarly, the metaphors used of rewards and punishments are diverse and include: God keeping accounts, hiring and firing, paying wages, harvesting crops, herding animals, and scourging slaves. Marshall is undoubtedly correct to suggest that to think of rewards as some quantifiable material benefit is to misunderstand the metaphor, for it would be wrong to imagine that something could be added to the bliss of knowing God. Conversely, he argues that when the New Testament speaks of judicially imposed punishment, or torment, for the condemned, that one need not imagine some extra punishment over and above being excluded from relationship with God.[251] For what greater reward could there be than to be with Christ, and what greater punishment than to be excluded from relationship with him?[252] Travis agrees: "To talk freely of punishment in the sense of retribution is to distort the Christian message and encourage misunderstanding. To speak of relationship or lack of relationship with God is to get to the heart of the matter."[253]

The limitation of human language often poses a challenge to theological understanding, so when the Bible speaks of God's wrath one is inevitably

---

243. Matt. 3:7; Luke 21:33; John 3:36; 1 Thess. 1:9–10; 2:14–16; 5:9; Rom. 1:18–32; 2:1–11; 3:5; 4:15; 5:9; 9:22–23; 12:19–21; Eph. 2:3; 5:6; Col. 3:6; Rev. 6:16–17; 11:18; 14:10, 19; 15:1, 7; 16:1; 16:19; 19:15.

244. 2 Thess. 1:6–10; Heb. 10:28–30; Jude 7; cf. Rom. 12:19; 1 Thess. 4:6; Luke 18:7–8.

245. Rom. 12:19; 2 Thess. 1:6; 2:9–12; Rom. 6:23; cf. 1 Cor. 3:17; Gal. 6:7–8; Rom. 1:27, 32.

246. Luke 16:28; Rev. 20:10.

247. Matt. 24:51; Luke 12:46.

248. Destruction, death (*olethros*): 1 Thess. 5:3; 2 Thess. 1:9. Death (*thanatos*): Rom. 1:32; 6:21–23; 7:5; 8:6; 1 Cor. 15:21–22; 15:56; 2 Cor. 2:16; 7:10; James 1:15; 1 John 5:16; Rev. 2:11; 20:6; 20:14; 21:8. Annihilation, ruin, destruction (*apoleia*): Matt. 7:13; John 17:12; Acts 8:20; Rom. 9:22–24; Phil. 1:28; 3:19; 2 Thess. 2:3; 1 Tim. 6:9; Heb. 10:39; 2 Pet. 2:1; 3:7, 16.

249. Matt. 5:22; 13:42, 50; 24:41; Mark 9:47–48; Luke 17:29–30; 2 Thess. 1:8; Heb. 10:27; 2 Pet. 3:7; Rev. 11:5; 18:8; 19:20; 20:9–10, 14–15; 21:8.

250. Matt. 8:12; 22:13; 25:30.

251. Marshall, *Beyond*, 190.

252. See Blomberg, "Degrees," 26–34.

253. Travis, *Christ*, 169.

caught up in an attempt to appreciate the essence of the metaphor. Burrow approvingly quotes Bowne, who claims that all metaphorical language is "literally false, but we use it in the hope that it will be taken, not for what it says, but for what it means."[254] Thus, we seek to embrace the deep and abiding truth about God that the metaphor presents, distinguishing between the letter and the spirit, and between the truth and the expression.[255]

There is no necessary contradiction between the belief that God loves all people and that he directs his wrath towards those who do evil. Rather, it can be argued that there would be a contradiction if it were claimed that God truly loves yet does not become angry when people violate the human rights of others. Such "tough" love, would be a just love and would undoubtedly include a retributive element, for as Burrow claims, "a love without justice can be sentimental, naïve, and wishy-washy. On the other hand, justice without love can be impersonal, crude and insensitive . . . Divine love and wrath are not traits that cancel, but rather enhance each other."[256] Even so, the biblical evidence demonstrates that divine anger is an act, which lasts for a moment, but divine love is permanent.[257] For example, "'In a surge of anger I hid my face from you for a moment, but with everlasting kindness I will have compassion on you,' says the LORD your Redeemer" (Isa. 54:8).[258] That is, God becomes angry with human injustice and violence and failure to love one's neighbor, precisely because God loves, and is Love. Indeed, God's wrath should not be regarded as an emotional flare-up of divine temper, but as a part of his persistent care for his creation.

Conclusion

This chapter has addressed the theological viability of posthumous salvation through reviewing the attributes of God, especially divine love and justice. In this section it was firstly determined that God is not divided into parts (divine simplicity), whereby one quality (e.g. love) competes with another

254. Burrow, "Love," 387, cites Bowne, *Atonement*, 9.

255. Asmon, "Wrath," 350, asserts that "one should be careful not to equate God's wrath fully with human anger," even though human anger is the metaphor through which God's holy wrath is verbally communicated. Human anger is often irrational, excessive, and unjust (see Gen. 4:6; Prov. 29:11, 22).

256. Burrow, "Love," 396.

257. Burrow, "Love," 400.

258. See also Mic. 7:18 "Who is a God like you, who pardons sin and forgives the transgression of the remnant of his inheritance? You do not stay angry forever but delight to show mercy," and Ps. 30:5 "For his anger lasts only a moment, but his favor lasts a lifetime; weeping may remain for a night, but rejoicing comes in the morning."

quality (e.g. justice) for preeminence. Rather, God's love should always be just and his justice always loving, with all of the divine attributes thought of as complementary with each other and in perfect harmony. Never should God's love allow something that his justice would not, nor should his justice demand something that his love would not. It was further argued that if love is a part of God's essence, then he cannot act in unloving ways to anyone, even his enemies. The time-honored practice of appealing to heaven as a proof of God's love and to hell as proof of his justice, is both naïve and misleading.

With this framework in place, the love and justice of God were examined in an attempt to appraise the feasibility of posthumous salvation. It was established that there is good reason to believe that God's love is both unconditional and unlimited, through demonstrating the viability of belief in the universality of both election and the Atonement. Although the deficiencies of limited election and atonement were exposed, especially their arbitrariness, it remains doubtful that those with a bias towards a more Reformed theology will be convinced by this short appraisal. However, my purpose in this section is to merely evaluate the theological feasibility of posthumous salvation through an examination of God's nature, not to necessarily prove it beyond doubt.

Then, a case was made for Christ as the "hound of heaven" who seeks lost sinners "until he finds them," and to suggest that death as a boundary to God's love would appear to be both artificial and unfounded. Furthermore, God is described as a Good Father, and being infinitely good it is reasonable to believe that he would do anything and everything within his power to reach his lost children with salvation, including, it was suggested, offering a postmortem opportunity.

After this, the doctrine of God's justice was appraised, and divine justice as "retribution" was measured against the concept of divine justice being "restorative." Both ideas were critiqued, and the latter was offered as a possible alternative to the more traditional view of divine justice being essentially punitive. The traditional view of hell as being a place of punishment against a person's will was shown to be deficient, even intolerable, especially when compared to the progressive view which holds that one's alienation from God is due entirely to one's free choice in rejecting God. This latter view also allows for a postmortem opportunity, with some proponents supporting the view that hell's gates are locked on the inside. It was also suggested that although conditional immortality provides a more cogent model for understanding the justice of God, one is still left with the question of whether God's "justice" of destruction or ceasing to be is compatible with God's eternal love. Pinnock suggests that the view of hell as destruction is more just than the view of an everlasting conscious torment, which is unquestionably correct. However, Pinnock's view itself needs to be challenged, as "more just" does not necessarily mean that such a view is essentially "just."[259]

The restorative model of divine justice was evaluated through five subsections, namely: in the ministry and teaching of Jesus; in Paul's thought; as a "righting of wrongs"; as forgiveness; and how this model of justice might be understood in the light of the retributive elements in the Bible.

It was argued that whilst the Scriptures fail to offer any direct or explicit statement on the question of posthumous salvation, there are numerous, more implicit and indirect, indications of the persistence and determination of God's love and forgiveness as demonstrated through Christ. For example, Jesus invited his hearers to respond to wrongdoing in ways that transcended the principle of retaliatory justice of equivalence ("an eye for an eye") in preference for "turning the other cheek."[260] Since this precept displays God's will and purpose for humans, one can safely argue that God himself is opposed to retaliatory justice and that the proper response to an offence committed, is forgiveness. On another occasion, Christ discarded the current practice of limited forgiveness for limitless forgiveness,[261] which is also indicative of how Christ might act towards sinful humans at the *eschaton*. It would be difficult to believe that Christ himself would not act in accordance with his own precept when he fulfils his role as Judge. Furthermore, Jesus abandoned the prevailing understanding of a restricted duty to love through charging his disciples not merely to love those who love them, but to love their enemies also that they should be perfect "as your heavenly Father is perfect."[262] This saying clearly links the morality of Christian disciples to the nature of God himself. Jesus himself exemplified this on the cross as he prayed for his persecutors, "Father, forgive them, for they do not know what they are doing."[263] This cry from the cross also begs the question, "If Jesus could treat his persecutors and enemies with such overwhelming forgiveness, could he not also have the same attitude of heart towards, especially, those who through no fault of their own have not heard the gospel?"

In the appraisal of restorative justice, Paul's understanding on justice was also assessed. It was demonstrated that the metaphor of justice is used considerably in Paul's letter to the Romans. It was shown that whilst

259. Pinnock, *Unbounded*, 93.

260. Matthew 5:38–42.

261. Matthew 18:21–22.

262. Matthew 5:43–48.

263. Luke 23:34.

there is a punitive element in Paul's teaching on justice, it is imperative to recognize the Hebraic concept of covenant justice based on relationship, rather than impose a Western notion of retributive justice on the text. It was shown that Paul's understanding of justice is influenced by the Old Testament which associates God's righteousness/justice with his love, generosity, liberation from oppression, and forgiveness, and is virtually synonymous with salvation of his people. It was argued that Paul, in Romans, views God's righteousness/justice as being demonstrated in an act of eschatological deliverance, through the death and Resurrection of Christ, restoring justice to the world, and to all who believe in Christ.

Furthermore, it was also shown that although human language is an imperfect and blunt instrument in conveying metaphysical truths, it would be wrong to think of either love or justice as something different to the normal human understanding of those words and concepts when one uses them in reference to God. Therefore, it is to be believed that should God condemn anyone who had no opportunity to receive Christ, such an action would be regarded as unjust, by the normal usage of the word and concept of justice, and would also contravene his love.[264]

It was further argued that God's justice needs to be thought of as a good thing and something to be celebrated, rather than feared, for God's justice will be meted out at the Judgment, when God himself will right the wrongs of the systematic injustice and evil in our world, redressing the balances. An attempt was made at understanding how such justice works in God's economy through forgiveness, by way of three simple analogies which attempted to illustrate the relationship between God's love and justice.[265] It is proposed that viewing God's justice as being met through forgiveness is theologically plausible and would add support to the concept of postmortem opportunity for salvation. Furthermore, it was demonstrated that divine wrath in no manner contradicts God's love or justice, for God's wrath is to be viewed as an essential ingredient of his love. Rather, there would be a contradiction if it was claimed that God truly loves, yet does not become angry when people violate the human rights of others. It was argued that God's wrath is contingent upon human sinfulness and should not be thought of

264. St. Paul provides a wonderful description of love in 1 Cor. 13:4, "Love is patient, love is kind. It does not envy, it does not boast, it is not proud. It is not rude, it is not self-seeking, it is not easily angered, it keeps no record of wrongs. Love does not delight in evil but rejoices with the truth. It always protects, always trusts, always hopes, always perseveres."

265. Talbott's story of the televangelist and his daughter; the proposal of using Peter's earthly reinstatement by Christ as a possible model of the Judgment; the Truth and Reconciliation Commission of South Africa.

as a permanent attribute of the nature of God, or as his final word. Wright argues that "God's justice is his love in action" and "God's love is the driving force of his justice."[266]

Retributive justice is inherently reactive, a response to something that has happened. If the final judgment were essentially retributive in character, it would then be compelled by something that is external to God: the existence of sin. Conversely, restorative justice is motivated by something within God's own nature, his love for humanity.[267] Marshall contends: "Those individuals who face destruction do so by their own choosing, not because God's retributive justice demands their demise. Restoration, not retribution, is the hallmark of God's justice and is God's final word in history."[268]

Finally, a typical objection to the concept of posthumous salvation asks, why did Jesus not teach such an important subject more explicitly? Or even, why did Jesus not communicate this more clearly to his own disciples? However, in response, it might be argued that Jesus instructed them in as much as they could accept and understand at that time. Jesus explicitly declared to them at the Last Supper, "I have much more to say to you, more than you can now bear" (John 16:12). At this time, his disciples had considerable difficulty in even understanding his death and subsequent Resurrection, so anything beyond that, such as the concept of posthumous salvation, would have been both unnecessary and incomprehensible to them. Even the apostle Paul, who had such awesome revelations of Christ (Gal. 1:11–12; 2:2; 2 Cor. 12:1–4) and whose epistles are included in the New Testament canon, confessed that he, with others, saw "but a poor reflection" but when perfection comes, "we shall see face to face. Now I know in part; then I shall know fully, even as I am fully known" (1 Cor. 13:11–12).

It is to be accepted that the argument from silence can work in both directions, that is, we have no record of Jesus teaching the concept of posthumous salvation, nor do we have any of Christ's teaching which suggests that this was an antithesis to what he believed. The parable of the rich man and Lazarus is often quoted as offering such proof, though, as was shown in chapter 3, it is not legitimate to draw such conclusions from this parable. The viability of postmortem opportunity therefore lies in the broader theological debate.

Whilst it is recognized that an exhaustive study in many of these areas is impossible, given the space restrictions of this chapter, it has been shown that as far as the nature of God is concerned, God's justice should

266. Wright, *What Saint Paul*, 110–1.
267. Marshall, *Beyond*, 189.
268. Marshall, *Beyond*, 199.

be thought of as complementary with divine love and not thought of as an obstacle to postmortem opportunity for salvation, which is, at the very least, a theologically feasible proposition.

5

Practical Evaluation of Posthumous Salvation

Introduction

In the two previous chapters, the concept of posthumous salvation was evaluated from both a biblical and a theological perspective. Chapter 3 concluded that there was no room for dogmatism when attempting to understand the passages that advocates and opponents use to support or challenge this concept. The claim that posthumous salvation is not explicitly taught in the Bible was found to be essentially correct, though, as previously stated, this was to be balanced through stating that it was not necessarily in conflict with biblical doctrine. Chapter 4 concentrated on a test-case theological argument which is significant for the concept of posthumous salvation, with special attention being focused upon the impartiality and eternity of God's love and on God's justice in a way that maintained the unity (or simplicity) of divine attributes. Traditionally, God's mercy and justice have been viewed as distinct, if not contrary or conflicting, characteristics within the being of God.

It was shown that as far as the nature of God is concerned, it is theologically feasible to think of God's love and God's justice as complementary. Divine justice as retributive was measured against the concept of divine justice being restorative, with the latter being offered as the preferred alternative to the more traditional view. As a consequence, it was contended that this model helps to maintain the unity of God's nature and allows for the possibility of postmortem opportunity for salvation.

Given this conclusion in chapter 4, chapter 5 will now focus upon the missiological and pastoral implications of a belief in a postmortem opportunity for salvation. At this point it is important to emphasize that this chapter's objective is not to prove or disprove the concept of posthumous salvation, but only answer how such a belief, if acceptable, will work in practice. For example, will such a belief damage the Christian gospel, reduce its urgency, or lull unbelievers into a false sense of security causing them to procrastinate on the challenge to decide for Christ? Furthermore, the question of how an acceptance of the concept of posthumous salvation might possibly be beneficial to the gospel will also be explored. It will be shown that utility does not establish truth, an argument that works both for and against this model.

Missiological evaluation of posthumous salvation

This section will include an evaluation of the impact of a belief in postmortem opportunity for salvation upon Christian evangelism and mission.

Cutting the nerve of mission

Firstly, it is important to emphasize that posthumous salvation is not universalism by another name, as many adherents of this model, as discussed in chapter 2, are not universalists, for they believe that God respects, and will not disregard, a person's free-will decision to receive or reject salvation.[1] However, some arguments that are raised against universalism, such as its undermining the urgency of evangelism, would be equally relevant to the discussion on posthumous salvation, as both views contend that death is not the end of one's opportunity for a decision for Christ.[2] Michael Griffiths likened universalism to a Trojan horse that "gained entrance into Christendom and threatens to destroy missionary motives and hinder the effectiveness of Christ's soldiers and their readiness to continue to battle."[3] Similarly, Van Engen states, "The universalist perspective threatens missionary motivation, reduces missional urgency, and emasculates the biblical

1. Cook, "Is Universalism," 395–409, deals with this question and asks whether posthumous salvation will lead by implication to universalism which might in turn be recognized as an evangelical option in a few decades' time much in the way that the "unmentionable" doctrine of conditional immortality became acceptable to evangelicals. He further argues for the rational consistency of Pinnock's position as a believer in posthumous salvation, but is not a universalist. Evangelical theologians, Fackre, Pinnock, Wright, and Bloesch, along with Cook, do not believe that universalism is the necessary product of posthumous salvation as they all believe that God will not override human free will. See also, Gray, "Post-Mortem Evangelism," 141–50, who supports the notion that a person cannot freely and rationally choose hell, once its nature is clear, and where hell is understood to be a place of continuing sin.

2. See Downes, "Will we all be saved?" 30; Packer, "Problem," 171 [169–78].

3. Griffiths, *Confusion*, 116.

message."[4] Fackre, himself an advocate of posthumous salvation, is aware of such allegations and asks, "If a patient and pursuing Christ can call in eternity those who have not heard the gospel in time, why the need to proclaim the gospel to all the world? Doesn't eschatological evangelization cut the nerve of mission? The answer is a resounding 'No!'"[5] Fackre's and others' reasons will be discussed later.

Alternatively, the writers of the Evangelical Alliance's report, *The Nature of Hell*, maintain that they would find it difficult to believe that advocates of any "second chance" theory could espouse a zeal for missions, claiming that "the doctrine of post-mortem repentance runs a very real risk of delegating back to God a responsibility which he has very deliberately assigned to us." They further contend that "although God may well save some who have not responded explicitly to the gospel, we cannot afford to make this 'wider hope' the basis for our missiology."[6] It is clear from these references that the report's authors indicate that to believe in a "second chance" theory, one is somehow weak on evangelism, though many advocates of posthumous salvation, such as Fackre, would contest such an inference.[7]

The eternal consequences of not accepting Christ within the limits of one's earthly life is a view that is widely accepted as the orthodox position in evangelical or conservative Christianity, as was observed in the Congress on World Mission at Chicago in 1960, which declared, "In the years since the war, more than one billion souls have passed into eternity and more than half of these went to the torment of hell fire without even hearing of Jesus Christ, who He was, and why he died on the cross at Calvary."[8] The motivation for mission has traditionally, and largely, been the urgency to "snatch others from the fire" (Jude 23) and to proclaim the gospel to them before it is too late.[9] Often such preaching has included anecdotal examples of those who procrastinated over the gospel invitation, and whose lives were consequently "demanded" from them by God before they had another opportunity, somewhat akin to the parable Jesus told of the rich fool (see Luke 12:20). As a young pastor I remember a more senior evangelist colleague repeat such an account with vivid detail, and to great effect, at the end of his

4. Van Engen, "Effect," 186.

5. Fackre, "Divine Perseverance," 93.

6. Hilborn, *Nature of Hell*, 118.

7. Fackre, "Divine Perseverance," 93–94.

8. Hick, *God*, 29–31, quoting from Percy, *Facing*, 9.

9. This is a verse that I have heard on many occasions in prayer meetings and sermons, and was a part of the terminology used by many Pentecostal churches up to the late 1980s, and possibly in some places even now. For more examples, see Blanchard, *Whatever*, 296; Packer, *Problem*, 7, 15; Dowsett, *Not Fair!*, 51.

evangelistic sermon. That evening there were more "decisions for Christ" than normal, and he later informed me, "That story always gets them!" Furthermore, quotes from famous pioneer evangelists, who themselves were motivated by the thought of saving people from an eternity without Christ, were (are) sometimes employed to add force to the message of urgency. For example, the motivation of Hudson Taylor's missionary enterprise in China was the 360 million dying without the gospel; and William Booth, founder of the Salvation Army, maintained that if only his officers could spend one night in hell, the effectiveness of their mission would be considerably strengthened.[10] Jay Wesley Richards, who according to MacDonald, offers "a more sophisticated version" of the urgency motive for missionary activity, and the need to respond to the gospel this side of death, by asking, "what missionary would be willing to die in his or her own blood at the hands of pagan tribes if the salvation of such tribes were in no way dependent on such risk?"[11]

It is better not to tell them

Nash uses a further argument against belief in postmortem opportunity for salvation, and suggests that if postmortem opportunity for salvation is a possibility, then it would be better that missionaries do not proclaim the gospel in this life, which might be refused and rejected, but wait until that person would receive full revelation of God at the judgment. Nash, rather disdainfully of advocates of posthumous salvation, claims that it would be better not to jeopardize the eternal hope of the evangelized by instructing them in this life, as "once they hear and reject the gospel, they are condemned."[12] Erickson, commenting on the implications of the concept of posthumous salvation for mission, makes a similar point, contending that "if hearing [the gospel] within this life disqualifies one from any opportunity to hear after this life, we are not necessarily doing persons a favor by telling them the good news now. It would actually be better for them in the long run if they did not hear until later."[13] It is important to understand that Erickson's statement is in response to Pinnock who asks whether those who have re-

10. See Dowsett, *Not Fair!*, 55.

11. MacDonald, *Evangelical*, 170, who cites Richards, "Pascalian," 216. Richards's focus is universalism, but as stated previously, both views would contend that death is not the end of one's opportunity for a decision for Christ, making his words equally relevant for posthumous salvation.

12. Nash, "Restrictivism," 135.

13. Erickson, *How Shall*, 267. See also Berkhof, *Systematic Theology*, 693, who makes the same point.

fused God in this world might have a second chance to believe in him. His response to this latter question is essentially negative; even though he claims that divine mercy is immeasurable, he presumes that the person who has decided against God throughout his/her life will not be inclined to choose him afterwards. Pinnock uses Hitler as an example of his theory, stating unequivocally, that "there is no way that Hitler will change his mind. God might want him to, Christians may even want him to, but a man like Hitler is not going to want to. Heaven would be the worst place he could imagine," yet he simultaneously claims that "those who are drawn to the concept of a post-mortem encounter are right to think that no one who really wants it will be deprived salvation." Whilst Pinnock's theory of Hitler continuing to resist God at the Judgment is uncertain, one might be tempted to test Pinnock's logic by the scenario of replacing Hitler with a kindly old grandmother, who remained agnostic throughout her life.[14]

Therefore, the claim of Erickson, and possibly Nash, that it would be better for proponents of posthumous salvation not to evangelize now in order for sinners to hear the message in the afterlife, is to be understood in the context of a rebuttal of Pinnock's view that "no hope can be offered to those declining God's offer to them in Christ."[15] Yet it would be wrong for Erickson or Nash to suggest that all advocates of posthumous salvation would view this model as an opportunity only for those who have not previously heard, but not for those who had previously rejected the gospel message.

Wright contends that those who are deprived of the opportunity to respond to Christ in life are provided that opportunity postmortem, but "this is not so much a 'second chance' as a first opportunity."[16] However, he continues by emphasizing that the language of chances which suggests "barely minimal ways of satisfying 'fair play'" are not always helpful as it does not accurately portray the grace of God which extends to undeserving human beings.

Other motivations for mission

As discussed above, the motivation for mission in evangelical or conservative Christianity is often focused on the concept of saving a person within the span of this life, which supposedly constitutes their only opportunity for salvation.[17] It is, therefore, claimed that to allow for postmortem opportunity

14. Pinnock, *Wideness*, 173–5.
15. Pinnock, *Wideness*, 168.
16. Wright, *Radical*, 99.
17. See Boettner, *Reformed*, 119; Dowsett, *Not Fair!*, 39; Fernando, *Christian's*

is to stifle and suppress the missionary mandate. Nash further argues that he fails to see how anyone might regard himself an example of compassion for the unevangelized by offering them a false hope about their future.[18] Packer, like Nash, argues that the urgency of evangelism in this life is undermined and is "guaranteed to ruin souls."[19] Packer's comment is a little ironic since he, as a five point Calvinist, faces a similar objection. To put it crudely, if God will save the elect anyway, why bother proclaiming the gospel to the unevangelized? Commenting on Augustinian theology in general, Pinnock states, "Under such a deterministic scheme, it is hard to find much motivation for any human action, missionary or otherwise."[20]

However, against such a line of reasoning, Pinnock suspects that the motivation for missions has been "narrowed down to this one thing: deliverance from wrath." He further argues that "we have made it the major reason for missions when it is not," and objects "to the notion that missions is individually oriented, hellfire insurance." He contests that "sinners are not in the hands of an angry God. Our mission is not to urge them to turn to Jesus because God hates them and delights in sending them to hell," and reminds his readers that Jesus did not come to condemn the world, but to save it (John 3:17), for the mission of the church is "to announce the wonderful news of the kingdom of God" (Mark 1:14–15). He further contests that "it is a travesty to maintain that the primary motive of missions is to rescue souls from hell" as "missions are part of God's strategy for transforming the world and changing history."[21] The writers of *Nature of Hell* argue similarly that those who hold traditional values of hell need to remember that the proclamation of the gospel is an invitation to abundant life before it is a warning against eternal damnation.[22]

Pinnock is not alone in disputing "deliverance from wrath" as the primary motivation for missions, as other wider hope theologians also prefer to understand mission in a more positive way as expressed below.[23]

Attitude, 132; Gundry, "Salvation," 342–4.

18. Nash, "*Response*," 101.

19. Packer, "Problem," 171, 178.

20. Pinnock, *Wideness*, 177. See also MacDonald, *Evangelical*, 169, who makes the same observation.

21. Pinnock, *Wideness*, 177–8.

22. *Nature of Hell*, 117, though no biblical references are provided.

23. See Ellenberger, "Is Hell," 217–27 [226]; Sanders, *No Other*, 207; Green, *Evangelism*, 76–78.

Motivated by Christ's command

The first disciples were commanded by Christ to go into all the world and make disciples and to baptize in the name of the Father, and of the Son, and of the Holy Spirit.[24] Moreover, the last words of Christ to his disciples, before his ascension, emphasized mission, through Jesus instructing them that when the Holy Spirit comes on them, they will receive power to "be my witnesses in Jerusalem, and in all Judea and Samaria and to the ends of the earth" (Acts 1:8). The remainder of Acts describes the Spirit-filled disciples of Christ fulfilling this command to mission. Such direct commands from the Lord are not lost on advocates of posthumous salvation, for even if they had no other reason to reach out evangelistically to others, the command of Christ would surely be enough. Sanders adds, "If the explicit instructions of our Lord are not motivation enough for evangelicals to engage in missions, then perhaps they are not as committed to the authority of Jesus as they claim."[25]

Ellenberger contends that Paul was motivated to evangelize through a wide array of factors, which included his sense of obligation to God. Ellenberger develops this point by emphasizing that Paul's obligation to God could be seen by: his discharging a trust that God had committed to him (1 Cor. 9:16–17); his being obedient to the divine commission (Rom. 1:1, 5); his fear of disappointing his beloved master (2 Cor. 5:11); his speaking as Christ's ambassador (2 Cor. 5:20); and also his desire for reward for his labor in the gospel (1 Cor. 3:8–9).[26]

Motivated by the blessing of knowing Christ

Green claims that the early Christians were motivated to evangelize because of a "profound sense of indebtedness."[27] Paul speaks of his indebtedness in his letter to the Romans, asserting "I am bound both to Greeks and non-Greeks, both to the wise and the foolish. That is why I am so eager to preach the gospel," (Rom.1:14–15).[28] Such indebtedness exhibited itself in Paul's passion to reach those lost, for Christ, so that they might experience the same salvation that he had received. This is evidenced in his writing to the

24. See Matt. 28:18–20; also, Mark 16:15; Luke 24:47–48; Acts 1:8.

25. Sanders, *No Other*, 284.

26. Ellenberger, "Is Hell," 221.

27. Green, *Evangelism*, 77.

28. The RSV translates this phrase, "I am under obligation," with the NLT translating, "For I have a great sense of obligation."

Corinthians, "Though I am free and belong to no man, I make myself a slave to everyone, to win as many people as possible" (1 Cor. 9:19) and "I have become all things to all men, so that by all possible means I might save some. I do this for the sake of the gospel, that I may share in its blessings" (1 Cor. 9:22–23).

However, the motivation to share the gospel with others is more than an obligation, for Paul instructs the Corinthian believers that "Christ's love compels us" (2 Cor. 5:14). Such love for his own people motivated him to write to the Roman believers that he was willing to be damned if it meant salvation for others (Rom. 9:1–3). Green claims that those early Christians were not prepared to selfishly bask in God's love, but were stimulated to share that love with others out of their own sense of gratitude and love. He writes, "Believers do not evangelize because they have carefully calculated the probabilities of universalism, annihilation, or unending torment . . . They go because they have fallen in love with the great Lover. They go because they have been set free by the great Liberator. They love him and they want that love to reach others. It is far too good to keep to themselves."[29]

Fackre, similarly, maintains that the person who has come to faith in Christ will desire to share the good news of Christ. He states, "A basic motivation for evangelism is this joy in the Lord. We've heard the good news, and we want to pass it on. No belief in the divine perseverance after death is going to still this story."[30] He further asserts that life in this world is much richer "when one has the confidence and consolations of the gospel."[31]

Motivated by the judgment to come

Paul was also mindful of, and motivated by, the coming judgment of the Lord.[32] He writes to the Corinthians: "We make it our goal to please him . . . For we must all appear before the judgment seat of Christ, that each one may receive what is due to him for the things done while in the body, whether good or bad . . . since, then, we know what it is to fear the Lord, we try to persuade men." (2 Cor. 5:9–11). For Paul, to please Christ was to comprise of living in accordance with God's will and purpose, including being obedient to his calling as apostle to the Gentiles.[33] From the above text, it would also appear that Paul is encouraging the work of evangelism on the

29. Green, *Evangelism*, 78.

30. Fackre, "Divine Perseverance," 94, see also Sanders, *No Other*, 284.

31. Fackre, "Divine Perseverance," 94.

32. See for example, Rom. 2:1–16.

33. Acts 9:15; Gal. 2:7; 1 Thess. 2:4; 1 Tim. 1:11.

basis that one day each believer will be accountable for the manner in which they proclaimed the gospel.

Judgment by works was held in tension with Paul's justification by faith, for in the 2 Corinthians chapter 5 passage we find both Paul's confidence for those who are "in Christ," who were forgiven (v. 19) and righteous (v. 21) as well as being assured that they have a "building from God" (v. 1), and Paul's teaching that all believers will "appear before the judgment seat of Christ." Barnett contests that "the sure prospect of the judgment seat reminds the Corinthians—and all believers—that while they are righteous in Christ by faith alone, the faith that justifies is to be expressed by love and obedience . . . and by pleasing the Lord."[34]

Furthermore, those who embrace the possibility of posthumous salvation also recognize that all people, believers and unbelievers, will one day stand before Christ the Judge, and even though there might be opportunity to receive Christ's salvation at that juncture, the judgment is nevertheless a serious matter where all people will give account for their earthly lives. In chapter 4, I proposed how this judgment might be understood, asserting that the judgment will be no soft option, for all sinners will be confronted by the perfect Son of God and will be faced with the damaging effects of their sin on God and others. Such a realization that the judgment will be a time of anguish and torment, would in itself be a powerful motivation to share the gospel with others.[35]

Utility does not establish truth

Whilst the questions above on how a postmortem opportunity for salvation might affect the motivation for missions is important, one needs to note that this is not the most important criterion, for, as Sanders points out, the argument for "utility does not necessarily establish truth."[36] That is, even if a belief in restrictivism were to lead to a more fervent missionary zeal, it

34. Barnett, *Second Epistle*, 277. Barnett proposes the possibility "that some at Corinth held to a super-spirituality associated with an over-realized eschatology leading to a less than earnest approach to their responsibilities during the present age" which caused Paul to remind them of their coming judgment. He further contends that one's confidence of being "with the Lord" (v. 8) is to be held in tension with the "fear of the Lord" (v. 11).

35. Even some universalists, like MacDonald and Ferre, embrace a concept of punishment and hell. MacDonald argues that hell is to be treated seriously and "to be avoided at all costs." This comment is based on an understanding of hell which is real but is not forever, see MacDonald, *Evangelical*, 166. See also Ferre, "Universalism," 24.

36. Sanders, *No Other*, 283–4.

does not necessarily mean that restrictivist theology is correct. Conversely, if belief in posthumous salvation, or any other wider hope theory, were conclusively shown to suppress or demotivate mission, then this in itself would not be proof that posthumous salvation was false, or indeed, if the concept of posthumous salvation were shown to be a more compassionate response to the bereaved, equally, does not make it true.[37] MacDonald claims: "Whilst I would not desire to diminish the motive for missions, if the prime motivation is a false one, we should not hang on to it just for its pure pragmatic value."[38]

Nigel Wright contends that "we engage in mission because the Christian gospel is true, it enables human beings to find liberation and fulfil their destiny, because through it people receive the Spirit of the messianic age and come themselves to participate in his mission of redemption, and because through the gospel people learn how to give glory to God, Father, Son and Spirit. This seems to be enough motivation to be going on with."[39]

Wright further argues that without Christ, people are lost and are alienated from their own destiny. The gospel conveys a truth about God that invites them to enter into the life of God through being participators in the Holy Spirit into the messianic community of believers. He continues by emphasizing that the motive which undergirds missionary outreach "is not the fear that without it people will go to hell . . . but the love and generosity which are instilled into our hearts by the missionary Spirit of God and which seek to reclaim what has been lost. The ultimate motivation is to bring glory to God, to serve that work whereby his splendor, beauty and goodness are made known and the world and its inhabitants are restored to their true equilibrium and creative fruitfulness now and in the age to come."[40]

It might further be argued, that the concept of one needing to make a decision for Christ in the confines of this life only, with no opportunity postmortem, could actually be a stumbling block to evangelism in a post-Christendom world.[41] I have personally witnessed how Christianity has been marginalized in the UK through a creeping secularism over many decades with school children no longer being aware of even the basic tenets of the Christian faith. Therefore, when the gospel is presented to people in this context, who have not heard, or been encouraged to have respect for, the Christian faith, they often evaluate Christianity more robustly, critiquing its

37. Sanders, *No Other*, 284. For a similar argument, see Van Engen, "Effect," 186–7.
38. MacDonald, *Evangelical*, 171–2.
39. Wright, *Radical*, 100.
40. Wright, *Radical*, 101–2.
41. I am writing essentially in the context of the UK.

rationale and "justice" more acutely than previously. Whilst not suggesting that the church of past generations has been negligent in its apologetic, there was generally in society a greater acceptance of the authority of the Church and the Bible in spiritual matters. Postmoderns are not content with this, and rightly challenge the authority and credibility of the gospel message as it has been traditionally proclaimed. As discussed in chapter 1, such challenges also come partly through globalization.[42] That is, for much of the history of the world, most people lived their lives without coming into contact with people of different races and cultures, but now, through international travel, immigration, television, and the World Wide Web, people are exposed to others as never before. It was, therefore, far easier to make generalized statements concerning the salvation of the "alien and stranger" who was once detached and remote. Now, however, that person has become integrated into society, being known personally as a friend or family member.

Perhaps one of the most repeated statements concerning the restrictivist view of salvation that one needs to respond to the message of the gospel within the limits of one's life, is "It's not fair!" followed by a range of possible scenarios. As a church pastor engaged in regular evangelistic conversations for over twenty-five years, I would suggest that it is restrictivist theology that acts as a greater hindrance to the gospel message than any disincentive apparently caused through wider hope theologians diminishing the urgency for mission. Though, as discussed earlier, the usefulness or convenience of an argument does not establish its legitimacy.

Pastoral evaluation of posthumous salvation

The loss of a loved one, especially when s/he did not embrace the Christian faith, can bring a significant emotional and spiritual challenge to family and friends. This challenge is also felt, acutely, by those involved in pastoral ministry who are required to bring comfort and support to the bereaved. As discussed in chapter 1, clergy are often content with allowing the family to embrace an uneasy hope that God will accept their loved one into heaven, a view that most clergy would not contradict on the basis of agnosticism, for who really knows where a person might have stood in regard to his/her faith? Also, as previously discussed, when the question of the deceased's resting place is put more directly to clergy there are many ways in which the questions are deflected without needing to convey a pessimistic reply to the loved ones. There is no suggestion that clergy are being less than sincere

42. See Chapter 1 comments on globalization.

in this, for most would recognize the immense difficulties they face in trying to be true to their theological understanding at the same time as being compassionate to the bereaved.

Such pastoral responses which enable clergy, on occasions, to "get out of a tight spot," cause many, more contemplative clergy, to remain ill at ease over the superficiality of their reply. A few years ago I was confronted by a pastoral situation where a church member suffered a double bereavement. A brother and nephew (father and son) of this church member died within days of each other, the nephew being only a teenager. The church member was angry with God and utterly confused, as is often observed at such times, and spoke of her own sadness and guilt for not being able to share the gospel with them *in time*. She was instructed quite emphatically by the more immediate family members not to speak about God to her dying brother, a request which she felt obliged to obey. When offering pastoral counsel and support, it was clear that her understanding of the gospel opportunity as being limited to this life caused her great pain, as now, for her, all hope for salvation had been extinguished. Whilst a detailed theological response would have been wholly inappropriate at that moment, I asked her if she believed that God loved her brother. She responded positively. I then asked her, "Does God love your brother eternally and unconditionally?" To which she again responded positively. It was then suggested that God would not love her brother any less one minute after his heart had stopped beating than he had one minute before his death. Whilst this kind of pastoral response fell short of an explicit explanation of postmortem opportunity, the implication was not lost on her. Almost immediately her spirit lifted and a tangible sense of peace became evident. She did not ask any further questions of whether God would provide opportunity for salvation, or whether such an opportunity could be refused by her brother. She seemed content to embrace the hope that rested on God's love for her brother.

MacDonald argues similarly, contending that in the case of a Christian mother at the funeral of her son who had rejected his Christian upbringing, traditional theology offers no hope at all, "for it is more or less certain that her son will be condemned to hell with no hope of redemption."[43] At such times there will be a grasping of straws of how her son *might* have trusted God when he attended church as a young boy, or that *maybe* he turned to the Lord in his dying moments, as he would have had the way explained to him in earlier life. MacDonald is correct to suggest that those who think that people believe the gospel because it provides them with a "comfort

---

43. MacDonald, *Evangelical*, 172. He states a case for universalism, but this is irrelevant here as both universalism and posthumous salvation allow for a postmortem opportunity for salvation.

blanket" of an eternal bliss would do well to consider such a scenario where Christian belief would be more a source of torment than comfort. He further suggests that the alternative of liberal theology is no better as it offers a feeble promise of eternal life based on little more than the niceness of God, which seems to suggest that it does not really matter if one responds to the Lord, or how one lives on earth.

The funeral service of a person who was clearly not a Christian also offers a considerable dilemma to those officiating, for the unequivocal, evangelistic gospel message which is appropriately preached in a church service, would appear to be wholly inappropriate given the sensitivities of the pastoral situation. Stoddart writes: "Publicly acknowledging the breadth of this grey area . . . would be perceived as blunting the gospel or, in the eyes of some of his congregation, 'going liberal.'"[44]

Stoddart claims that the pastoral questions over the death of a non-Christian family member are left "largely unaddressed by the evangelical community" resulting in many of its own members encountering intense distress at the prospect of a person they have loved being eternally lost. Such distressed members of the evangelical community, he claims, "are left huddled together in that pale light of insufficient answers to questions that they have taken considerable courage to voice in the silence of their own heart let alone voice to the minister they hear preaching of hell in his evangelistic sermons."[45] Stoddart's own story relates of how he was introduced to a conservative evangelical faith at the age of fifteen and felt unable to voice his concerns about his deceased "unsaved" father to his evangelical friends. For him, at that time, it was a tension of either rejecting the foundation of biblical authority upon which his "own salvation from hell was based" to release (in his own mind) his father from the possibility of hell, or, to choose to believe in hell and live with the suspicion that his father was there.[46] He chose to remain silent on the issue rather than have to make a decision on this dilemma.

In a later article for the Guardian newspaper, Stoddart asks, "If you believe (or are told you should believe) your grandmother is going to hell because she is not a Christian, how do you deal with that? Do you dehumanise her or psychologically distance yourself in order to accept her fate? How is it possible to go about daily life while believing that your loved-one has entered eternal suffering? When most hell-believing Christians are likely to encounter the death of 'non-Christian' loved-ones it is striking that it is

44. Stoddart, "Bespoke," 22. See also Stoddart and Pryce, "Observed," 129–53.
45. Stoddart, "Hell," 6.
46. His own words, Stoddart, "Hell," 6.

a subject rarely tackled. No one talks about this aspect. There is something of a conspiracy of silence."[47] Indeed, as MacDonald argues, the traditional beliefs can bring torment, rather than comfort to the loved-ones of the deceased through limiting the opportunity of salvation to this life only.

Conclusion

As discussed above, the concept of posthumous salvation does not necessarily reduce the urgency for proclaiming the gospel, or lull unbelievers into a false sense of security causing them to procrastinate on the challenge to decide for Christ, despite allegations to the contrary. Salvation is to be thought of not merely as an insurance against the judgment of God, but as an eternal relationship with one's Creator which commences during one's earthly life. The gospel is not to be reduced to cognitive information about Jesus, and salvation is much more than a rescue from the eternal consequences of not accepting Christ, for "it involves being a part of the people of God, participating in a covenantal relationship, and working for the *shalom* of the kingdom in all of society."[48] Furthermore, the traditional focus on the need for decision before death in order to receive salvation, and shun damnation, has been demonstrated to be neither the only, nor primary, reason for mission.

Through this chapter, other reasons for mission have been emphasized, which include: the motivation to be obedient to the command of Christ to take his gospel into the whole world; to proclaim the gospel out of a profound sense of indebtedness to God; and, the stimulus of both Christ's love and one's joy in the Lord. That is, those who have heard and received the good news of Christ will want to share it with others. As Jesus taught, "out of the overflow of the heart the mouth speaks" (Matt. 12:34). Furthermore, a person's fear of the Lord and recognition that s/he will one day be required to stand before the Judgment seat of Christ and give an account for his/her life will provide a considerable incentive for evangelization.

As also discussed in this chapter—though not to argue conclusively the case for posthumous salvation—the pastoral sensitivities that arise at a time of bereavement can often be difficult for clergy to deal with transparently. Many clergy recognize that the unequivocal evangelistic gospel message, which might seem so appropriate to a church service, is wholly inappropriate in a funeral home when one is ministering to the a bereaved family, especially where the Christian faith of their loved one was, at best, uncertain.

47. MacLeod, "St. Andrews researcher questions belief in hell."
48. Ellenberger, "Is hell," 226.

Whilst accepting, as already stated, that utility does not establish truth, if the concept of posthumous salvation is to be received as a theologically acceptable model, as in chapter 4, then pastorally and missiologically, it is in no way inferior to the traditional theology. Rather, it presents a model that would offer a more cogent and compassionate approach to the Christian faith, and a more robust apologetic where God is not viewed as arbitrary or unjust, and where a gospel offering hope beyond the grave should be thought of as truly good news.

6

Conclusion

Summary

The previous chapters have addressed the research question of whether there is grace, or salvation, beyond the grave for those who have either not heard or have heard but not responded to the gospel message before death. Traditionally, within evangelical/conservative circles, the answer to this question has been negative. Chapter 1 focused especially on setting the scene contextually, emphasizing why such a question is regarded as one of the "hottest topics on the agenda of theology."[1] This was firstly done through highlighting the not insignificant difficulties associated with traditional theology in a pastoral context, especially where the deceased was not a believer. This was followed by an appraisal of the revival of interest in the destiny of the unevangelized, which included the impact of globalization and the advent of a postmodern worldview with its critical questioning of metanarrative and truth claims. The more recent challenges from pluralistic theologians, Roman Catholicism, and conservative Protestantism were also described before the chapter concluded by laying down two theological axioms, namely God's universal salvific will, and the particularity and finality of salvation through Christ, as foundational to this work.[2]

The second chapter provided an overview to the common approaches in dealing with the question of the destiny of the unevangelized, setting the subject of posthumous salvation in its wider context. Following the works

---

1. Pinnock, *Wideness*, 7.

2. As stated previously, the first axiom of universality would be challenged mostly by restrictivists, especially by those who hold the reformed position. The second axiom of particularity would receive most opposition from liberals who would defend the universality of God's salvific will but jettison a high Christology.

of Race and D' Costa, the threefold typology of exclusivism, inclusivism, and pluralism was explained, though an in-depth critique of the various wider hope views was beyond the constraints of this chapter. The rationale for posthumous salvation, which is placed within the exclusivism section was summarized, emphasizing that (1) one's eternal destiny is not necessarily determined at death, and (2) explicit faith in Christ is necessary for salvation.[3]

As discussed, much of the more recent debate has focused on the unevangelized and has largely ignored the pastoral theology aspect. For, it is one thing to establish a strong polemic in discussing the salvation of those who are personally unknown in some far-reached part of the world, but another thing altogether to provide answers to the often difficult questions that bereaved families sometimes ask. In this context, it was argued that the concept of posthumous salvation offers the most coherent and convincing response to the question of the unbeliever's eternal destiny.[4]

In chapter 3 the biblical passages which purportedly support or undermine the concept of posthumous salvation were evaluated. Whilst it was concluded that there is no room for dogmatism, the passages and verses that have been traditionally used by advocates and opponents of this concept were shown to neither unambiguously confirm nor deny posthumous salvation. Pinnock was essentially correct in his claim that the scriptural evidence for postmortem opportunity for salvation was not abundant.[5]

Pinnock also proved to be correct by contesting that the strength of posthumous salvation lies in its theological argument, as was established in chapter 4.[6] This chapter concentrated on a test-case theological argument which has a significant and close connection with the concept of posthumous salvation, namely God's attributes, especially divine love and justice. It was concluded that it is theologically feasible to consider God's attributes of mercy and justice as complementary, rather than contradictory, with the concept of *restorative* justice being the preferred alternative to the more traditional position of *retributive* justice which is essentially punitive. This,

---

3. This is because the concept of posthumous salvation contends that Jesus is both an ontological and epistemological necessity.

4. Though, again, it is to be emphasized that utility does not establish truth; an argument that can work for and against this concept. The primary focus of raising the missiological and pastoral questions is to discover whether posthumous salvation somehow undermines or destabilizes the Christian faith, not in order to provide an argument for its feasibility per se.

5. Pinnock, *Wideness*, 169.

6. Pinnock, *Wideness*, 169.

in turn, helped to maintain the unity of God's nature and also support the notion of postmortem opportunity for salvation.

Chapter 5 concentrated on missiological and pastoral implications of posthumous salvation. It was concluded that a belief in this notion would not necessarily reduce the urgency for proclaiming the gospel, or cause unbelievers to procrastinate on making a decision for Christ. It was contended that missionary motivation should not be reduced to the fear of the eternal consequences of one not turning to Christ whilst on earth. Other motivations include: obedience to the command of Christ; profound indebtedness to God; the love of Christ; the joy of the Lord; and the awareness of one needing to stand before the Lord to give account at the Judgment. Furthermore, whilst recognizing that the usefulness or convenience of an argument does not establish the legitimacy of that argument, a belief in posthumous salvation would enable clergy to minister to and comfort the bereaved family more effectively through offering a more rational and empathetic approach to pastoral ministry. It is contended that it would also offer a more robust apologetic, where God is not viewed as capricious or unreasonable, and where a gospel offering the possibility of salvation beyond the grave should be thought of as truly good news.

Contribution to the discussion

As discussed in chapter 2, the majority of advocates of posthumous salvation do not agree with the concept of salvation through general revelation, or implicit faith.[7] For them, salvation requires an explicit faith, and if no opportunity is given for such an explicit faith response during one's life, then it must be available following death, in the light of a God who is defined as Love and who desires the salvation of all people. Alternatively, inclusivists argue for implicit faith being salvific, for according to them general revelation brings enough knowledge of God for a person to respond to the light that they have received. For them, death brings the end of that opportunity. This book treads a more conciliatory pathway between these two, often quite distinct, approaches to the destiny of the unevangelized, by arguing for a "both and" rather than an "either or" approach, on the basis that God would surely use all means and methods available to bring about his salvific purposes in the world.

Considerable work has been focused in the area of Theology of Religions in recent decades in an attempt to answer the question of the salvation of those who have not heard the gospel message. The same is not true for

7. See also Appendix A.

those who are "closer to home," who might have some knowledge of the Christian faith, whether it be from a school assembly, a church baptism, a wedding or funeral, the customary church visit at Christmas, or being brought up in a Christian family. Other related questions would involve the accountability of someone who had heard a distorted gospel message or, who has heard the truth, but from someone who was a hypocritical scoundrel, whose life disqualified his message. Whilst this book goes beyond the typical arguments involving those who are unreached with the gospel message, and attempts to provide some cogent and compassionate answers that might be of assistance in the context of pastoral ministry, I would freely admit that I have barely scratched the surface of this subject. This would require future research.

Those who have criticized the concept of posthumous salvation have often done so by attempting to undermine the exegesis of 1 Peter 3:19—4:6 frequently used by advocates of posthumous salvation. As was discussed, at length, in chapter 3, the Petrine passage has caused considerable debate and it has been claimed that such a contentious and controversial passage should not be used as the basis for the concept of posthumous salvation. Erickson, for example, spends more than half of his fourteen page paper entitled "Is there opportunity for salvation after death?" dealing with this one passage, concluding, "It is strange to rest a doctrine about the eternal destiny of humans on such an obscure passage."[8] Erickson's rebuttal of the concept of posthumous salvation on the basis that it rests on this "obscure passage" is mistaken, for although the majority of the advocates of posthumous salvation quote the Petrine passage as an evidence for salvation after death, this present work has argued that it neither stands nor falls on this passage. I have sought to move the debate on posthumous salvation away from this problem passage, claiming that its critics are correct in their concerns that such an ambiguous passage should not be used to offer proof of this concept. Rather, the answers are to be found in theology, as Pinnock claims.

This work has sought to move the discussion on the theological viability of posthumous salvation forward through an argument based on the simplicity of God and by contending that restorative justice offers a more cogent and coherent model than the traditional model based on retributive justice. I am not aware of any other work that has explicitly connected these subjects in the manner of this work.

Compared with other wider hope views, the theory of posthumous salvation has received comparatively little interest or consideration. It is

---

8. Erickson, "Is there," 144.

hoped that this book will have a catalytic effect to encourage further conversation and research into this concept, which though popular in the nineteenth century, has now largely lost its former appeal.

Further work

As suggested in the previous section, further research on how death is to be understood in the pastoral context of evangelical churches would be of benefit to this discussion. Having served in pastoral ministry for more than a quarter of a century, I am painfully aware of the "conspiracy of silence" over the death of loved ones whose faith was, at best, uncertain.[9] Qualitative analysis of this subject from the perspective of both the clergy and laity would make interesting reading, and possibly reveal the divergence of one's theological understanding from one's practical application at a time of family bereavement of loved ones who did not share their faith.

Last word

In evaluating the orthodoxy, or otherwise, of the concept of posthumous salvation, it is important to ask whether one is required to deny any aspect of orthodox Christianity other than the belief that death seals one's eternal destiny. This line of reasoning for establishing the legitimacy of posthumous salvation follows that of Robin Parry, aka Gregory Macdonald, who convincingly argues his point for Christian universalism.[10] Likewise, I am confident that belief in posthumous salvation is compatible with belief in Creation, the Fall, Redemption, the Trinity, the inspiration of Scripture, the centrality of Christ as the unique Savior of the world, the Incarnation, the Resurrection of Christ, the fulfilling of the Great Commission, and more. Moreover, posthumous salvation is not only no threat to orthodoxy, but it is contested that it provides a more compelling understanding of the nature of God's attributes, in that his love and his justice are complementary, rather than conflicting.

Parry, who propounds a Christian universalism, asks with transparent openness, "What if I am wrong?" That is, what damage might have been done to others and to the gospel through his honest questioning of traditional theology in favor of universalism? Both his question and his answer

---

9. Stoddart's term, as quoted by Donald MacLeod, "St. Andrews researcher questions belief in hell," www.guardian.co.uk (5th Dec. 2005). I am quite aware of the truth of Stoddart's claim.

10. MacDonald, *Evangelical Universalist*, 175–7.

have relevance to the validity of posthumous salvation too. What if I am wrong? Would a belief in posthumous salvation undermine the gospel, or hurt others, or dishonor God, or lead people away from a Trinitarian Christian faith? Would such a false hope damage a person's faith, or diminish one's understanding of God, or undermine the authority of the Bible? The answer must also be "no!"

Parry further argues that "belief in universalism is most certainly *not* a requirement for Christian orthodoxy, but neither does it amount to an exclusion from orthodoxy *even if it is wrong*"[11] which, at the very least, can also be claimed for a belief in postmortem opportunity for salvation. That said, the arguments, biblical, theological, and pastoral, presented in the pages of this book, offer a challenge to traditional understandings through an alternative vision which maintains the unity of God in a way that the traditional model does not, and provides a compelling narrative of God's universal salvific will and the particularity and finality of the person and work of Christ.

When comparing the traditional view which seals one's eternal destiny at death with the concept of posthumous salvation, as described in this book, Parry's question is pertinent: "Which vision has the strongest view of divine love? Which story has the most powerful narrative of God's victory over evil? Which picture lifts the atoning efficacy of the cross of Christ to the greatest heights? Which perspective best emphasizes the triumph of grace over sin? Which view inspires worship and love of God bringing him honor and glory? Which has the most satisfactory understanding of divine wrath? Which narrative inspires hope in the human spirit?"[12] The answer to these questions would, to me at least, appear obvious. Even so, the sentiment of St. Paul continues to act as a warning against dogmatism: "Now we see but a poor reflection as in a mirror; then we shall see face to face. Now I know in part; then I shall know fully, even as I am fully known" (1 Cor. 13:12).

This sentiment is memorably personalized in Sheldon Vanauken's book *Severe Mercy*, when he recalled of the time he had spoken with his friend C. S. Lewis, who had been influential in both Vanauken and his wife "Davy" becoming Christians. "Davy" subsequently struggled with a serious illness which eventually took her life. In the midst of sorrow, Vanauken sought out Lewis, and they exchanged letters, eighteen of which are published in his book. Reminiscing of one occasion when he and Lewis were about to part ways, he writes: "We talked, I recall, about death or, rather, awakening

11. MacDonald, *Evangelical Universalist*, 176. His italics.

12. MacDonald, *Evangelical Universalist*, 176–7. He uses it in the context of Christian universalism, but here the same quote is used in the context of posthumous salvation.

after death. Whatever it would be like, we thought, our response to it would be, 'Why, of course! Of *course* it's like this. How else could it have possibly been?' We both chuckled at that."[13]

---

13. Vanauken, *Severe Mercy*, 125. Original italic.

Appendix A

General Revelation and Salvation

THEOLOGIANS LIKE ANDERSON ARGUE that if general revelation is salvific then the concept of posthumous salvation becomes redundant.[1] That is, if someone can come to saving faith in Christ, without reference to Christ in this life, then postmortem opportunity would be superfluous. In this Appendix, associated questions of the importance of explicit faith in Christ for salvation and how much one is required to know of the gospel message in order to be saved, will be raised.

Understanding general revelation

In a Christian context, the term *revelation* refers to God's self-disclosure, and is normally classified into two categories of general revelation and special revelation.[2] Erickson offers the following definitions: "General revelation is God's communication of himself to all persons at all times and in all places. Special revelation involves God's particular communications and manifestations of himself to particular persons at particular times, communications and manifestations that are available now only by consultation of certain sacred writings."[3] More specifically, general revelation is tradition-

1. Anderson, *Christianity*, 154, appears not to consider the possibility of posthumous salvation for those who have not responded to general revelation. See also Nash, *Is Jesus the Only Savior?* 149; Carson, *Gagging*, 299–300.

2. Berkouwer, "General and Special Divine Revelation," 13–24, addresses the question of whether it is correct to press the distinction between these two categories and whether to do so permits a "proper view of the wonder of the one divine revelation," 13.

3. Erickson, *Christian Theology*, 178. For an extensive discussion of the doctrine of general revelation, see Demarest, *General Revelation*. Tiénou , "Eternity in Their

175

ally understood to be communicated through observation of the created order, divine providence in history, and through the moral and spiritual qualities of humankind.[4] For the purpose of this section, the question of how much Christian truth can be gleaned from general revelation, apart from special revelation, and how much information must one know and believe to be saved, is paramount. These questions are very important since the vast majority of people who have ever lived have not been recipients of special revelation.

Is general revelation salvific?

The question of whether general revelation is salvific is crucial in understanding the differentiation between the exclusivist and inclusivist positions. Exclusivists, who include proponents of posthumous salvation, believe that Jesus Christ is both an ontological and epistemological necessity for salvation. Thus, there is no salvation outside of Christ, but one also needs to know of Christ's person and work and make an appropriate explicit response.[5] Inclusivists, conversely, believe that whilst there is no salvation outside of Christ, one does not necessarily need to know the details of Christ's life and ministry. All one needs to do is to make an implicit faith response to the light that one has through general revelation, as described above. Thus, salvation for the inclusivist equates to Christ being an ontological necessity, but not an epistemological one. Erickson poignantly phrases the issue as to whether one must know about Christ and his atoning death to be saved, or

---

Hearts," 213, emphasizes that though the Bible is a record of God's special revelation, it does not record all of God's specific ways of making himself known to humans throughout history, and that it is "inaccurate to suggest that if an idea is not in the Bible, it cannot be special revelation."

4. *Created order*: Ps. 19:1; Rom. 1:20; *Divine providence in history*: Job 12:23; Pss. 47:7–8; 66:7; Isa. 10:5–13; Dan. 2:21; Acts 17:26; *Moral and spiritual qualities*: Rom. 2:11–16. See Grudem, *Systematic Theology*, 122–3; Erickson, *Christian Theology*, 179–80. Demarest, "General Revelation," 944–5, refers to general revelation being divided into two categories, "internal" which refers to the "innate sense of deity and conscience," and "external" which refers to nature and providential history.

5. For example, Lindsell, *Christian Philosophy*, 107, states, "General revelation, to be a vehicle of salvation, must insist that God is revealed sufficiently so as to restore the broken relationship with man . . . this much is perfectly evident: general revelation is totally insufficient as a vehicle for salvation." Similarly, Demarest claims that "the light they do possess is too fragmentary and distorted to illume the path that leads to a saving knowledge of God," in *General Revelation*, 259.

whether it is sufficient to believe in a deity that is powerful, holy, and good, and to cast oneself on the mercy of this God.[6]

Even amongst those who do not believe that general revelation is salvific, there is significant diversity in how general revelation is viewed, from Barth, who refused to acknowledge any revelation independent of Christ, to Berkouwer, who claims that general revelation was "never intended to assert that true knowledge of God is possible through the natural light of reason," and Demarest who believes that objective and reliable information can be known about God through general revelation, which in turn is rejected by rebellious human beings.[7] He further claims that "since knowledge of God is mediated to all by general revelation, human accountability is firmly established."[8]

Using a similar argument to Demarest, Henry questions that if human beings are incapable of drawing valid conclusions about God from general revelation, then should God hold them blameworthy and culpable? He asks whether God's judgment on such people would be morally tolerable.[9] He further argues that the notion of general revelation providing only a "misty pseudo-knowledge of God would . . . impugn God's justice for condemning a person on the basis of ignorance."[10] Henry censures Van Til for not doing justice to the "epistemic potency of general revelation" which Van Til believes as functioning only to condemn human beings, not illuminate them.[11] Whilst Henry disagrees with Van Til's view of general revelation, his conclusion that general revelation is not able to save is firmly in agreement with Van Til. Henry's view differs in that he believes that although general revelation attests God's eternal power and moral majesty, it renders rebellious humankind guilty for revolting against the light they have been given. He claims that general revelation is unable to provide fallen humanity with a "comprehensive and reliable view of God" which is to be found in the Bible. He further likens the fate of unredeemed humans who have

---

6. Erickson, *How Shall*, 122.

7. Barth, *Church Dogmatics*, vol. 2, part 1, 93, 105. Berkouwer, "General and Special Divine Revelation," 15. Henry alleges that Berkouwer, "grossly exaggerates the pagan ignorance of God," in Henry, "Is It Fair?," 249. According to Calvin, general revelation offers an objective and genuine revelation of God which human sin obscures resulting in failure to recognize the truth. However, following faith and salvation a person is enabled to perceive the truth found in general revelation. Calvin refers to this as seeing through the spectacles of faith. See Calvin, *Institutes*, Book 1, Chapter 6, Section 1, 39.

8. Demarest & Lewis, *Integrative*, 246.

9. Henry, "Is It Fair?" 249.

10. Henry, "Is It Fair?" 250. See also Demarest, *General Revelation*, 145.

11. Henry, "Is It Fair?" 251. See also Van Til, *Defense*, 87.

not heard the name of Christ as similar to those angels for whom no provision for salvation has been made.[12] He continues, "God is not obliged to save any morally rebellious creature. His non-provision of redemption for some fallen humans does not compromise his justice, any more than does his non-provision of redemption for all fallen angels. God is not obliged to redeem all or any rebels; his elective intervention is a voluntary expression of holy love."[13]

Sproul, in accordance with Calvinist tradition, states unequivocally that general revelation is inadequate for salvation by contesting those who assume that the unevangelized are innocent.[14] In citing Romans 1:19–21, he affirms that general revelation is "clear and unambiguous" and that the problem is not that humans do not know of God, but that they refuse to acknowledge what they know to be true. He asserts that "the revelation is sufficient to render man inexcusable," emphasizing that an unevangelized person living in some remote area, isolated from the gospel, will not be judged for not accepting Christ; rather, that person will be held accountable according to the light s/he had, including the law of God written on their hearts (Rom. 2:15).[15] He concludes, stating that all unevangelized will be condemned if they reject the Father through general revelation, yet he also declares that God's only remedy for sin is through the gospel of Christ which is proclaimed by human messengers (Rom. 10:14–15). He argues that it is, therefore, imperative that the church take up its mandate to proclaim the gospel of Christ.

A major criticism of this restrictivist view of general revelation is that it is sufficient for condemnation, but insufficient for salvation.[16] Sproul's position, quoted above, appears to suggest that the unevangelized are justly condemned by rejecting the light of general revelation, but since salvation is only through Christ, even an acceptance of that revelation would prove insufficient for salvation. Sanders, a proponent of the wider hope outlook, questions that if a person's "rejection of the truth of general revelation is

12. Consigned to judgment without mercy, see 2 Pet. 2:4.

13. Henry, "Is It Fair?" 253.

14. Sproul, *Reason to Believe*, 47–59; chapter entitled, "What about the Poor Native Who Never Heard of Christ?"

15. Sproul, *Reason to Believe*, 52.

16. Exclusivists believe in both the ontological and epistemological necessity of Christ, which also includes advocates of the concept of posthumous salvation, whilst restrictivists, more specifically, restrict the opportunity for salvation to this life. It might be argued that, even if most proponents of posthumous salvation do not believe that general revelation is salvific, they, at least, allow for a wider hope through the postmortem opportunity.

counted as an implicit rejection of Jesus, then why is it that an individual's conviction of sin and desire for God through the leading of the Holy Spirit are not counted as implicit acceptance of Jesus?" He also questions, "If infants can be saved through the work of Christ even though they never hear about Christ, why can unevangelized adults not be saved in the same manner?"[17]

Clark contends that the saying of "*ignorance is no excuse* applies only in cases where a person *ought* to know the law and through culpable negligence does not."[18] He illustrates this point by stating that a speeding motorist could not plead ignorance to the police, claiming that s/he did not know the speed limit for the road. However, he proposes that when a person is innocently ignorant, one assumes that such ignorance may be a valid excuse. Clark claims that this concept is in line with Paul's argument in Romans 1:18–23.

> "The wrath of God is being revealed from heaven against all the godlessness and wickedness of men who suppress the truth by their wickedness, since what may be known about God is plain to them, because God has made it plain to them. For since the creation of the world God's invisible qualities—his eternal power and divine nature—have been clearly seen, being understood from what has been made, so that men are without excuse. For although they knew God, they neither glorified him as God nor gave thanks to him, but their thinking became futile and their foolish hearts were darkened. Although they claimed to be wise, they became fools and exchanged the glory of the immortal God for images made to look like mortal man and birds and animals and reptiles."

Paul argues that no one is ignorant and that no one is without excuse, but that is all that Paul contends. Paul is silent as to whether there might be people who are "not permanently rebellious, but who have responded positively by God's enabling grace to the glimmers of light they have seen in natural revelation."[19] Clark contends that the two responses to Paul's silence are (a) the belief that God does not desire all persons to have opportunity for salvation, and regards those who are without excuse to be people who have not received special revelation, but are condemned through not responding to general revelation, and (b) the belief that it is the godless and wicked and those "who suppress the truth by their wickedness" (v. 18) who are without

17. Sanders, *No Other*, 70.
18. Clark, "Is Special Revelation," 39. Italics his.
19. Clark, "Is Special Revelation," 40.

excuse. If one admits that one requires special revelation in order to be saved, with general revelation merely causing humans to be without excuse, then Clark is also correct in asserting that "God expects them to do the impossible (to exercise faith in Christ) and then condemns them eternally for failing to do it."[20] The point that Clark again conveys is that the above verses (Rom. 1:18–23), although consistent with the claim that general revelation is not salvific, indicate the possibility that salvation is feasible for those who respond positively to the light of general revelation.[21] He further poignantly questions, "How could God create human beings whom he presumably loves and then use them *only* to display the divine glory through their damnation? Does it make sense to say that God gives the damned enough light through general revelation to render them without excuse (and so to bring it about such that it is their fault they are damned) when the light of general revelation is not sufficient for them to be anything but damned, and when the God who can give them special revelation will not lift a finger on their behalf?"[22] Moody questions "What sort of God is he who gives man enough knowledge to damn him but not enough to save him?"[23]

Sanders concurs with Clark, contesting those who claim there is sufficient information in the created order to condemn but not to save. He asserts that revelation, whether general or special, does not save, for it is God who condemns or saves, and he uses any means he so desires in order to reach those he loves. Sanders continues by challenging the dualistic approach that some theologians hold of God, namely, the one who is known through creation, damns, and the one known through the Bible, saves.[24] Similarly, Tiénou states, "If the question is, does general revelation save? the answer is no. Revelation does not save, Jesus Christ does! Yet Scripture never rules out the possibility that some might come to a saving knowledge through general revelation."[25]

The New Testament story of Cornelius remains a major battleground between exclusivist and inclusivist theologians, with exclusivists claiming that Cornelius was unsaved before Peter's visit and inclusivists asserting that he was a true believer.[26] Inclusivists maintain that Peter presented Cornelius

20. Clark, "Is Special Revelation," 40.

21. Clark, "Is Special Revelation," 40–41.

22. Clark, "Is Special Revelation," 44. His italic.

23. Moody, *Word of Truth*, 59.

24. Sanders, "Inclusivism," 42, 105.

25. Tiénou, "Eternity" 215.

26. See Acts 10:1–48. Detailed arguments for/against Cornelius being a true believer before Peter's visit, although worthy of mention, are beyond the scope of this Appendix.

with the fullness of salvation that comes from a personal relationship with Christ. Erickson appears to remain open to the possibility of Cornelius being a true believer before Peter's visit, though he asserts that it cannot be argued that his coming to salvation would be on the basis of general salvation alone.[27]

A central tenet of inclusivist theology is that people are saved not by the content of their theology, but by faith in God.[28] Pinnock contends that "people cannot respond to light that did not reach them. They can only respond to revelation that did."[29] He claims that Abraham, for example, despite conceptual shortcomings, was saved by genuinely trusting in God. "What God was looking for in Abram was faith, not a certain quotient of knowledge . . . for who has perfect knowledge? Whose knowledge of the things of God is not surrounded by oceans of ignorance?"[30] Pinnock further claims that anyone who is "informationally premessianic" is in the same spiritual situation as the Old Testament people of faith.[31] Anderson, similarly, from experience and observation, believes that it is indisputable that "some of the great Muslim mystics have sought the face of God with a wholesomeness which cannot be questioned."[32] Restrictivist theologians challenge inclusivists, like Pinnock and Anderson, by claiming that it is wrong to compare Old Testament believers with the unevangelized as the former benefitted from special, not general, revelation.[33] Anderson agrees

27. Erickson, *How Shall*, 155–6. He claims that Cornelius is described as a "God fearer" which is a technical term for a Gentile who attended synagogue service, but was not a full proselyte and had not been circumcised. If this is true, then he would have been exposed to the same special revelation that the Jews had and epistemologically his status would have been the same as Old Testament believers. He further makes mention of the angel that visited him; such an appearance signifying special revelation. On "God fearer," see Perkin, "God-fearer," 1:888.

28. Heb.11:6 states, "And without faith it is impossible to please God, because anyone who comes to him must believe that he exists and that he rewards those who earnestly seek him."

29. Pinnock, *Wideness*, 158. Pinnock argues that one does not need to confess the name of Christ in order to be saved as Old Testament characters such as David, Job, Abraham et al. did not know the name of Christ.

30. Pinnock, *Wideness*, 160. It is noteworthy that Abraham was saved by believing that God was true to his promise and he would have a son, see Gen. 15:6 and Rom. 4:3.

31. Pinnock, *Wideness*, 161. Anderson makes the same point in *Christianity*, 144.

32. Anderson, *Christianity*, 152.

33. Henry, *Revelation*, 369. Erickson, *How Shall*, 155, challenges inclusivists like Pinnock, Sanders, and Richardson, over their use of people like Melchizedek as an example of a "holy pagan" who was outside of the covenant nation of Israel, yet supposedly saved by general revelation. Erickson rightly asks how we might know whether Melchizedek's revelation was general or special, for God might have appeared to him in

with Henry on his point of the Old Testament believers having responded to special revelation, even though it was incomplete. He, however, argues that the similarity between Old Testament believers and the unevangelized lies in the fact that neither had heard of the atoning work of God through the death of his Son.[34] Anderson leaves open the possibility of true followers of other religions receiving God's mercy through the working of his Spirit in their hearts which will bring them in some manner to realize their sin and need for forgiveness.[35]

It is recognized that the scholarly discussion on whether general salvation is salvific is much more extensive than the brief summary above, though for the purpose of this section, a definitive answer, if one were ever possible, is not necessary. The important question for this section is whether the concept of posthumous salvation becomes redundant if it is proved that general revelation provides enough "light" for salvation, or put another way, can posthumous salvation and inclusivism be wider hope partners and allies rather than opponents in the discussion of the destiny of the unevangelized?

Is posthumous salvation made redundant?

Advocates of both posthumous salvation and inclusivism believe in a wider hope for humanity. That is, God desires the salvation of all, and that salvation is only through Christ. Inclusivists allow for universal opportunity through the means of general revelation being potentially salvific, and that any implicit faith is required before death. Proponents of posthumous salvation, conversely, deny the possibility of general salvation being salvific, though allow for the opportunity of salvation after death.[36] An example of the divergence of views on the matter of general revelation and salvation is found in *What About Those Who Have Never Heard?*.[37] Fackre argues that

the way he appeared to Abraham.

34. Anderson, *Christianity*, 152–3.

35. Anderson, *Christianity*, 148–9. He affirms that he does not doubt "that there may be those who, while never hearing the gospel here on earth, will wake up, as it were, on the other side of the grave to worship the One in whom, without understanding at the time, they found the mercy of God," 154.

36. For example, Bloesch, *Future*, 121, who asserts that "the universal awareness of God made possible by the light in nature and conscience is the basis of misunderstanding, not understanding, of God." In Bloesch, *Essentials*, 1:244, he further argues that the claim that someone can be saved apart from the knowledge of the gospel is "pernicious" for the Christian faith.

37. A book that represents three arguments to the question, namely, from Restrictivist theologian, Ronald H. Nash, advocate of posthumous salvation, Gabriel Fackre, and Inclusivist John Sanders, who is also the book's editor. Each author is invited to

explicit faith is required and that all who do not have opportunity to exercise such faith before death will have the opportunity postmortem.[38] Sanders's inclusivism maintains that God makes salvation available to the unevangelized through an implicit faith response during this life to the light they had received, whilst also allowing for a postmortem encounter with Christ, but only as a confirmation of their implicit faith.[39] This differs to the view of Fackre, and other proponents of posthumous salvation, in that Sanders and Pinnock believe that any postmortem encounter will be for the purpose of confirming the decision that one has made to general revelation during this life and not as a response to evangelization.[40]

The postmortem views of Sanders and Pinnock are coherent with their inclusivism for all they appear to be saying is that those who are saved through their response to general revelation in this life will have their knowledge of God "updated" when they enter his presence after death.[41] If, as inclusivists claim, Cornelius was a true believer before his meeting with Peter (Acts 10:1–49), and that Peter brought to Cornelius the fullness of salvation that comes from a personal relationship with Christ, and not salvation itself, then, such a model provides Sanders and Pinnock with a credible biblical model for their views. All one is required to believe is that the updating of one's knowledge of God and the fullness of salvation happens not in this life but is delayed to the other side of the grave.

The more challenging question is whether the views of those, like Fackre and Bloesch, who believe in postmortem *evangelism* in contrast to postmortem *confirmation*, can coexist with inclusivist views, or does inclusivism make posthumous salvation redundant?

---

present their case for their particular viewpoint and the other two contributors are then invited to critique the theological position presented. Whilst Sanders and Fackre appear to have much more in common (both being proponents of the wider hope), they cross swords over the subject of whether one requires general or special revelation to be saved.

38. Scriptures often quoted include: Mark 1:14–15; 16:15–16; John 3:16, 36; 1 John 2:23; Acts 11:14; and Rom. 10:9–10 which states, "If you confess with your mouth, 'Jesus is Lord,' and believe in your heart that God raised him from the dead, you will be saved. For it is with your heart that you believe and are justified, and it is with your mouth that you confess and are saved." Sanders correctly questions whether this verse teaches the necessity of confessing Jesus for salvation— that is, all this verse teaches is if you confess Jesus you are saved, but it says nothing of those who do not confess Christ, see Sanders, *What About*, 104.

39. Sanders, *What About*, 103–4.

40. See also p 44, Common Approaches to the Destiny of the Unevangelized.

41. Pinnock, *Wideness*, 172. Pinnock confesses that his views on postmortem encounter are not the same as Fackre and Bloesch who believe in postmortem evangelization, not confirmation, see Pinnock, "Inclusivist View," 148.

Though some authors believe that these two views are inconsistent, "superfluous," (Anderson) "logically incompatible," (Nash) or not a "well thought out theological synthesis" (Carson), such views are not inevitable, for it might be argued that God would use all means at his disposal in achieving his objective of reaching the lost with his offer of salvation.[42] That is, an all-wise, all-powerful, all-loving God would not need to limit himself to such humanly defined and narrow constructs as inclusivism or posthumous salvation. Could not God save the unevangelized through their implicit faith response to the light they received to then have their knowledge of God "updated," before or after death, *and* save those who had not responded to the misty half-light of general revelation whilst on earth through a postmortem opportunity? I am not aware of any theologian that explicitly makes this case, although there would appear to be no good theological reason why both views cannot be held in tension and as complementary to one another.

42. Anderson, *Christianity*, 154; Nash, *Is Jesus the Only Savior?*, 149; Carson, *Gagging*, 299–300.

Appendix B

Descensus in the Early Church

It is to be concluded that none of the biblical Descensus passages previously discussed in chapter 3, that are traditionally used to support the concept of posthumous salvation, actually offer concrete or explicit biblical corroboration for this belief.

The tradition of the Descensus is found in early church history. MacCulloch lists a number of early patristic references to the descent,[1] including Polycarp (early/mid-second century),[2] Justin Martyr (mid-second century),[3] the Shepherd of Hermas,[4] Irenaeus,[5] Tertullian,[6] and Hippolytus.[7] The Gnostic Marcion is also regarded as an important witness to the early

1. MacCulloch, *Harrowing*, 83–84, also cites, Ignatius's letters to Magnesians (c. 9), Philadelphians (c. 5), and Trallians (c. 9). It is uncertain that these are references to the Descensus.

2. *Letter to the Philippians* 1, see MacCulloch, *Harrowing*, 84, and Harris, "Ascent," 199. As with Ignatius, this is far from an explicit reference to the Descensus.

3. *Dialogue with Trypho*, (c. 72) cites an apocryphon which he claims the Jews deleted from the Book of Jeremiah, which was still to be found in some synagogue copies, stating, "The Lord God remembered His dead people of Israel who lay in the graves; and He descended to preach to them His own salvation." Justin also makes reference to Christ's descent (c. 99) by referring to the Jews' mistaken idea that Christ being put to death, would remain in Hades like a common man.

4. *Shepherd of Hermas Similitudes*, 9.15, 16, in which a preaching in Hades is ascribed, not to Christ, but to the apostles.

5 *Against Heresies*, 4.27.2.

6. Tertullian, *On the Resurrection of the Flesh*, opposed the current belief that Christ, by his descent emptied Hades so that the faithful should not go there. He claimed that all souls, good and bad, go to Hades. In any case, his opposition provides evidence that the teaching of the descent was commonplace. See MacCulloch, *Harrowing*, 93–94.

7. *Treatise on Christ and Antichrist*, 26, 45.

185

acceptance of the doctrine of the descent in the first half of the second century. Marcion gave the descent doctrine an unusual twist, teaching that the creator god of the Old Testament was inferior, with Marcion regarding the Old Testament heroes as villains and the villains as heroes.[8] In Marcion's thought, Christ descended to Hades to deliver the likes of Cain, the Sodomites, and the heathen.[9] Marcion, admittedly in an obtuse manner, also acts as a witness to the Descensus belief that was prevalent in his day.

Dalton contends that the view of Christ's descent was the most strongly represented amongst the early Fathers up until the time of Augustine, yet before Clement of Alexandria the 1 Peter 3:19 text is not connected with Christ's descent into the underworld.[10] Even Irenaeus, who Cross claims was "the most considerable theologian of the second century,"[11] accepted Peter's authorship, yet never quotes or alludes to 1 Peter 3:19 when he discusses Christ's descent. Selwyn writes, "The outstanding fact in the Patristic evidence before A.D. 190 is that despite the popularity of the doctrine of Christ's 'harrowing of hell,' 1 Peter 3:18ff is never quoted as authority for it. The conception of the *Descensus* current in the early Church proceeds on entirely different lines, and arose independently of 1 Peter 3:19f. Prior to the time of Clement of Alexandria . . . and Origen, this passage, so far as we know, was never referred to in connexion with the *Descensus*"; while Irenaeus "who regarded 1 Peter as authentic . . . never quotes the passage at all, nor, in dealing specially with the *Descensus*, does he even allude to it."[12]

Origen's apologetic against Celsus is especially noteworthy in providing his understanding of the descent of Christ. Origen replies to the taunt of pagan Celsus, who claimed that since Christ had no success in preaching to the living he went to try his luck in the world of the dead, with what appears to be a reference to 1 Peter 3:19, affirming that Christ did preach to the dead but that he converted only those who were willing to hear him.[13]

Christ's descent into hell (Hades) is included in the Apostles' Creed: that Christ "suffered under Pontius Pilate, was crucified, dead, and buried; He descended into hell. The third day He arose again from the dead; He ascended into heaven," though the phrase "he descended into hell" was not included in the earlier Roman form of the creed. The first appearance was found in a version by Rufinus in c. AD 390, being the only one to include

---

8. Trumbower, *Rescue*, 93.

9. MacCulloch, *Harrowing*, 86–87. See *Irenaeus Against Heresies*, 1.27.3.

10. Dalton, *Christ's Proclamation*, 28. See *Stromata* 6.6:38–39.

11. Cross, *Early Christian Fathers*, 10.

12. Selwyn, *First Epistle*, 340. Selwyn quotes from Loofs, "Descent to Hell," 4.648–63.

13. As cited by Dalton, *Christ's Proclamation*, 30.

this phrase before AD 650, and even he did not take the words to mean that Christ descended into the underworld, rather he understood the words to mean that Christ was buried.[14] Grudem is probably correct to question whether the term "apostolic" can be in any sense applied to this phrase, contending that this "late intruder into the Apostles' Creed" should be removed altogether as it never belonged there in the first place. His argument is based both on the phrase's dubious origins and also on its uncertain scriptural foundation, not believing that this doctrine is found anywhere in the Scriptures. Whilst admitting that teaching on the Descensus was apparently taught in early and mid-second-century Christianity, it remains an area of ambivalence and uncertainly in the biblical text, and one has sympathy with Grudem, certainly with respect to his views on its removal from the Apostles' Creed.[15] Erickson provides a fascinating anecdote in that in the late 1960s, the chaplain of Wheaton College decided that a series of messages should be delivered on the Apostles' Creed from the college chapel. Members of the department were asked to preach, each on a different phrase within the creed. However, no one was willing to preach on the phrase "descended into Hades" because no one believed in it. It was omitted from the series.

14. Grudem, "He did not," 103. He also notes that this phrase only appeared in one of the two versions of the Creed we have from Rufinus. It was not found in the Roman form of the Creed that he preserved.

15. Erickson, *How Shall*, 172.

Bibliography

Aalen, S. "St. Luke's Gospel and 1 Enoch." *New Testament Studies* 13 (1967): 1–13.

Abbott, T. K. *The Epistles to the Ephesians and to the Colossians*, International Critical Commentary. Edinburgh: Clark, 1897.

Abbott, W. M. ed. *The Documents of Vatican II*. New York: Guild, 1966.

Achtemeier, P. J. *1 Peter: A Commentary on First Peter*. Hermeneia: Fortress, 1996.

Adams, M. "Hell and the Justice of God." *Religious Studies* 11 (1975): 433–47.

Altstadt, R. A, and E. Wan. "The Salvation of the Unevangelized: What the Literature Suggests." Global Missiology 2 (January 2005). No pages. Online: http://ojs. globalmissiology.org/index.php/english/article/view/107

Anderson, J. N. D. *Christianity and Comparative Religion*. Downers Grove: IVP, 1977.

———. *Christianity and World Religions: The Challenge of Pluralism*. Downers Grove: IVP, 1984.

Anselm. "Cur Deus Homo." I:XXI. Online: http://www.ewtn.com/library/CHRIST/ CURDEUS.HTM.

Aquinas, T. "Question 52: Christ's Descent into Hell." No pages. Online: http://www. newadvent.org/summa/4052.htm#article2.

———. "Question 87. The Remission of Venial Sin." No Pages. Online: http://www. newadvent.org/Summa/2087.htm#article4.

Ashmon, S. A. "The Wrath of God: A Biblical Overview." *Concordia Journal* (2005): 348–58.

Augustine, "Letter 164 to Evodius." In *Letters 156–210, The Works of Saint Augustine: A Translation for the 21st Century*. Translated by R. J. Teske. New York: New City, 2004.

Baker, S. L. *Razing Hell*. Louisville: Westminster John Knox, 2010.

Bandstra, A. J. "'Making Proclamation to the Spirits in Prison': Another Look at 1 Peter 3:19." *Calvin Theological Journal* 38: (2003) 120–24.

Barclay, W. *The Letter to the Hebrews*: DSB. Edinburgh: Saint Andrew, 1985.

Barnett, P. W. *The Second Epistle to the Corinthians*, NICNT. Grand Rapids: Eerdmans, 1997.

Barrett, C. K. *A Commentary on the First Epistle to the Corinthians*, Harper's New Testament Commentaries. New York: Harper and Row, 1968.

Barth, K. *Church Dogmatics*. Edinburgh: T. & T. Clark, 1957.

Battle, M. *Reconciliation: The Ubuntu Theology of Desmond Tutu*. Cleveland: Pilgrim, 1997.

Bauckham, R. J. "Universalism: a historical survey." *Themelios* 4, no. 2 (1979): 48–54.

Bauckham, R. *The Fate of the Dead: Studies on the Jewish and Christian Apocalypses.* Leiden: Brill Academic, 1998.

Bavinck, H. *The Last Things: Hope for This World and the Next.* Edited by Bolt, J. Translated by Vriend, J. Carlisle: Paternoster, 1996.

Beare, F. W. *The Earliest Records of Jesus.* New York: Abingdon, 1968.

Beasley-Murray, G. *Baptism in the New Testament.* Grand Rapids: Eerdmans, 1994.

Beilby, J., and P. R. Eddy, eds. *The Nature of the Atonement: Four Views.* Downers Grove: IVP Academic, 2006.

Bell, R. *Love Wins.* London: Harper Collins, 2011.

Berkhof, L. *Systematic Theology.* Edinburgh: Banner of Truth, 1979.

Berkouwer, G. C. "General and Special Divine Revelation." In *Revelation and the Bible, Contemporary Evangelical Thought,* edited by C. F. H. Henry, 13–24. London: Tyndale, 1959.

Beveridge, Henry, translator. "John Calvin: Institutes of the Christian Religion." No pages. Online: http://www.reformed.org/master/index.html?mainframe=/books/institutes/

Bietenhard, H. "Hell." In *New International Dictionary of New Testament Theology,* edited by Brown C., 2:210. Grand Rapids: Zondervan, 1986.

Blanchard, J. *Whatever Happened to Hell?* Darlington: Evangelical Alliance, 1993.

Bloesch, D. G. "Descent into Hell (Hades)." In *Evangelical Dictionary of Theology,* edited by Elwell, W. A., 313–15. Basingstoke: Marshall Pickering, 1985.

———. *Essentials of Evangelical Theology.* 2 vols. San Francisco: Harper and Row, 1978.

———. *The Future of Evangelical Christianity: A Call for Unity amid Diversity.* Garden City: Doubleday, 1983.

Blomberg, C. L. "Degrees of Reward in the Kingdom of Heaven?" *Journal of Evangelical Theological Society* 35, no. 2 (1991): 26–34.

Bock, D. L. *Luke 9:51—24:53,* Baker Exegetical Commentary on the New Testament, vol. 2. Grand Rapids: Baker, 1996.

Boettner, L. "Purgatory." In *Evangelical Dictionary of Theology,* edited by Elwell, W. A., 897. Basingstoke: Marshall Pickering, 1985.

———. *The Reformed Doctrine of Predestination.* Grand Rapids: Eerdmans, 1954.

Borland, J. "A Theologian Looks at the Gospel and World Religions." *Journal of the Evangelical Theological Society* 33: (1990) 3–11.

Bowne, B. P. *The Atonement.* New York: Eaton & Mains, 1900.

Boyd, G. A., and P. R. Eddy. *Across the Spectrum: Understanding Issues in Evangelical Theology.* Grand Rapids: Baker Academic, 2002.

Boyd, W. J. P. "Gehenna—According to J. Jeremias." In *Studia Biblica 1978: II. Papers on the Gospels,* edited by E. A. Livingstone, 9–12. Sheffield: JSOT Press, 1980.

Braaten, C. "Lutheran Theology and Religious Pluralism." In *Religious Pluralism and Lutheran Theology,* edited by J. P. Rajashekar, 105–28. Geneva: Lutheran World Federation, 1991.

Bradley, J. T. *A Manual for Ministers.* Cheltenham: Greenhurst, n.d.

Bray, G. *Biblical Interpretation: Past & Present.* Leicester: Apollos, 1996.

———. "Hell: Eternal Punishment or Total Annihilation?" *Evangel* 10, no 2 (1992): 19–24.

Brinsmead, R. "Justification by Faith Re-Examined," *The Christian Verdict,* Special Issue, no.1, (1983): n.p.

Brown, R. M. "Some are Guilty, All Are Responsible: Heschel's Social Ethics." In *Abraham Joshua Heschel: Exploring His Life and Thought*, edited by J. C. Merkle, 123–41. New York: MacMillan, 1985.

Brown, R. *The Message of Hebrews: BST*. Leicester: Inter-Varsity Press, 1996.

Bruce, F. F. *1 and 2 Corinthians*, New Century Bible. London: Marshall, Morgan & Scott, 1971.

————. *Romans*, Tyndale New Testament Commentaries. Leicester: Inter-Varsity Press, 1983.

————. *The Epistle to the Hebrews*, NICNT. Grand Rapids: Eerdmans, 1990.

Brunner, E. *The Letter to the Romans*, London: Lutterworth Press, 1961.

Buis, H. "Hades" In *Zondervan Pictorial Encyclopedia*, vol. 3, edited by Tenney, M. C., 7–8. Grand Rapids: Zondervan, 1976.

Bultmann, R. *History of the Synoptic Tradition*. New York: Harper & Row, 1963.

Burrow, R. "The Love, Justice and Wrath of God." *Encounter* 59, no. 3 (1998): 379–406.

Butler, B. H. "Infant Salvation: An Ecumenical Problem." *Foundations* 14 (1971): 344–60.

Caird, G. B. *Saint Luke*. London: SCM, 1977.

————. "The Descent of Christ in Ephesians 4:7–11." In *Studia Evangelica*, edited by F. L. Cross, 2:535–545. Berlin: Akademie, 1964.

Calvin, J. *The Institutes of Christian Religion*. Edited by T. Lane and H. Osbourne, London: Hodder and Stoughton, 1986.

————. *Commentaries on the Catholic Epistles*. Grand Rapids: Eerdmans, 1948.

Carson, D. *The Difficult Doctrine of the Love of God*. Leicester: IVP, 2000.

————. *The Gagging of God: Christianity Confronts Pluralism*. Leicester: Apollos, 1996.

Chalke, S., and A. Mann. *The Lost Message of Jesus*. Grand Rapids: Zondervan, 2003.

Chambers, Talbot W., translator. "Homily 40 on First Corinthians (Chrysostom)." No pages. Online: http://www.newadvent.org/fathers/220140.htm.

Chapman, A., and B. Spong. eds. *Religion and Reconciliation in South Africa: Voices of Religious Leaders*. Philadelphia: Foundation, 2003.

Charles, R.H. translator. "Jubilees, 10:4–5." No pages. Online: http://www.pseudepigrapha.com/jubilees/10.htm.

Clark, D. K. "Is Special Revelation Necessary for Salvation?" In *Through No Fault of Their Own*, edited by W. V. Crockett and J. G. Sigountos, 35–45. Grand Rapids: Baker, 1993.

————. "Warfield, Infant Salvation, and the Logic of Calvinism." *Journal of the Evangelical Theological Society* 27 (1984): 459–64.

Cochrane, W. *Future Punishment or Does Death End Probation?* Melbourne: Bradley Garretson & Co., 1886.

Collins, G. N. M. "Infant Salvation." In *Evangelical Dictionary of Theology*, edited by Elwell, W. A., 559–60. Basingstoke: Marshall Pickering, 1985.

Cone, J. *Black Theology and Black Power*. Minneapolis: Seabury Press, 1969.

Congar, Y. *The Wide World My Parish: Salvation and Its Problems*. Translated by Donald Attwater. London: Darton, Longman and Todd, 1961.

Conzelmann, H. *1 Corinthians*, Translated by J. W. Leitch. Philadelphia: Fortress, 1975.

Cook, R. R. "Is Universalism an implication of the notion of post-mortem evangelism?" *Tyndale Bulletin* 45, no. 2 (1994): 395–409.

Craig, W. "No Other Name: A Middle Knowledge Perspective on the Exclusivity of Salvation through Christ." *Faith and Philosophy* 6 (1989) 172–88.

———. *The Only Wise God: The Compatibility of Divine Foreknowledge and Human Freedom*. Grand Rapids: Baker, 1987.

Cranfield, C. E. B. "The Interpretation of 1 Peter 3:19 and 4:6." *The Expository Times*, 69, no. 12 (1958) 369–72.

Creed, J. M. *The Gospel according to St. Luke*. London: Macmillan, 1953.

Crisp, O. "Augustinian universalism." *International Journal for Philosophy and Religion* 53 (2003): 127–45.

———. "Divine Retribution: A Defence." *Sophia* 42, no. 2 (2003): 36–53.

Crockett, W. ed. *Four Views on Hell*. Grand Rapids: Zondervan, 1997.

Crombie, Frederick, translator. "Contra Celsus, (Book II)." No pages. Online: http://www.newadvent.org/fathers/04162.htm.

Cross, F. *The Early Christian Fathers*. London: Gerald Duckworth, 1960.

Crossan, J. D. *In Parables: The Challenge of the Historical Jesus*. New York: Harper & Row, 1973.

D' Costa, G. *John Hick's Theology of Religions*. New York: University Press of America, 1987.

———. *Theology and Religious Pluralism: The Challenge of Other Religions*. Oxford: Blackwell, 1986.

Dalton, W. *Christ's Proclamation to the Spirits: A Study of 1 Peter 3:18—4:6*. Rome: Pontifical Biblical Institute, 1965.

Danaher, W. "Towards a Paschal Theology of Restorative Justice." *Anglican Theological Review* 89, no. 3 (2007): 359–73.

Davids, P. H. *The First Epistle of Peter*, NICNT. Grand Rapids: Eerdmans, 1990.

Davies, B. *An introduction to the Philosophy of Religion*. Oxford: Oxford University Press, 2004.

Davis, S. T. "Universalism, Hell, and the Fate of the Ignorant." *Modern Theology* 6, no. 2 (1990): 173–86.

de Romestin et al., translators. "Exposition of the Christian Faith." No pages. Online: http://www.newadvent.org/fathers/34043.htm.

Demarest, B. "General Revelation." In *Evangelical Dictionary of Theology*, edited by Elwell, W. A., 944–45. Basingstoke: Marshall Pickering, 1985.

———. *General Revelation*. Grand Rapids: Zondervan, 1982.

Demarest, B., and G. Lewis. *Integrative Theology*. Grand Rapids: Zondervan, 1987.

Derrett, J. D. M. *Law in the New Testament*. London: Darton, Longmann, and Todd, 1970.

Dezinger, H. *The Sources of Catholic Dogma*. Translated by Roy Defarrari. St. Louis: Herder, 1957.

Dodd, C. H. *The Epistle of Paul to the Romans*. London: Hodder and Stoughton, 1932.

———. *The Johannine Epistles*. London: Harper & Row, 1946.

Dods, Marcus, and George Reith, translators. "Dialogue with Trypho (Chapters 69–88)." No pages. Online: http://www.newadvent.org/fathers/01286.htm.

———. "Dialogue with Trypho (Chapters 89–108)." No pages. Online: http://www.newadvent.org/fathers/01287.htm.

Donahue, J. R. "Biblical Perspectives on Justice." In *The Faith that Does Justice: Examining the Christian Sources for Social Change*, edited by J. C. Haughey, 68–112. New York: Paulist, 1977.

Donelson. L. R. *I & II Peter and Jude*, The New Testament Library. Louisville: Westminster John Knox, 2010.

Donnelly, E. *Heaven and Hell*. Edinburgh: Banner of Truth, 2001.

Donnelly, J. P. "Limbo." In *Evangelical Dictionary of Theology*, edited by Elwell, W. A., 642–43. Basingstoke: Marshall Pickering, 1985.

Dorner, I. A. *A System of Christian Doctrine*. Edinburgh: T. & T. Clark, 1890.

Downes, G. "Will we all be saved?" *Christianity* (2011): 26–32.

Dowsett, D. *God, That's Not Fair!* Singapore: OMF, 1982.

Dunn, J. D. G. *The Theology of Paul the Apostle*. Edinburgh: T. & T. Clark, 1998.

Dupuis, J. "The Cosmic Christ in the Early Fathers." *Indian Journal of Theology* 15 (1966): 106–20.

Dyer, G. J. "The Unbaptized Infant in Eternity." *Chicago Studies* 2 (1963): 147.

Easton, B. S. *The Gospel according to St. Luke*. New York: Scribner, 1926.

Edwards, D. L. and J. Stott. *Essentials: A Liberal-Evangelical Dialogue*. Downers Grove: InterVarsity Press, 1988.

Edwards, J. *Works of Jonathan Edwards: Ethical Writing*, vol. 8. Edited by Paul Ramsey. New Haven and London: Yale University Press, 1989.

Ellenberger, J. D. "Is Hell a Proper Motivation for Missions?" In *Through No Fault of Their Own*, edited by W. J. Crockett and J. G. Sigountos, 217–27. Grand Rapids: Baker, 1993.

Elliott, J. H. *1 Peter*, Anchor Bible, vol. 37B. New York: Doubleday, 2000.

Enoch. First Enoch, Book 1. No pages. Online: http://www.ccel.org/c/charles/otpseudepig/enoch/ENOCH_2.HTM.

———. First Enoch, Book 2. No pages. Online: http://www.ancienttexts.org/library/ethiopian/enoch/1watchers/watchers.htm.

Erickson, M. J. "Is Hell Forever?" *Bibliotheca Sacra* 152 (1995): 259–72.

———. *Christian Theology*. Grand Rapids: Baker, 1998.

———. *How Shall They Be Saved? The Destiny of Those Who Do Not Hear of Jesus*. Grand Rapids: Baker, 1996.

———. "Is There Opportunity for Salvation After Death?" *Bibliotheca Sacra* 152 (1995): 131–44.

———. "The Fate of Those Who Never Hear." *Bibliotheca Sacra* 152 (1995): 3–15.

———. "The State of the Question." In *Through No Fault of Their Own*, edited by W. J. Crockett and J. G. Sigountos, 23–34. Grand Rapids: Baker, 1993.

Evans, L. H. *Hebrews*, The Communicator's Commentary. Milton Keynes: Word, 1986.

Fackre, G. "Divine Perseverance." In *What About Those Who Have Never Heard? Three Views on the Destiny of the Unevangelised*, edited by J. Sanders, 71–95. Downers Grove: IVP, 1995.

———. *The Christian Story: A Narrative Interpretation of Basic Christine Doctrine*. Grand Rapids: Eerdmans, 1984.

———. "The Scandals of Particularity and Universality." *Midstream* 22 (1983): 32–52.

Fairhurst, A. "Death and Destiny." *The Churchman* 95 (1981): 313–14.

Fee, G. D. *God's Empowering Presence*. Peabody: Hendricksen, 1994.

———. *The First Epistle to the Corinthians*, NICNT. Grand Rapids: Eerdmans, 1987.

Fee, G. D. and D. Stuart. *How to Read the Bible for all its Worth*. London: Scripture Union, 1991.

Feinberg, J. S. "1 Peter 3:18–20, Ancient Mythology, and the Intermediate State." *The Westminster Theological Journal* 48, no. 2 (1986): 303–36.

Fernando, A. *Crucial Questions About Hell*. Eastbourne: Kingsway, 1991.

———. *The Christian's Attitude Toward World Religions*. Wheaton: Tyndale House, 1987.

Ferre, N. "Universalism: Pro and Con." *Christianity Today* 7, no. 11 (1963): 24.

———. *Evil and the Christian Faith*. New York and London: Harper & Bros, 1947.

Fiddes, P. *Past Event and Present Salvation: The Christian Idea of Atonement*. London: Darton, Longman & Todd, 1989.

Field, T. P. "'The Andover Theory' of Future Probation." *The Andover Review* 7 (1887): 461–75.

Fisher, E. J. "Exploration and Responses: LEX TALIONIS in the Bible and Rabbinic Tradition." *Journal of Ecumenical Studies* 19, no. 3 (1982): 584–87.

Fitzmyer, J. *Romans*, Anchor Bible vol. 33. New York: Doubleday, 1993.

———. *The Gospel according to Luke*, Anchor Bible, vols. 28–28A. New York: Doubleday, 1985.

Forbes, G. W. *The God of Old: The Role of the Lukan Parables in the Purpose of Luke's Gospel*. Sheffield: Sheffield Academic Press, 2000.

Fowler, James A., "Universalism: Forms and Fallacies." Christ in you ministries (2004). No pages. Online: http://www.christinyou.net/pages/universalism.html.

Frame, J. M. "Second Chance." In *Evangelical Dictionary of Theology*, edited by Elwell, W. A., 991–2. Basingstoke: Marshall Pickering, 1985.

———. *The Doctrine of God*. Phillipsburg: Presbyterian and Reformed, 2002.

France, R. T. "Exegesis in Practice: Two Samples." In *New Testament Interpretation*, edited by I. H. Marshall, 264–81. Grand Rapids: Eerdmans, 1977.

———. *The Gospel of Matthew*: NICNT. Grand Rapids: Eerdmans, 2007.

Friedrich, G., translated by Bromiley, G. W., 10 vols., 1:148–49. Grand Rapids: Eerdmans, 1964–1976.

Geldenhuys, N. *The Gospel of Luke*, New London Commentary on the New Testament. London: Marshall, Morgan and Scott, 1977.

Gray, T. "Post-Mortem Evangelism: A Response to R. R. Cook." *Tyndale Bulletin* 46, no. 1 (1995): 141–50.

Green, J. B. *The Gospel of Luke*, NICNT. Grand Rapids: Eerdmans, 1997.

Green, M. *Evangelism Through the Local Church*. London: Hodder and Stoughton, 1990.

Grensted, L. W. "The Use of Enoch in St. Luke 16:19–31." *Expository Times* 26 (1915): 333–34.

Gressman, H. *Vom reichen Mann und armen Lazarus: eine literargeschichtliche Studie*, no. 7. Berlin: Verlag der königlich Akademie der Wissenschaft, 1918.

Griffiths, M. *The Confusion of the Church and the World*. Downers Grove: Intervarsity Press, 1980.

Grobel, K. ". . .Whose Name was Neves." *New Testament Studies* vol. 10, no. 3 (1964): 373–82.

Gruchy, J. de. *Reconciliation: Restoring Justice*. Minneapolis: Fortress, 2002.

Grudem, W. *1 Peter*, Tyndale New Testament Commentaries. Leicester: IVP, 1997.

———. "Christ Preaching Through Noah: 1 Peter 3:19–20 in the light of dominant themes in Jewish literature." In *1 Peter, Tyndale New Testament Commentaries*, 203–39. Leicester: IVP, 1997.

———. "He did not descend into Hell: A plea for following Scripture instead of the Apostles' Creed." *The Journal of the Evangelical Theological Society* 34, no. 1 (1991): 103–13.

———. *Systematic Theology*. Leicester: Intervarsity Press, 1994.

Guelich, R. A. *The Sermon on the Mount*. Waco: Word, 1982.

Gulley, P. and J. Mulholland. *If Grace is True*. San Francisco: Harper Collins, 2003.

Gundry, R. H. "Salvation According to Scripture: No Middle Ground." *Christianity Today* 22, (1977): 342–44.

Gunton, C. *The Actuality of Atonement*. Grand Rapids: Eerdmans, 1989.

Hanson, A. T. *The Wrath of the Lamb*. London: SPCK, 1959.

Harris, W. Hall, III. "The Ascent and Descent of Christ in Ephesians 4:9–10." *Bibliotheca Sacra* 151: (1994) 198–214.

Hart, T. "Universalism: Two Distinct Types." In *Universalism and the Doctrine of Hell*, edited by N. M. de S. Cameron, 1–34. Carlisle: Paternoster, 1992.

Haughey, J. C. "Jesus as the Justice of God." In *The Faith That Does Justice: Examining the Christian Sources for Social Change*, edited by J. C. Haughey, 264–90. New York: Paulist, 1977.

Hays, R. *The Moral Vision of the New Testament: A Contemporary Introduction to New Testament Ethics*. Edinburgh: T. & T. Clark, 1996.

Hendriksen, W. *Luke*, New Testament Commentary. Edinburgh: Banner of Truth, 1984.

———. *Matthew*, New Testament Commentary. Edinburgh: Banner of Truth, 1982.

Henry, C. F. H. *God, Revelation and Authority: God Who Stands and Stays*, vol. 6. Waco: Word, 1983.

———. "Is It Fair?" In *Through No Fault of Their Own*, edited by W. V. Crockett and J. G. Sigountos, 245–55. Grand Rapids: Baker, 1993.

Hermas, Shepherd of. "Similitude Ninth." No pages. Online: http://www.ccel.org/ccel/schaff/anf02.ii.iv.ix.html.

Heschel, A. J. *The Prophets*. New York: Harper, 1962.

Hewitt, T. *Hebrews*, Tyndale New Testament Commentaries. London: Tyndale, 1969.

Hick, J. "A Pluralist View." In *Four Views on Salvation in a Pluralistic World*, edited by D. L. Okholm and T. R. Phillips, 27–91. Grand Rapids: Zondervan, 1996.

———. *Death and Eternal Life*. New York: Harper and Row, 1976.

———. *God Has Many Names*. London: MacMillan, 1980.

Hilborn, David, ed. *The Nature of Hell: A Report by the Evangelical Alliance Commission on Unity and Truth Among Evangelicals (ACUTE)*. Carlisle: Paternoster, 2000.

Hillyer, N. *1 and 2 Peter, Jude*, New International Bible Commentary. Peabody: Hendrickson, 1992.

Hippolytus. "Treatise on Christ and Antichrist." No pages. Online: http://www.ccel.org/ccel/schaff/anf05.iii.iv.ii.i.html.

Hock, R. F. "Lazarus and Micyllus: Greco-Roman Backgrounds to Luke 16:19–31." *Journal of Biblical Literature* 106 (1987): 447–63.

Holmes, Peter, translator. "Against Marcion (Book 5)." No pages. Online: http://www.newadvent.org/fathers/03125.htm.

———. "On the Resurrection of the Flesh (Tertullian)." No pages. Online: http://www.newadvent.org/fathers/0316.htm.

Hubbard, M. "2 Corinthians." In *Zondervan Illustrated Bible Backgrounds Commentary*, vol. 3, edited by Arnold, C. E., 194–263. Grand Rapids: Zondervan, 2002.

Hudson, A. O. *Future Probation in Christian Belief*. Hounslow: Bible Fellowship Union, 1975.

Hughes, P. E. "Grace." In *Evangelical Dictionary of Theology*, edited by Elwell, W. A., 479–82. Basingstoke: Marshall Pickering, 1985.

Jeffrey, S., et al. *Pierced for Our Transgressions: Recovering the Glory of Penal Substitution*. Nottingham: Inter-Varsity Press, 2007.

Jeremias, J. "Hades." In *Theological Dictionary of the New Testament*, edited by Kittel, G. and Geoffrey W. Bromiley, 1:147–49. Grand Rapids: Eerdmans, 1964.

———. *The Parables of Jesus*. Translated by S. H. Hooke. New York: Charles Scribner's Sons, 1963.

Johnson, T. "A Wideness in God's Mercy: Universalism in the Bible." In *Universal Salvation?* edited by R. Parry and C. Partridge, 77–102. Carlisle: Paternoster, 2003.

Jülicher, A. *Die Gleichnisreden Jesu*. Tübingen: Mohr, 1910.

Keathley, K. "Salvation and the Sovereignty of God: The Great Commission as the Expression of the Divine Will." *Journal of the Grace Evangelical Society* (Spring 2006): 3–22.

Kellogg, S. H. "Future Probation." *The Presbyterian Review* 6, no. 22 (1885): 226–56.

Kelly, J. N. D. *The Epistles of Peter and of Jude*, Black's New Testament Commentary. Peabody: Hendrikson, 1969.

Kendall, R. T. *Once Saved, Always Saved*. London: Hodder and Stoughton, 1984.

Kidner, D. A. "Retribution and Punishment in the Old Testament in Light of the New Testament." *Scottish Bulletin of Evangelical Theology* 1 (1983): 3–9.

Kistemaker, S. J. *Peter and Jude*, New Testament Commentary. Grand Rapids: Baker, 1987.

Knight, G. A. F. "Is 'Righteous' Right?" *Scottish Journal of Theology* 41 (1988): 1–10.

Knight, G. W. "The Rich Man and Lazarus." *Review and Expositor* 94 (1997): 277–83.

Knitter, P. F. *No Other Name? A Critical Survey of Christian Attitudes toward the World Religions*. New York: Orbis, 1985.

Koch, K. "Is There a Doctrine of Retribution in the Old Testament?" In *Theodicy in the Old Testament*, edited by J. L. Crenshaw, 57–87. London: SPCK, 1983.

Kreitzer, L. "Luke 16:19–31 and 1 Enoch 22." *The Expository Times* 103 (1992): 139–42.

Küng, H. "The World Religions in God's Plan of Salvation." In *Christian Revelation and World Religions*, edited by J. Neuner, 25–66. London: Burnes and Oates, 1967.

Ladd, G. E. "Age, Ages." In *Evangelical Dictionary of Theology*, edited by Elwell, W. A., 19–21. Basingstoke: Marshall Pickering, 1984.

Landes, G. M. "Some Biblical and Theological Reflections on the Wrath of God." *The Living Pulpit* 2, no. 4, (1993): 10–11.

Lane, W. L. *Hebrews: A Call to Commitment*. Vancouver: Regents College Press, 2004.

Lange, J. *The First Epistle General of Peter*. New York: Charles Scribner, 1868.

Leckie, J. H. *The World to Come and Final Destiny*. Edinburgh: .T. & T. Clark, 1918.

Lewis, C. S. *Chronicles of Narnia: The Last Battle*. New York: Collier, 1970.

———. *The Problem of Pain*. New York: MacMillan, 1944.

Lightfoot, J. B., translator. "First Clement." No pages. Online: http://www.earlychristianwritings.com/text/1clement-lightfoot.html.

Lincoln, A. T. *Ephesians*, Word Biblical Commentary. Dallas: Word, 1990.

———. "The use of the Old Testament in Ephesians." *Journal for the Study of the New Testament* 14 (1982): 18–25.

Lindbeck, G. *The Nature of Doctrine: Religion and Theology in a Postliberal Age*. Philadelphia: Westminster, 1984.

Lindsell, H. *A Christian Philosophy of Missions*. Wheaton: Van Kempen, 1949.

Loofs, F. "Descent to Hell." In *Encyclopedia of Religion and Ethics*, edited by Hastings, J., 4.648–63. Edinburgh: T. & T. Clark, 1937.

Luckock, H. M. *The Intermediate State between Death and Judgment*. London: Longmans, Green and Co., 1896.

Luther, M. *Lectures on Galatians*, vol. 26 of Luther's Works, edited by Jaroslav Pelikan. St. Lois: Concordia, 1963.

———. "Letter to Hans von Rechenberg." In *Luther's Works* 43, 1522, translated by Martin H. Bertram. St. Louis: Concordia, 1968.

MacArthur, J. *Hebrews*, MacArthur New Testament Commentaries. Chicago: Moody, 1983.

———. *1 Corinthians*, MacArthur New Testament Commentaries. Chicago: Moody, 1984.

MacCulloch, J. A. *The Harrowing of Hell*. Edinburgh: T. & T. Clark, 1930.

MacDonald, G. *The Evangelical Universalist*. Eugene: Cascade, 2006.

MacLeod, Donald. "St. Andrews researcher questions belief in hell" (5th Dec. 2005). No pages. Online: http://www.theguardian.com/education/2005/dec/05/highereducation.uk2.

Marshall, C. D. *Beyond Retribution: A New Testament Vision of Justice, Crime and Punishment*. Grand Rapids: Eerdmans, 2001.

Marshall, I. H. "An Evangelical Approach to Theological Criticism." *Themelios* 13 (1988): 79–85.

———. "For All, All My Saviour Died." In *Semper Reforandum: Studies in Honour of Clark H. Pinnock*, edited by S. E. Porter and A. R. Cross, 322–46. Carlisle: Paternoster, 2003.

———. *The Gospel of Luke*, NIGTC. Exeter: Paternoster, 1978.

———. "The New Testament does not teach Universal Salvation." In *Universal Salvation?* edited by R. Parry and C. Partridge, 55–76. Carlisle: Paternoster, 2003.

Martin, R. P. *Ephesians, Colossians and Philemon: Interpretation, A Bible Commentary for Teaching and Preaching*. Louisville: Westminster John Knox Press, 1992.

McCormack, B. "Grace and Being: The Role of God's Gracious Election in Karl Barth's Theological Ontology." In *The Cambridge Companion to Karl Barth*, 92–110. Cambridge: Cambridge University Press, 2000.

McGrath, A. E. "'The Righteousness of God' from Augustine to Luther." *Studia Theologica* 36 (1982): 63–78.

McLaren, B. D. *The Last Word and the Word After That*. San Francisco: Jossey-Bass, 2005.

McVeigh, M. "The Fate of Those Who've Never Heard? It Depends." *Evangelical Missions Quarterly* (October 1985): 370–79.

Michaels, J. R. *1 Peter*, Word Biblical Commentary. Waco: Word, 1988.

Moltmann, J. "Destructive Judgment is a Godless Picture." No pages. Online: http://www.indybay.org/newsitems/2009/06/28/18604450.php.

———. *The Coming of God: Christian Eschatology*. Minneapolis: Fortress, 1996.

Moo, D. J. "Romans." In *Zondervan Illustrated Bible Backgrounds Commentary*, vol. 3, edited by Arnold, C. E., 2–99. Grand Rapids: Zondervan, 2002.

Moody, D. *The Word of Truth*. Grand Rapids: Eerdmans, 1981.

Moore, William, and Henry Austin Wilson, translators. "On the Soul and the Resurrection (St. Gregory of Nyssa)." No pages. Online: http://www.newadvent.org/fathers/2915.htm.

Morgan, G. C. *The Acts of the Apostles*. New York: Revell, 1924.

Morgan, R. *Romans*, New Testament Guides. Sheffield: Sheffield Academic, 1995.

Morris, L. *Luke:* Tyndale New Testament Commentaries. Leicester: Inter-Varsity Press, 1983.

———. *The Cross in the New Testament.* Exeter: Paternoster, 1966.

Mott, S. C. "The Partiality of Biblical Justice." *Transformation* 10, no. 1 (1993): 23–29.

Mounce, R. *A Living Hope: A Commentary on 1 and 2 Peter.* Grand Rapids: Eerdmans, 1982.

Nash, R. H. "Response to Fackre." In *What About Those Who Have Never Heard? Three Views on the Destiny of the Unevangelised,* edited by J. Sanders, 96–101. Downers Grove: IVP, 1995.

———. "Restrictivism." In *What About Those Who Have Never Heard? Three Views on the Destiny of the Unevangelised,* edited by J. Sanders, 105–39. Downers Grove: IVP, 1995.

———. *Is Jesus the Only Savior?* Grand Rapids: Zondervan, 1994.

Neitzsche, F. *The Anti-Christ.* Translated by R. Hollingdale. Harmondsworth: Penguin, 1969.

Neuner, J. and H. Roos, *The Teaching of the Catholic Church as Contained in Her Documents.* Edited by Karl Rahner. Translated by Geoffrey Stevens. Staten Island: Alba, 1967.

Nolland, J. *Luke 9:21—18:34,* Word Bible Commentary, vol. 35B. Dallas: Word, 1993.

O' Donnell, K. *Postmodernism.* Oxford: Lion, 2003.

Okholm, D. L. and T. R. Phillips, eds. *Four Views on Salvation in a Pluralistic World.* Grand Rapids: Zondervan, 1996.

Olley, J. W. "Righteousness—Some Issues in Old Testament Translation into English." *The Bible Today* 38 (1987): 309–13.

Osei-Bonsu, J. "The Intermediate State in Luke-Acts." *IBS* 9 (1987): 115–30.

Outler, A. ed. *John Wesley.* New York: Oxford University Press, 1964.

———., translator. "Enchiridion." No pages. Online: http://www.ccel.org/ccel/pearse/morefathers/files/augustine_enchiridion_02_trans.htm#C25

Packer, J. I. "Can the Dead Be Converted?" *Christianity Today* (January 11, 1999): 82.

———. "Evangelicals and the Way of Salvation: New Challenge to the Gospel—Universalism, and Justification by Faith." In *Evangelical Affirmations,* edited by K. S. Kantzer and C. F. H. Henry, 107–36. Grand Rapids: Zondervan, 1990.

———. *Knowing God.* London: Hodder and Stoughton, 1975.

———. *The Problem of Eternal Punishment.* Disley: Orthos, 1990.

———. "The Problem of Universalism Today." In *Celebrating the Saving Work of God,* edited by J. I. Packer, 169–78. Carlisle: Paternoster, 1998.

———. *What Did the Cross Achieve? The Logic of Penal Substitution.* Leicester: TSF Monograph, 1974.

Pannenberg, W. *Jesus: God and Man.* Philadelphia: Westminster, 1968.

———. *Systematic Theology,* vol. 3. Translated by G. W. Bromiley. Edinburgh: T. & T. Clark, 1998.

———. *The Apostles' Creed in the Light of Today's Questions.* Philadelphia: Westminster, 1972.

Parry, R. A. and C. H. Partridge, eds. *Universal Salvation? The Current Debate.* Carlisle: Paternoster, 2003.

Percy, J. O. ed. *Facing the Unfinished Task: Messages Delivered at the Congress on World Mission.* Grand Rapids: Zondervan, 1961.

Perkin, H. W. "God-fearer." In *Baker Dictionary of the Bible*, edited by Elwell, W. A., 1:888. Grand Rapids: Baker, 1988.

Pietersma, A. *The Apocryphon of Jannes and Jambres the Magicians, Religions in the Graeco-Roman World.* Leiden: Brill, 1994.

Pinnock, C. H. "An Inclusivist View." In *Four Views on Salvation in a Pluralistic World*, edited by D. L. Okholm and T. R. Phillips, 93–141. Grand Rapids: Zondervan, 1996.

———. *A Wideness in God's Mercy: The Finality of Jesus Christ in a World of Religions.* Eugene: Wipf and Stock, 1997.

———. "God limits His Knowledge." In *Predestination and Free Will: Four views of Divine Sovereignty and Human Freedom*, edited by D. Basinger and R. Basinger, 143–62. Downers Grove: InterVarsity, 1986.

———. ed. *The Grace of God and the Will of Man.* Grand Rapids: Zondervan, 1989.

Pinnock, C. H. and R. C. Brow. *Unbounded Love—a Good News Theology for the 21st Century.* Carlisle: Paternoster, 1994.

Piper, J. "How Does a Sovereign God Love? A Reply to Thomas Talbott." *The Reformed Journal* 33 (1983): 9–13.

———. *Let the Nations Be Glad: The Supremacy of God in Missions.* Leicester: IVP, 1994.

———. *The Justification of God: an exegetical and theological study of Romans 9:1–23.* Grand Rapids: Baker, 1993.

Plummer, A. *A Critical and Exegetical Commentary on the Gospel according to St. Luke.* Edinburgh: T & T Clark, 1901.

Plumptre, E. H. *A Bible Commentary for English Readers*, vol. 6, edited by Ellicott. C. J. London: Cassell, n.d.

———. *The Spirits in Prison.* London: Isbister, 1884.

Race, A. *Christians and Religious Pluralism: Patterns in the Christian Theology of Religions.* Marynoll: Orbis, 1982.

Rahner, K. *Theological Investigations.* Translated by Karl and Boniface Kruger. Baltimore: Helicon, 1969.

Ramm, B. "Will All Men Be Finally Saved?" *Eternity* (August 1964): 21–33.

Reichenbach, B. "Freedom, Justice and Moral Responsibility." In *The Grace of God, the Will of Man*, edited by C. Pinnock, 277–303. Grand Rapids: Zondervan, 1989.

Reicke, B. *The Disobedient Spirits and Christian Baptism.* Copenhagen: Egnar Munsksgaard, 1946.

Reitan, E. "Human Freedom and the Impossibility of Eternal Damnation." In *Universal Salvation?* edited by R. Parry and C. Partridge, 125–42. Carlisle: Paternoster, 2003.

Richards, J. W. "A Pascalian Argument Against Universalism." In *Unapologetic Apologetics*, edited by W. A. Dembski and J. W. Richards, 207–20. Downers Grove: InterVarsity, 2001.

Richardson, A. *Christian Apologetics.* London: SCM, 1947.

Richardson, D. *Eternity in Their Hearts.* Ventura: Regal, 1981.

Rissi, M. *Die Taufe für die Toten.* Zurich: Zwingli Verlag, 1962.

Roberts, Alexander, and James Donaldson, translators. "The Epistle of Ignatius to the Magnesians." No pages. Online: http://www.newadvent.org/fathers/0105.htm.

———. "The Epistle of Ignatius to the Philadelphians." No pages. Online: http://www.newadvent.org/fathers/0108.htm.

———. "The Epistle of Ignatius to the Trallians." No pages. Online: http://www. newadvent.org/fathers/0106.htm.

———. "Epistle of Polycarp to the Philippians." No pages. Online: http://www. newadvent.org/fathers/0136.htm.

Roberts, Alexander, and William Rambaut, translators. "Against Heresies (Book I, Chapter 27)." No pages. Online: http://www.newadvent.org/fathers/0103127.htm.

———. "Against Heresies (Book IV, Chapter 27)." No pages. Online: http://www. newadvent.org/fathers/0103427.htm.

Robinson, J. A. T. *In the End, God.* New York: Harper and Row, 1968.

Ryrie, C. *Dispensationalism Today.* Chicago: Moody, 1965.

Sanders, J. "Inclusivism." In *What About Those Who Have Never Heard? Three Views on the Destiny of the Unevangelised,* edited by J. Sanders, 21–55. Downers Grove: IVP, 1995.

———. "Is Belief in Christ Necessary for Salvation?" *Evangelical Quarterly* 60 (1988): 241–59.

———. *No Other Name.* London: SPCK, 1994.

———. "Response to Fackre." In *What About Those Who Have Never Heard? Three Views on the Destiny of the Unevangelised,* edited by J. Sanders, 102–6. Downers Grove: IVP, 1995.

Schaff, P. and H. Wace, eds. *Nicene and Post Nicene Fathers,* 2nd series, vol. 5. Edinburgh: T. & T. Clark, 1892.

Schleiermacher, F. D. E. *The Christian Faith.* Edinburgh: T. & T. Clark, 1928.

Selwyn, E. G. *The First Epistle of Peter.* Grand Rapids: Baker, 1981.

Smyth, E. C. "Probation after Death." *The Homiletic Review* 11 (1886): 286–87.

———. *The Andover Heresy.* Boston: Cupples, Upham & Company, 1887. Republished by Bibliobazaar in 2008.

Smyth, N. *Dorner on the Future State.* New York: Charles Scribner's Sons, 1883.

Sproul, R. C. *Reason to Believe.* Grand Rapids: Zondervan, 1982.

Stedman, R. C. *Hebrews,* IVP New Testament Commentary. Leicester: Inter-Varsity Press, 1992.

Stoddart, E. "Bespoke Theology for the Bereaved?" *The Bible in Transmission* (Winter 2008): 20–22.

———. "Hell—A Practical Theological Enquiry." PhD diss., University of Aberdeen, 2001.

Stoddart, E. and G. Pryce. "Observed Aversion to Raising Hell in Pastoral Care: The Conflict between Doctrine and Practice." *Journal of the Evangelical Theological Society* 18, no. 2 (2005): 129–53.

Stott, J. *The Message of Ephesians:* BST. Leicester: Inter-Varsity Press, 1979.

———. *The Message of Romans,* BST. Leicester: IVP, 1994.

Strange, D. "A Calvinist Response to Talbott's Universalism." In *Universal Salvation?* edited by R. Parry and C. Partridge, 145–68. Carlisle: Paternoster, 2003.

———. "Clark H. Pinnock: The Evolution of an Evangelical Maverick." *Evangelical Quarterly* 71, no. 4 (1999): 311–26.

———. *The Possibility of Salvation Among the Unevangelised, An Analysis of Inclusivism in Recent Evangelical Theology.* Carlisle: Paternoster, 2002.

Strauss, M. "Luke." In *Zondervan Illustrated Bible Backgrounds Commentary,* vol. 1, edited by Arnold, C., 318–515. Grand Rapids: Zondervan, 2002.

Strong, A. H. *Systematic Theology: A Compendium and Commonplace Book.* Philadelphia: Judson, 1907.

Talbott, T. "A Pauline Interpretation of Divine Judgement." In *Universal Salvation?* edited by R. Parry and C. Partridge, 32–52. Carlisle: Paternoster, 2003.

———. "Punishment, Forgiveness and Divine Justice." *Religious Studies* 29 (1993): 151–68.

———. "Reply to my Critics." In *Universal Salvation?* edited by R. Parry and C. Partridge, 247–66. Carlisle: Paternoster, 2003.

———. The Inescapable Love of God. n.p.: Universal, 1999.

Tasker, R. V. G. *The Biblical Doctrine of the Wrath of God.* London: Tyndale, 1951.

Taylor, S. "Future Probation: A Study in Heresy, Heterodoxy, and Orthodoxy." Paper presented to ATLA 2004 Annual Conference.

Thackeray, H. St. John. *The Septuagint and Jewish Worship.* London: Oxford University Press, 1921.

Tiénou, T. "Eternity in Their Hearts." In *Through No Fault of Their Own*, edited by W. V. Crockett and J. G. Sigountos, 209–16. Grand Rapids: Baker, 1993.

Tillich, P. *Love, Power and Justice.* New York: Oxford University Press, 1960.

Travis, S. H. *Christ and the Judgement of God: The limits of Divine Retribution in New Testament thought.* Milton Keynes: Paternoster, 2008.

Trueblood, E. *Philosophy of Religion.* New York: Harper & Row, 1957.

Trumbower, J. A. *Rescue for the Dead: The Posthumous Salvation of Non Christians in Early Christianity.* New York: Oxford University Press, 2001.

Tutu, D. *No Future Without Forgiveness.* New York: Doubleday, 1999.

Unger, W. "The Destiny of Those Who Have Never Heard: A Bibliographical Essay." *Direction* 23, no. 1 (1994): 54–63.

Van Engen, C. "The Effect of Universalism on Mission Effort." In *Through No Fault of their Own*, edited by W. V. Crockett and J. G. Sigountos, 183–94. Grand Rapids: Baker, 1991.

Van Til, C. *The Defense of the Faith.* Nutley: Presbyterian & Reformed, 1967.

Vanauken, S. *A Severe Mercy.* London: Hodder and Stoughton, 1979.

Volf, M. *Exclusion and Embrace: A Theological Exploration of Identity, Otherness, and Reconciliation.* Nashville: Abingdon, 1996.

von Rad, G. *Old Testament Theology.* 2 vols. London: SCM, 1962.

von Soden, H. ed. *Hand-Kommentar zum Neuen Testament, vol. 3: Die Briefe an die Kolosser, Epheser, Philemon; die Pastoralbriefe.* Frieburg: Mohr, 1893.

Wallis Robert Ernest, translator. "Epistle 72." No pages. Online: http://www.newadvent.org/fathers/050672.htm.

Walls, J. *Hell: The Logic of Damnation.* Notre Dame: University of Notre Dame Press, 1992.

———. "A Philosophical Critique of Talbott's Universalism." In *Universal Salvation?* edited by R. Parry and C. Partridge, 105–24. Carlisle: Paternoster, 2003.

Ward, K. *Re-thinking Christianity.* Oxford: Oneworld, 2007.

———. *The Word of God: The Bible after modern scholarship.* London: SPCK, 2010.

———. *What the Bible really teaches: A challenge for fundamentalists.* London: SPCK, 2004.

Warfield, B. B. "Annihilationism." In *Studies in Theology*, 447–50. New York: Oxford University Press, 1932.

———. *Studies in Theology.* New York: Oxford University Press, 1932.

Wenham, D. *The Parables of Jesus.* London, Hodder and Stoughton, 1989.

Wenham, J. *Facing Hell: An Autobiography.* Carlisle: Paternoster, 1998.

Wesley, J. *The Works of John Wesley.* 3rd edition, 14 vols. Peabody: Hendrickson, 1986.

Wiersbe, W. W. *Hebrews: Be Confident.* Amersham: Scripture Press, 1987.

Wilken, R. "Religious Pluralism and Early Christian Theology." *Interpretation* 4 (1986): 379–91.

Wilson, William, translator. "The Stromata (Clement of Alexandria)." Book 6. No pages. Online: http://www.newadvent.org/fathers/02106.htm.

Wright, Nigel, *The Radical Evangelical:Seeking a Place to Stand.* London: SPCK, 1996.

Wright, N. T. *Surprised by Hope.* London: SPCK, 2007.

———. "The Cross and the Caricatures." No pages. Online: http://www.fulcrum-anglican.org.uk/articles/the-cross-and-the-caricatures/.

———. "Towards a Biblical View of Universalism." *Themelios* 4, no. 2 (1979): 54–58.

———. *What Saint Paul Really Said.* Oxford: Lion, 1997.

Yoder, P. B. *Shalom: The Bible's Word for Salvation, Justice, and Peace.* Newton: Faith and Life, 1987.

Zerbe, G. M. *Non-Retaliation in Early Jewish and New Testament Texts: Ethical Themes in Social Contexts.* Sheffield: Sheffield Academic, 1993.

Printed in Great Britain
by Amazon.co.uk, Ltd.,
Marston Gate.